*Women of the Mexican
Countryside, 1850-1990*

CREATING SPACES ✿ SHAPING TRANSITIONS

Women of the Mexican Countryside, 1850–1990

Edited by
Heather Fowler-Salamini
& Mary Kay Vaughan

The University of Arizona Press / Tucson & London

The University of Arizona Press
Copyright © 1994
The Arizona Board of Regents
All Rights Reserved

98 97 96 95 94   5 4 3 2 1

Library of Congress Cataloging-in-Publication Data

Women of the Mexican countryside, 1850–1990 : creating spaces, shaping
    transitions / edited by Heather Fowler-Salamini and Mary Kay Vaughan.
        p.   cm.
    Includes index.
    ISBN 0-8165-1415-1 (acid free paper). —
    ISBN 0-8165-1431-3-(pbk. : acid free paper)
    1. Rural women—Mexico—History.   2. Women peasants—Mexico—
    History.   3. Women in rural development—Mexico.   I. Fowler-Salamini,
    Heather, 1940–   . II. Vaughan, Mary K., 1942–   .
    HQ1462.W66   1994   94-10179
    305.42′0972—dc20   CIP

Parts of Chapter 5 are reprinted here with the permission of the University of
Texas Press from *Soldaderas in the Mexican Military: Myth and History* (1990).

Parts of Chapter 7 are reprinted with the permission of St. Martin's Press from
Being Indian in Hueyapan: A Study of Forced Identity in Contemporary Mexico
(1975).

Parts of Chapter 12 are reprinted with the permission of El Colegio de México,
from Soledad González Montes, "Los ingresos no agropecuarios, el trabajo
remunerado femenino y la transformación de las relaciones intergenéricas e
intergeneracionales de las familias campesinas," in *Textos y pretextos. Once
estudios sobre la mujer* (1991).

Contents

Tables

Acknowledgments

At the U.S.–Mexican Historians' Conference held in San Diego in September 1990, we organized the first panel on rural women in the conference's twenty-five-year history. The excitement generated among the presenters and the audience gave rise to this book.

We began by inviting scholars from a variety of disciplines to present papers on women of the Mexican countryside at a conference organized by the Latin American Studies Program of the University of Illinois-Chicago in April 1992. At the conference, entitled "Crossing Borders, Creating Spaces: Mexican and Chicana Women, 1848–1992," researchers studying women in Mexico exchanged ideas, information, and perspectives with scholars studying Mexican women in the United States. For support for this conference we are grateful to Louise Año Nuevo Kerr, then associate vice chancellor for academic affairs at the University of Illinois-Chicago; Alice Dann, director of the UIC Center for Research on Women and Gender; Rafael Nuñez Cedeño, director of Latin American Studies at UIC; the Office of Teaching Excellence and Faculty Development at Bradley University; the John D. and Catherine T. MacArthur Foundation; and the Illinois Humanities Council. We are also indebted to Asunción Lavrín, Guillermo de la Peña, Friedrich Katz, and Carmen Ramos-Escandón for their insightful commentary on the papers.

As editors, we share a common experience and debt. When we first met, we found that we had both been influenced and inspired as undergraduates at Cornell University by Edward Whiting Fox, a professor of European history. He taught us to view history as an exhaustive inquiry into the socioeconomic underpinning of political events. His teaching persuaded both of us to pursue graduate studies in history, although we did not know each other at the time. Curiously, when we met a decade later we had both chosen Mexican history as our field of specialization.

Our efforts to put together this volume owe much to the constant encouragement of Silvia Arróm, Asunción Lavrín, and Carmen Ramos-Escandón. Francie Chassen-López has been with us from the volume's inception and contributed invaluable criticism at all stages. Harold Feinberg and Leonardo Salamini, our husbands, gave their personal support from the sidelines, commented on our work, and were witnesses to our frequent long-distance conversations and meetings. Yvonne, Alicia, and Alexey, our children, took an active interest in this project, inquiring about its progress and giving up valuable time with us to ensure its completion. This book is thus something of a two-family project.

We must also thank two anonymous readers for the University of Arizona Press for their very helpful suggestions. Neicy Zeller translated two of the essays from Spanish. Mary Ellen Grawley and Melinda Conner provided invaluable assistance in the preparation and copyediting of the manuscript, respectively. Finally, we thank Joanne O'Hare and Judith Wesley Allen of the University of Arizona Press for facilitating the publication process in every way.

Introduction

When the magnificent muralists of the Revolution of 1910 painted the Mexican people making their entrance onto the stage of history as brown, militant, and courageously defiant of oppression, they painted the women of the countryside in modes of changeless subordination—their backs bent over *metates* grinding corn, their faces shrouded behind rebozos, tears of grief and suffering falling from their wide, dark eyes, torsos bowed by the weight of gigantic loads of fruits and flowers, hands clasped and heads lowered in prayer and supplication. These women were necessary to the historical action of men as marginal appendages and background supports. They were witnesses, helpers, and lovers. They were mothers and mourners.

Today, as the twentieth century closes, Mexican women of the countryside capture our attention as historical actors—as factory and field workers, migrants, community activists, artists, artisans, merchants, managers, and heads of households. Their increasing visibility prompts us to question the marginality depicted for them in revolutionary iconography and to delve into the past to understand their roles and experiences—the knowledge, skills, and customs they have accumulated, discarded, and reworked over time. In the 1970s and 1980s, researchers began to uncover urban women's trajectory since colonial times.[1] This volume is a pioneering effort to make women of the countryside visible as they trek through the tumultuous transition from fledgling agrarian republic to industrialized nation-state,

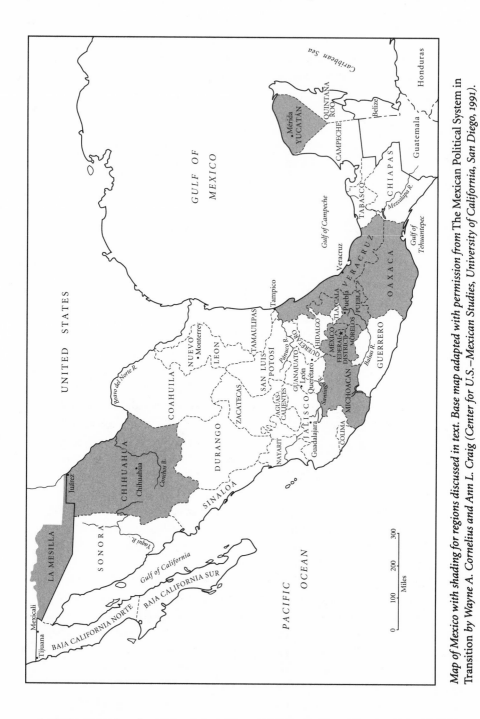

Map of Mexico with shading for regions discussed in text. Base map adapted with permission from The Mexican Political System in Transition by Wayne A. Cornelius and Ann L. Craig (Center for U.S.–Mexican Studies, University of California, San Diego, 1991).

from the middle of the nineteenth century to the present. Our task is difficult because rural women wrote less, spoke less, and are less present in the archival record than rural men or urban women. We build, however, on three richly developed areas of research: Mexican community studies, gender studies, and rural history.

Mexican community studies have recognized rural women's work and social roles since Robert Redfield and Oscar Lewis studied Tepoztlán in the 1920s and 1940s. Their focus on the family made women's activities complementary within a patriarchal structure. As social scientists in the 1960s and 1970s abandoned Redfield's and Lewis's implicit optimism about modernization, the pioneering work of Lourdes Arizpe, Arturo Warman, and Cynthia Hewitt de Alcántara made rural women more visible as vital but exploited income earners in peasant households squeezed by the pressures of commercialization and capitalization.[2]

Since the 1960s, prominent scholars of gender in Mexico and Latin America, including Lourdes Arizpe, Lourdes Benería, Susan Bourque, Carmen Diana Deere, Magdalena León, Gita Sen, Fiona Wilson, and Kay Warren, have challenged three assumptions about the rural household as a unit of production.[3] First, in terms of the gender division of labor, they emphasize men's primary control over most agricultural tasks but highlight women's contribution to both reproduction and production. While women meet household needs in food procurement and preparation, child care, nursing, and household maintenance, they also engage in a variety of productive activities, including harvesting, animal husbandry, cottage industries, wage labor, and marketing. Second, feminist scholars probing the reasons for women's subordination within families have found that patriarchal values persist despite capitalist development and vary in their impact and expression according to class, race, ethnicity, marital status, and age. Third, these scholars challenge developmentalists' arguments that both rural men and women benefit from the expansion of capitalism. On the contrary, the penetration of capitalism takes advantage of the surplus of cheap female labor at the same time that women must become increasingly engaged in income-producing activities to ensure the survival of their peasant families. Women's work—considered no more than a complement to men's labor—is severely undervalued, and they appear to be even more marginalized by the development process than their male counterparts.[4]

Although scholars of rural gender practices primarily study household economy and gender ideology since the 1960s, historians of rural Mexico focus on social structure and movements in the context of long-term economic processes and the dynamics of state formation.[5] They study conquest, settlement, and frontier expansion and analyze the impact of capitalist growth on regional variations in land and labor allocation and social differentiation. Although historians have shown how people from diverse sectors of the countryside acted on and shaped the processes of state formation and market penetration, only a handful have noticed women as actors. Scholars reconstructing the histories of great landowning families mention marriage alliances as elements in strategies for accumulating wealth and power, and several note the astuteness of widows who maintained family fortunes.[6] In his pathbreaking study of rural indigenous and mestizo communities in central and southern Mexico in the colonial period, William Taylor focuses on women as victims of domestic violence, leaders of community revolts, and energetic traders and processors of *pulque,* the alcoholic beverage of rural central Mexico.[7] Leticia Reina and Paul Vanderwood recognize female religious figures as oracles and symbols igniting millenarian uprisings: Agustina Gómez Checheb of the Chamula Maya in 1869, and Santa Teresa de Cabora in the rebellion at Tomochíc, Chihuahua, in 1892.[8] Many others have celebrated the Virgin of Guadalupe as the patroness of popular struggle from the late eighteenth century through the Revolution of 1910.

Among historians, John Tutino was the first to adopt the anthropologists' notion of a peasant household productive unit that ascribes an essential economic role to women.[9] When Luis González y González opened rural studies to social history by combining the historian's skills with the community studies tradition, he began to etch a more detailed picture. In the cattle-ranching society of western Mexico, "la mujer trabajadora," he notes, performed more manual labor than the ranchero himself. In addition to her household tasks, she ground corn, stoked the fire, bleached beeswax, made cheese, and wove clothing and blankets.[10] Ramón Gutiérrez has delved into deeper levels of sociocultural history. Combining the insights and concepts of social and symbolic anthropology with the archival skills of the historian, he makes gender, family, and sexuality central to his analysis of Spanish-Indian relations in New Mexico from 1538 to 1846.[11]

The essays by historians, anthropologists, and sociologists collected in this volume elucidate the roles of women and gender relations as rural families negotiated the transition from an agrarian to an industrial society between 1850 and 1990. Each essay is a work in interdisciplinary scholarship. The historians are indebted to the social scientists, who in turn have added a historical dimension to their work. This collaboration is necessary to uncover women's history. Social scientists documenting women in the present have advantages over historians, who often must rely on accounts that ignore women or see them through dismissive male lenses. Social scientists can speak directly with their subjects; rural women of the past cannot speak directly to us, and they left behind little in the way of written records. Women have been traditionally excluded from or marginalized in the areas where the written historical record is strong: in war, politics, intellectual life, property ownership, and large-scale commerce. Social scientists today can observe women in the spaces of everyday life not easily captured in the written record. Moreover, their observations of and dialogues with rural women both enrich and are enriched by the conceptual and analytical framework rapidly evolving in the field of gender studies.

On the other side of the coin, as historians draw from gender studies they make important contributions to scholarship. Behind their attachment to the written record is a concern for daily life as it was integrated into larger, long-term processes of change. Historians are wary of fixed notions of the past or rigid starting points for the dynamics of today. They tend to be skeptical of the propositions that patriarchy existed unmitigated until yesterday, that capitalism began in 1940, and that rural life was idyllic before Coca Cola.

The essays in this volume are divided into three chronological periods. Part 1 focuses on how rural women negotiated the processes of state formation and economic growth from 1850 to 1910. After a period of civil war (1854–67), the dictatorship of Porfirio Díaz (1876–1910) introduced rural Mexico to a process of rapid market penetration that involved the privatization of vast areas of public lands and communal properties, the building of railroads and port facilities, and the influx of foreign capital. Although this process created opportunities for entrepreneurship, capital accumulation, and mobility for women as well as for men, it intensified strains and pressures on the household unit of production by threatening its resource base in land. Economic necessity prompted changes in the familial organization of labor and forced women into new areas of paid and unpaid work.

The essays in Part 2 explore the sociopolitical effects of the Revolution of 1910 on rural women during the years of civil war (1910–17) and state construction (1917–40). The consolidation of the revolutionary state rested on agrarian reform, which prevented the destruction of many farming households threatened by Porfirian economic growth. Although men dominated war, politics, and reform during the Revolution and afterward, new spaces for women were created as well, through both formal processes such as education and informal ones such as increased mobility.

Part 3 deals with rural women since 1940 as they have confronted rapid urbanization and industrialization. Since 1940, the proportion of Mexicans living in the countryside has fallen from 78 to 40 percent. Especially after 1960, a series of factors including population growth, soil exhaustion, declining terms of trade, and a renewed concentration of resources in the hands of a few undermined the viability of peasant agriculture and presented new challenges and opportunities to rural women.

Throughout the period under study, the ways rural women shape transitions and carve spaces for themselves within the context of patriarchal gender ideology and macrostructural constraints are examined at four levels. At one level, women are depicted as individuals navigating periods of economic expansion and contraction by changing their work patterns and venues, migrating and trading, and buying and selling property and goods. They endure the violence and deprivation of wars and revolution, to which they make vital contributions. As artists, they draw upon generations of accumulated knowledge and craftsmanship to fashion their gardens and kitchens into social and spiritual spaces, transcending mere economic utility.

At the second level, many of the essays situate women within the context of the rural household. Rural families vary according to social class, property ownership, and productive assets, but most of the essays focus on the peasant household as an evolving unit of production and consumption. Peasant households populated the Mexican countryside in both indigenous and mestizo regions in the mid-nineteenth century. Units of subsistence production, they utilized family labor and marketed only small surpluses. Peasant households earned a living as smallholders, tenant farmers, and sharecroppers; as resident peons and day or seasonal laborers; and by supplementing subsistence farming with artisan production, trade, and migratory labor.[12] These families must be distinguished from families of higher economic status—those owning haciendas, plantations, or ranchos that produced large marketable surpluses and employed nonfamily labor.

A third venue for defining women's spaces is the community. In the opening essay in the collection, Florencia Mallon presents a concept of community based on principles of democratic patriarchy in which the oldest men control politics, property, production, and religion. Women and younger men accept subordination in return for the elders' safeguarding of community welfare. Mallon applies this concept to indigenous agrarian villages in the Puebla sierra in the mid-nineteenth century. Mallon and other contributors to this volume emphasize the fact that political events and economic processes constantly oblige communities, like families, to renegotiate their relations with the outside world. They also compel communities to redefine their internal relations, including those of class, gender, and age.

Region is the fourth venue for examining women and gender in the Mexican countryside. A region is defined as a geographic space larger than a locality but smaller than a nation-state, with a boundary setting off some economic, political, or cultural system which mediates interactions with outside forces.[13] The essays in this book show that gender roles are differentially constructed within regional socioeconomic systems.

These essays are initial efforts at tracking the experiences of Mexican rural women over the long term, and they suggest the need to modify assumptions and explore new perspectives in five areas: (1) the impact of capitalist penetration and modernization on women's incorporation into the labor force; (2) the changing nature and changing conceptualization of the rural household; (3) evolving constructions of gender ideology and patriarchy; (4) revolutionary processes, resistance, and sociopolitical movements as these intersect with gender identity; and (5) methodologies and conceptualizations in Mexican rural studies.

The essays support the contention that capitalist penetration of the countryside and modernization led to significant female incorporation into the labor force, especially in the least advantaged sectors. In consonance with other scholars, the authors agree that this incorporation drew on and often reinforced ideological notions of women's inferiority and complementarity while enhancing their income-earning capacity.

The essays provide new insights on eight issues. First, they suggest that women were active in agricultural production, property ownership, and related rural income-producing activities before modern capitalist growth. Second, the authors date modern capitalist development in Mexico and its impact on women not from 1940, its favored point of departure for most feminist scholars, but from 1880, when the building of railroads, political stabilization, and legal reforms opened the country to foreign capital and trade. Third, they argue that rural women's incorporation into this process as income earners depended on a variety of regional factors, including prior traditions of gendered labor, gender ideology, and the organization and nature of the family economy as it intersected with market forces.

Fourth, the essays by Francie Chassen-López and Heather Fowler-Salamini stress how social differentiation accompanying land tenure changes and market penetration enabled some women, as family members or single heads of household, to move to more privileged and lucrative levels of property ownership and opportunity while other women had little choice but to take up low-paid, low-status work in the fields or in agricultural processing or to commercialize their domestic skills. Fifth, Piedad Peniche Rivero's essay on henequen haciendas in Yucatán uncovers women's hidden contribution to the profitability of this famous export industry, which supplied International Harvester Company with the binder twine used to harvest North American wheat. Appropriating Mayan matrimonial customs, hacienda owners lent money to male workers to cover the bridewealth for women, thus binding male productive labor in conditions of debt slavery while also securing unpaid female labor to maintain the peon's household— and the hacendado's.

Sixth, the essays by Chassen-López, Fowler-Salamini, and Patricia Arias pinpoint migration, urbanization, and frontier settlement in the late nineteenth century as critical in creating women's economic spaces, whether these were carved out at home to make ends meet in the absence of a migrant husband, or in response to opportunities for land acquisition and trade in newly opening regions, or under the duress of forced migration to tropical plantations. Demographic movement as a critical variable linked to women's economic activities was probably not new; the linkage between male out-migration and women's participation in agriculture has been demonstrated for the colonial period as well.[14] The intimate relationship between twentieth-century women's work and migration is examined in the essays by Arias, Raquel Rubio Goldsmith, Gail Mummert, Maria da Glória Marroni de Velázquez, and Soledad González Montes.

Seventh, the essays suggest that events and processes not directly related to capitalist production facilitated rural women's income-earning activities in the first half of the twentieth century. The revolutionary upheaval in 1910 loosened social structures and constraints on movement. In rural schools women learned new skills, activities, and values. The *molino de nixtamal* (mechanized corn mill) introduced between 1930 and 1950 eliminated the long hours women had spent grinding tortillas.[15] In the same period, the building of highways and roads and the expansion of cheap public transportation facilitated women's travel under secure conditions. The essays by Mary Kay Vaughan, Judith Friedlander, González, Rubio Goldsmith, and Marroni highlight these enabling processes and events, which opened new spaces for women's work at a time when the peasant household could no longer support itself by agriculture alone.

Finally, although feminist scholars have insisted on the subordinate and disadvantaged position of women workers, Arias suggests that global trends in production, including the ruralization of industry, are making rural women more employable than men in certain regions of Mexico. Food processing and *maquiladora* industries in rural areas have relied heavily on women's labor. Arias, Mummert, and González challenge two powerful stereotypes in developmentalist models: the identification of industry with cities and the identification of industrial employment with men.

The second realm of scholarship to which these essays contribute concerns the changing nature of the rural household and its conceptualization. For decades, a debate has raged among "campesinista" scholars and their "decampesinista" counterparts about the survival of the peasant household. Campesinistas such as Arturo Warman and Rodolfo Stavenhagen hold that the Mexican peasantry resisted full proletarianization within the framework of dependent capitalist development by adopting new economic strategies combining self-provisioning with commerce and wage labor.[16] Feminist analyses have enriched the campesinista argument by documenting the critical contribution of women's productive and reproductive work to household income.[17] Implicit in the debate, which has been framed within the context of the post-1960 agrarian crisis, is the notion of a rural household moving away from being primarily a unit of agricultural production and becoming instead a consuming unit drawing wage income from varied sources, including family farming. As the *peasant* household becomes increasingly divorced from agricultural self-sufficiency, it is more convenient to employ the term *campesino* household, a catchall describing low-income rural people in Mexico.

The essays in this collection provide historical depth to this evolution by reconceptualizing the peasant household and focusing on women's contribution to its maintenance. Fowler-Salamini argues that the peasant household is better conceived historically as Deere has defined it: as a heterogeneous family farming unit whose multiple income earners, including women, contribute to family income.[18] The essays in this volume show the historical flexibility of households in responding to macrostructural pressures. Faced with the exigencies of capitalist penetration during the Porfiriato, families adopted a variety of survival tactics, including migration, wage labor, and trade. During the Revolution, as Elizabeth Salas shows, peasant women literally reconstituted their households on and around the battlefields. Between 1910 and 1940, the peasantry struggled to shore up the household unit of production. The tenacity and flexibility of the household, combined with state policies (land reform, education, infrastructural development), contributed to its survival as a primarily agricultural unit until the post-1960 crisis forced a rapid deployment of labor outside the family parcel. Arias traces the historical roots of women's nonagricultural remunerative activities, which have become increasingly vital to household survival since 1960.

A gendered perspective promotes a better understanding of variation and evolution in household organization. Patrivirilocality, or the shared residence of the head of household and his wife and their sons and sons' wives and children, is usually assumed for the family farming economy, and yet the essays show how commonplace female-headed households are and have been as a result of mortality, abandonment, or male migration.[19] In the colorful story of Doña Zeferina Barreto, presented here by Friedlander, the female-headed household is the preferred choice. Further, the authors point to changes in the practice of patrivirilocality as part of the transition from agricultural self-sufficiency to a diversified campesino economy. Several essays note a shortening of the period during which young married couples live with their in-laws. González documents a number of changes in household organization in Xalatlaco, México, as women have increased their income-earning capacity: proliferation of female-headed households, males living with wives' families, and married women returning to their family homes with or without their husbands.

The third area of debate to which this collection contributes concerns changing constructions of gender and patriarchy. Arias argues that rural women have not been able to transform their increased economic power into social or political power. Multiple sociocultural and ideological mechanisms are brought into play to preserve male privileges and female subordination.[20] But the notion of gender as a social construction implies flexibility and change. Arias herself argues that patriarchal norms governing women's behavior vary regionally. González suggests that as the peasant household evolves from one based on family agriculture and organized by the patriarch to a campesino household dependent on a variety of income-producing activities, power relations shift in favor of women and youth. The diversified campesino household, which cuts across ethnic and regional lines, is the focus of González, Marroni, Mummert, and JoAnn Martin. Their essays demonstrate how women's income-earning capacities combine with their invasion of new cultural and institutional spaces (factories, markets, school, travel, recreation, store ownership, and politics) to produce an often tortuous renegotiation of gendered power, spaces, and roles. Women have increased their power in household management and decision making, in determining family size, in the choice of marriage partners and living arrangements, in control over their own earnings, and in community and workplace politics. Even though patrivirilocality persists, the writers note a decline in mother-in-law hegemony, spearheaded by older women themselves, who disapprove of the long-standing custom of daughter-in-law servitude. Wives in Xalatlaco and Quiringüicharo, Michoacán, have also become much less tolerant of male abuse.

Fourth, these essays contribute much-needed insight into processes of revolution, rebellion, and resistance as these intersect with gender identity in Mexican history. Historians have long appreciated the importance of war in Mexican state formation and the fact that rural rebellion has been part of every significant transformation from the conquest to the Revolution of 1910.[21] The essays in this volume offer a fresh understanding of war as social process and ideological construction. Mallon and Salas describe women's essential wartime roles as food providers, and, in the Revolution of 1910, as spies, smugglers, and combat soldiers. Viewed from a gendered understanding of social process, wars were uprooting and terrifying for women, who suffered violence, kidnapping, rape, and abandonment. Conversely, war opened opportunities and weakened social constraints for women just as it did for men. Viewed from the ideological perspective provided by Mallon and Salas, however, the Revolution—like the wars and rebellions that preceded it—engendered a discursive celebration of male prowess that trivialized women's contributions.[22]

Although the essays here essentially support Alan Knight's populist conception of the Revolution as a rural upheaval confronting the destructive forces of Porfirian modernization, they go further and introduce a gender dimension.[23] The Revolution emerges as a patriarchal event. The experience of prolonged armed mobilization tended to heighten pretensions to patriarchal privilege and power. The fact that politicians emerged from the armies solidified men's domination of politics. Much has been written from an urban feminist perspective about the Revolution's limited contribution to women's rights.[24] Women could not vote in national elections until the 1950s; nor were they immediately entitled to receive land. However, Friedlander, Vaughan, González, and Martin suggest that during the Revolution and its aftermath, economic processes requiring women's increased participation, social processes increasing their mobility, and ideological processes that opened arenas for activity, identity, and learning widened women's spaces and subtly altered the patriarchal norms governing women's behavior.

In recent years, resistance to domination has become a major focus for scholars. The instances of resistance described in these essays bring a refreshing gender perspective to processes implicitly viewed as masculine. At the individual level, the women described by Rubio Goldsmith and Marroni invest their creative energies and skills in the construction of private spaces—household gardens in northern Mexico and Arizona and dual kitchens in Atlixco, Puebla. In these domains they assert their social power, forge their identity, and protect their dignity in the face of domination, abuse, hardship, and unwanted change. In war, soldiers such as Angela Jiménez from Oaxaca and La China from Morelos took command—sometimes with cool aplomb, and sometimes in rage—to avenge abuses inflicted by men. Doña Zeferina Barreto of Morelos takes pride in her ability to resist demanding urban employers, greedy brothers, bandits, and unwanted suitors as she constructs her highly autonomous sense of identity.

The essays also describe women's participation in collective movements—their struggle to preserve communal integrity in mid-nineteenth-century Oaxaca and Puebla and their resistance to the government's antireligious policies in the 1930s. In these movements women acted to preserve customs, values, and traditional spaces. Indeed, the major political mobilization of rural women in the Mexican Revolution may well have been their successful defense of the Catholic religion against government campaigns to curb it as a backward ideology.[25] But women in collective movements promote change as well. Marroni notes their increasing involvement in campaigns for community services in rural Atlixco, and Mummert refers to trade union struggles among strawberry packing plant workers in Michoacán.[26]

In the final essay in the collection, Martin examines questions of gender identity as they intersect with social movements and the social-ideological construction of community in the town of Buena Vista, Morelos. Martin's narrative illustrates how the relatively closed community, visualized by Mallon in the book's first essay, has been penetrated by capitalist growth and modernization in ways that have altered gender relations and deepened class fissures. The women of Buena Vista organized themselves to subvert the notion of democratic patriarchy and to assert their collective obligation to intervene in politics in order to preserve community and family welfare from male irresponsibility and corruption. Their discursive articulation and invasion of a new space reflected their accumulated power in the household as skillful income generators and managers of the purse strings in a mixed economy no longer dependent on subsistence agriculture. Over time, the Buena Vista women's organization fragmented, and several members joined the class-based and male-dominated Committee to Defend Communal Land, obliging the latter group to alter its perceptions of gender identity, behavior, and roles.

Although Martin is concerned primarily with the dynamics of gender identity and its continual reconstruction across political and social spaces and competing discursive formations, her essay poses a series of unresolved questions related to politics and social movements. Is rural women's political involvement an occasional act of crisis intervention, or is it becoming more commonplace and consistent? To what extent does women's presence in formerly all-male political arenas alter gender behavior, perception, roles, and identity for both men and women? Must women form autonomous women's organizations and make horizontal linkages with other women's organizations in order to construct a strong arena for entry into the decision-making process?[27] What impact has the urban-based, middle-class professional women's movement had on women's politics in rural Mexico?

Finally, the essays in this volume suggest new methodological approaches and conceptual alternatives for the study of rural women and gender. In their essays about nineteenth-century women the historians imaginatively scrutinize written accounts and archival sources to make women visible: travelers' accounts, including those of anthropologists, agricultural experts, and botanists; hacienda and war records; census data; and untapped municipal and state archival materials related to land distribution, judicial hearings, and statistics. Chassen-López's and Fowler-Salamini's meticulous critiques of census data from a gendered perspective should ease the work of future scholars. The more contemporary essays integrate written sources with oral interviews and participant observation. Oral history and interviewing emerge as indispensable tools for illuminating the dynamics of power within and between usually invisible or dimly perceived social spaces.[28]

Conceptually, these essays differ in the importance they give to Marxist and class analysis and feminist and postmodernist frameworks. Perhaps the most important conceptual contribution of the essays taken as a whole derives from the authors' efforts to understand the interaction between historical agency at the microlevel and macrostructural forces. None of the essays makes a crude linkage between female earnings and empowerment. The economic is mediated by the social construction of gender, which is itself a source of constant tension and struggle. Critical to understanding processes of change is the notion of space. Working outside the home involves more than the income it yields. As Mummert succinctly argues, it involves the penetration of new spaces, of new cultural and social milieus where women learn new activities, values, and skills, forge new identities, and empower themselves. The interaction within and between gendered spaces is at the heart of constantly renegotiated identities, roles, and behaviors. The kind of change that takes place through these negotiations may not be the kind feminists hope for, but neither is it the negation of change promoted by the guardians of tradition. Through local-level negotiations where the exigencies and opportunities introduced by macrostructural forces meet the power of cultural constructs and social groups, women create spaces and shape the transitions that have altered the Mexican countryside since 1850.

NOTES

1. See Silvia Arrom, *The Women of Mexico City: 1790–1857* (Palo Alto: Stanford University Press, 1986); Asunción Lavrín, ed., *Sexuality and Marriage in Colonial Latin America* (Lincoln: University of Nebraska Press, 1989); Carmen Ramos Escandón, "Mujeres trabajadoras en el México porfiriano: Género e ideología del trabajo femenino, 1876–1911," *Revista Europea de Estudios Latinoamericanos y del Caribe* 48 (1990):27–46; Patricia Seed, *To Love, Honor and Obey in Colonial Mexico: Conflicts over Marriage Choice, 1574–1821* (Palo Alto: Stanford University Press, 1988).

2. See Oscar Lewis, *Life in a Mexican Village. Tepoztlán Revisited* (Urbana: University of Illinois Press, 1951); Robert Redfield, *Tepoztlán* (Chicago: University of Chicago Press, 1930); Lourdes Arizpe, *Parentesco y economía en una sociedad nahua* (Mexico City: Instituto Nacional Indigenista, 1973); Arturo Warman, *Y venimos a contradecir* (Mexico City: Casa Chata, 1976); Cynthia Hewitt Alcántara, "Modernization and Changing Life Chances of Women in Low Income Rural Families," Mimeograph, Economic Commission for Latin America (ECLA), May 1979.

3. Gender, in the words of Lourdes Beneria and Marta Roldán, refers to a socially constructed "network of beliefs, personality traits, attitudes, feelings, values, behaviors, and activities differentiating men and women"; see *The Crossroads of Class and Gender* (Chicago: University of Chicago Press, 1987), 11–12.

Important works on gender and rural society in Latin America include, among many others, Lourdes Beneria and Gita Sen, "Accumulation, Reproduction and Women's Role in Economic Development: Boserup Revisited," *Signs* 7.2 (1981):279–98; Susan Bourque and Kay Warren, *Women of the Andes: Patriarchy and Social*

Change in Rural Peru (Ann Arbor: University of Michigan Press, 1981); Carmen Diana Deere and Magdalena León de Leal, eds., *La mujer y las políticas agrarias en América Latina* (Bogotá, Colombia: Siglo XXI Editores, 1986), translated as *Rural Women and State Policy. Feminist Perspectives on Latin American Agricultural Development* (Boulder: Westview Press, 1987); Deere, *Households and Class Relations. Peasants and Landlords in Northern Peru* (Berkeley: University of California Press, 1990); Fiona Wilson, "La mujer y las transformaciones agrarias en América Latina: Revisión de algunos conceptos que fundamentan la investigación," in Deere and León, *La mujer y las políticas agrarias,* 265–90.

On gender in rural Mexico, see, among others, Arizpe, *Parentesco y economía;* Arizpe, "Mujer campesina, mujer indígena," *América Indígena* 35.3 (1975):575–86; Josefina Aranda Bezuary, ed., *Las mujeres en el campo* (Oaxaca: Instituto de Investigaciones Sociológicas de la Universidad Autónoma Benito Juárez, 1988); Beverly Newbold de Chiñas, *Mujeres de San Juan: La mujer zapoteca del Istmo en la economía* (Mexico: Sepsetentas, 1975); Brenda Rosenbaum, *With Our Heads Bowed: The Dynamics of Gender in a Mayan Community* (Austin: University of Texas Press, 1993); Lynn Stephen, *Zapotec Women* (Austin: University of Texas Press, 1991).

On the peasant household unit of production, see Eric Wolf, *Peasants* (Englewood Cliffs, N.J.: Prentice-Hall, 1966); Marshall Sahlins, *Stone Age Economics* (Chicago: Aldine, 1972); A. V. Chayanov, *The Theory of Peasant Economy* (Homewood, Ill.: Richard D. Irwin, 1965).

4. See, e.g., Lourdes Arizpe and Josefina Aranda, "The 'Comparative Advantages' of Women's Disadvantages: Women Workers in the Strawberry Export Agribusiness in Mexico," *Signs* 7.2 (1982):453–73; Marta Roldán, "Subordinación genérica y proletarización rural: Un estudio de caso en el Noreste Mexicano," in *Debate sobre la mujer en América Latina y el Caribe. Las Trabajadoras del Agro,* vol. 2, ed. Magdalena León (Bogotá: Asociación Colombiana para el Estudio de la Mujer, 1982), 75–90; Kate Young, "Modes of Appropriation and the Sexual Division of Labor: A Case Study from Oaxaca, Mexico," in *Feminism and Materialism. Women and Modes of Production,* ed. Annette Kuhn and Ann Marie Wolpe (London: Routledge and Kegan Paul, 1978), 124–54.

5. See the valuable collection of essays edited by Friedrich Katz, *Riot, Rebellion and Revolution. Rural Social Conflict in Mexico* (Princeton: Princeton University Press, 1988); John Tutino, *From Insurrection to Revolution in Mexico: Social Bases of Agrarian Violence, 1750–1940* (Princeton: Princeton University Press, 1986).

6. See, e.g., Edith Couturier, "Women in a Noble Family: The Mexican Counts de Regla, 1750–1830," in Lavrín, *Latin American Women: Historical Perspectives,* 129–49; John Tutino, "Power, Class, and Family: Men and Women of the Mexican Elite, 1750–1800," *The Americas* 39.3 (1983):359–81.

7. William Taylor, *Drinking, Homicide and Rebellion in Colonial Mexico* (Stanford: Stanford University Press, 1979), 38, 53–54, 79, 85–97, 116.

8. Leticia Reina, *Las rebeliones campesinas en México (1819–1906)* (Mexico City: Siglo XXI, 1980), 45–60; Paul Vanderwood, "Santa Teresa: Mexico's Joan of Arc," in *The Human Tradition in Latin America. The Nineteenth Century,* ed. Judith Ewell and William H. Beezley (Wilmington, Del.: Scholarly Resources, 1989), 215–32.

9. "Family Economies in Agrarian Mexico, 1750–1850," *Journal of Family History* 10.3 (1985):259–62.

10. *San José de Gracia. Mexican Village in Transition* (Austin: University of Texas Press, 1974), 49. See also Guillermo de la Peña, "Ideology and Practice in Southern Jalisco: Peasants, Rancheros, and Urban Entrepreneurs," in *Kinship Ideology and Practice in Latin America*, ed. Raymond Smith (Chapel Hill: University of North Carolina Press, 1984), 204–34.

11. Ramón A. Gutiérrez, *When Jesus Came, the Corn Mothers Went Away. Marriage, Sexuality, and Power in New Mexico, 1500–1846* (Stanford: Stanford University Press, 1991).

12. Eric Wolf, *Peasant Wars of the Twentieth Century* (New York: Harper and Row, 1969), xiv; Guillermo de la Peña, "Commodity Production, Class Differentiation, and the Role of the State in the Morelos Highlands: A Historical Approach," in *State, Capital and Rural Society, Anthropological Perspectives on Political Economy in Mexico and the Andes*, ed. Benjamin S. Orlove, Michael W. Foley, and Thomas F. Love (Boulder: Westview Press, 1989), 98, fn. 3.

13. See Eric Van Young, "Are Regions Good to Think?" in *Mexico's Regions. Comparative History and Development*, ed. Eric Van Young (San Diego: Center for U.S. Mexican Studies, 1992), 3.

14. Correspondence with Raymond T. Buve, April 1993.

15. See Arnold Bauer, "Millers and Grinders: Technology and Household Economy in Meso-America," *Agricultural History* 64.1 (1990):1–17; Dawn Keremitsis, "Del metate al molino: La mujer mexicana de 1910 a 1940," *Historia Mexicana* 33 (1983): 285–303; and Oscar Lewis, *Life in a Mexican Village*, 323.

16. For a discussion of the decampesinista-campesinista debate, see Alcántara, *Anthropological Perspectives on Rural Mexico* (London: Routledge and Kegan Paul, 1984), 156–65. For the campesinista argument, see Rodolfo Stavenhagen, "Capitalism and the Peasantry in Mexico," *Latin American Perspectives* 5.3 (1978):27–37; Arturo Warman, *Ensayos sobre el campesinado en México* (Mexico City: Nueva Imagen, 1980). For the decampesinista argument, see Roger Bartra, *Campesinado y poder politico en México* (Mexico City: Era, 1982).

17. See, among others, Carmen Diana Deere, "What Difference Does Gender Make? Rethinking Peasant Studies," in *Women and Agriculture in the Third World*, ed. Simi Afonja (London: Macmillan, forthcoming), 13–15; Arizpe and Aranda, "The 'Comparative Advantages' of Women's Disadvantages," 453–73; Stephen, *Zapotec Women*, 144–55.

18. See Deere, *Household and Class Relations*, 95–147.

19. See the essays by Mummert and Arias in this volume; correspondence with Raymond T. Buve, April 1993; Robert McCaa, "Women's Position, Family, and Fertility Decline in Parral (Mexico) 1777–1930," *Annales de Demographie Historique 1989* (Paris: Societé de Demographie Historique, 1989), 233–43.

20. Arias is not alone in maintaining that women's increased economic capacity does not translate into empowerment within the household; Lynn Stephen makes the same argument in *Zapotec Women*.

21. See, e.g., Katz, *Riot, Rebellion and Revolution*, 3.

22. On revolutionary iconography as a celebration of male power, see Ilene V. O'Malley, *The Myth of the Revolution: Hero Cults and the Institutionalization of the Mexican State, 1920–1940* (Westport, Conn.: Greenwood Press, 1986), 62, 113–44.

23. Alan Knight makes the case for the peasantry's determining role in the Revolution in "The Mexican Revolution: Bourgeois? Nationalist? Or Just a "Great Rebellion'?" *Bulletin of Latin American Research* 4.2 (1985):1–37.

24. The most comprehensive recent work on women in the Revolution is Ana Lau and Carmen Ramos Escandón, *Mujeres y Revolución, 1900–1917* (Mexico City: Instituto Nacional de Estudios Históricos de la Revolución Mexicana, 1993); see also Shirlene Soto, *Emergence of the Modern Mexican Woman. Her Participation in Revolution and Struggle for Equality, 1910–1940* (Denver: Arden Press, 1990), 54–58; Anna Macias, *Against All Odds: The Feminist Movement in Mexico to 1940* (Westport, Conn.: Greenwood Press, 1982).

25. See especially Barbara Ann Miller, "The Roles of Women in the Mexican Cristero Rebellion: Las Señoras y las Religiosas," *The Americas* 40 (1984):303–24; and Marjorie Becker, "Torching La Purísima, Dancing at the Altar: The Construction of Revolutionary Hegemony in Michoacán, 1934–1940," in *Everyday Forms of State Formation: Revolution and the Negotiation of Rule in Modern Mexico,* ed. G. Joseph and D. Nugent (Durham, N.C.: Duke University Press, 1994).

26. See also essays and reports by María del Carmen Magallon C., Carola Carbajal R., Fausto Díaz M., David A. López V., Carmen Velasco H., and Gallia Arrillaga, in Aranda, *Las mujeres en el campo,* 409–47.

27. Stephen, *Zapotec Women,* 243–49.

28. For a stunning illustration, see Ruth Behar, *Translated Woman: Crossing the Border with Esperanza's Story* (Boston: Beacon Press, 1993).

PART ❀ ONE

Women, Communities, and Agriculture in Nineteenth-Century Mexico

1

Exploring the Origins of Democratic Patriarchy in Mexico: *Gender and Popular Resistance in the Puebla Highlands, 1850–1876*

Florencia Mallon

*I*n April 1985, when I first drove over the winding, narrow dirt road that leads to Xochiapulco, it became obvious why it had been possible for guerrillas to maintain their resistance activities in the area. The red earth on the jagged hillsides was covered with luxuriant vegetation, and clumps of evergreen and deciduous trees were everywhere. In the afternoon the clouds slowly dropped down, covering and caressing the mountaintops with billowy white. Old documents that described the frequent fogs and rain and the harsh nature of the terrain suddenly made a great deal of sense. This was clearly a region where successful and continuous occupation would have been nearly impossible for those who did not know the ground intimately and did not have social and family networks on which to rely.[1]

Between 1850 and 1874, Xochiapulco was the center of a guerrilla movement involving a significant sector of the indigenous peasantry in the Puebla highlands. Initially, guerrillas from a core area of Nahua and Totonac villages in the central and northern part of the sierra—including Tetela de Ocampo, Tenampulco, and Tuzamapan—had fought local conservatives and other liberals for control of local revenues and municipal government, and for more autonomous access to land and markets. Between 1861 and 1867 they resisted the invasion of French troops and the army of Emperor Maximilian. Finally, after the defeat of the empire in 1867 and continuing into the mid-1870s, the same guerrillas fought against the reconstituted Mexican state,

3

attempting to win for themselves the rewards and political participation they felt they deserved for defending their country.

Though they never received the recognition they desired, the indigenous guerrillas of the Puebla highlands were not defeated. Repeatedly throughout these years, fielding only a thousand men—most armed only with garrotes—the guerrillas fought French, Austrian, and Mexican armies to a stalemate. As their enemies clearly understood, the secret of the guerrillas' success lay in the consistent support they received from their communities. And Xochiapulco, perched on a narrow hilltop between two ravines that rapidly climb on both sides once again to form two other mountain ranges, was the quintessential stronghold of the movement.[2]

During my initial visit to the village I saw how stubbornly and dramatically the resistance had been preserved in local historical memory. An exhibit of Austrian bones was on display in a cabinet in the municipal building along with a cannon captured from enemy soldiers. The municipal secretary, a wizened old man with a wool hat perched on his head and a dog at his feet, informed me that to talk of the French Intervention would take weeks, and frankly, he had too much work. The villagers knew where the trenches had been in the forest and took me on a tour.[3]

I also met Donna Rivera Moreno, a retired schoolteacher who taught me more than anyone else about the nature of local consciousness. Considered an eccentric by the village population, Donna Rivera lived alone and supported herself through healing, her pension, and some subsistence agriculture. She had a suspicious, critical attitude toward everything and everyone, born almost surely of her own partial marginalization (as a single, independent woman) from local community life. At the start, she wanted very little to do with me and almost did not open her door.

She changed her mind when she discovered that I was studying the guerrilla resistance in Xochiapulco. Her eyes filled with tears at the idea that someone from the outside should be interested in the sacrifices made by her village. From that moment on, our common interest in Xochiapulco's history established a bond between us. She encouraged me to visit her again and stay with her. When I returned a month later, she took me on a tour of the village and its lands. She fed me and fussed over me. She guessed I was pregnant before I knew myself. And after careful negotiations, and with all kinds of special provisions, she finally allowed me access to her most precious possession: a manuscript in which she had collected the local visions of the guerrilla movement and Xochiapulco's role in national politics.[4]

My friendship with Donna Rivera Moreno forced me to confront a paradox. On the one hand, all my research on the guerrilla movement in the Puebla highlands pointed to the exclusion of women from significant political or military roles; yet, on the other hand, the movement among the region's indigenous peasantry was truly popular in that it encouraged local peasants to develop their own vision of the Mexican nation and of social justice, a vision that Donna Rivera's manuscript made clear had survived even to the present day.[5] Thus, despite the invisibility and subordination of women within it, the guerrilla movement seems to have involved and inspired women as well as men. The purpose of this essay is to unravel these two seemingly contradictory strands—the exclusion of women from the guerrilla movement and its popularity among both women and men. Ultimately, my purpose is to understand why Donna Rivera, a critical-minded and independent woman, took it upon herself to become the movement's spokesperson.

The secret to solving this puzzle lies, in my opinion, in understanding how a movement that marginalizes women—and whose very success is predicated, at least in part, on the continued subordination and marginalization of women—can nevertheless offer them something sufficiently attractive to elicit their active involvement and support. In the Puebla highlands between 1855 and 1874, even as they were defined as outsiders to combat, women from the villages involved in the popular resistance participated in constructing a vision of the good society which, following Judith Stacey, I am calling "democratic patriarchy."[6] In the Sierra de Puebla, this vision involved the idea that the "good" family—one in which the patriarch held most of the power but everyone was tied to everyone else by a *reciprocal* bond of mutual responsibility and obligation—was the model for organizing the community and, by extension, the nation. Clearly, such a vision was not egalitarian; yet at the same time, everyone's rights were respected, and everyone had the obligation to work for the welfare of all.

The particular vision of democratic patriarchy I have discovered for the Puebla highlands during the mid-nineteenth century is ethnically specific, based on locally contested and constructed concepts of community and community responsibility. A negotiated compromise among different groups in village society, it emerged with the new possibilities for alliance and political discourse created by the Liberal Revolution of 1855. As had been the case during earlier periods of transition and crisis, the 1855 Revolution and the resistance to the French Intervention opened up new possibilities within communities. In their ongoing generational struggles with their more prestigious elders, younger, indigenous, and less economically powerful men found that they could gain access to prestige by serving in the national guard battalions—not through the established channels of communal officeholding, but through physical bravery, loyalty, and direct connections to the liberal state. The national guard's institutional link to the liberal army, and thus to the local branches of the liberal state, also provided an alternate route to mediation with the outside. Both internally and externally, therefore, the liberal movement organized around the village national guard battalions presented a new conjuncture in the ongoing construction of communal politics.[7]

National guard soldiers and their leaders occupied this dual space in local political culture with a great deal of creativity and dynamism. On the one hand, they combined local indigenous concepts of community and collective responsibility with radical definitions of liberal citizenship, nurturing a democratic vision of how society should be organized. According to this perspective, elected municipal officials should be responsible to all of the community's citizens, distributing tax and labor obligations, as well as revenues, in an equal manner. On the other hand, the national guards used their position in local society, and the ideology of reciprocity that stood at the center of communal consensus, to conceptualize a more egalitarian relationship to the central state. At the state and national levels, the people should have the right to choose their own representatives and to demand responsiveness and access to political and economic participation for all. As defined by the national guards of highland Puebla, then, the nation was made up of all its citizens, and the state had an equal obligation to underwrite the prosperity of all.[8]

Democratic patriarchy thus emerged from the interaction of communal hegemony and liberal struggle. At its very center stood ongoing negotiations among male villagers over the sources and legitimation of local power and prestige. In these negotiations, national guardsmen held new access to state power and controlled the local means of violence and self-defense. Yet any reference to or use of communal solidarity by national guards had to go through the *pasados* (elders), the custodians of "legitimate" communalism who were themselves the very embodiment of communal notions of justice—of the concepts of reciprocity and responsibility contained in the idea of the good patriarch. This mutual recognition of power and influence underlay the construction of democratic patriarchy.[9]

But equally important to the concept was the oxymoronic tension between democracy and patriarchy. Democracy, in this case, meant the extension of influence and prestige to men who had previously been on the fringes of the system of communal power. Patriarchy signified the ongoing exclusion of women from this expanded definition of citizenship. And the oxymoronic tension was also present in the social and cultural struggles through which democratic patriarchy, as an emerging form of popular political culture, was built.

Democratic patriarchy was not only a negotiation among men, it was also an attempt by village peasants, women and men, to bridge the practical and ideological gap between their own dynamic and contested concepts of mutuality and justice and the new possibilities emerging along with the Liberal

Revolution. Literally in the heat of battle, the men and women of the Puebla highlands struggled to make theirs the ideas of individual freedom and equality contained within nineteenth-century liberalism. Situating these ideas in a context of indigenous communalism and reciprocity, highland peasants tempered the individualism and strengthened the promises of equality. In so doing they fashioned a liberal vision quite distinct, in class and ethnic terms, from the vision held by many citified intellectuals. At the same time, however, their vision was a gendered one in which the possibility of equality was necessarily mediated through existing patriarchal traditions and relationships.

During the conflictual two decades between the Liberal Revolution and the start of the Porfiriato in 1876, highland peasants participated in a pro-tracted guerrilla struggle to put their own stamp on the process of nation-state formation. Within this struggle, however, women and men—as well as different ethnic groups within the peasantry—had distinct ideas about where the conflicts of the period should lead. In this essay I will analyze the gender dynamic in these different ideas. At the end I will apply my analysis to a gendered understanding of political struggles, especially as it might pertain to an understanding of the Mexican Revolution of 1910.

Gender and Popular Resistance in the Puebla Highlands

In her study of women and the military, Cynthia Enloe argues that the establishment of a clear distinction between home front and battlefield is central to the maintenance of military power. This distinction, however, is difficult to discern in practice: combatants and noncombatants, women and men, exist in close proximity to each other in wartime. Civilians engaged in the support tasks necessary to maintain an army have often outnumbered soldiers in military campaigns. So how does one define the battlefield, that terrain over which the military should have complete control? Enloe's his-torical description of these definitions puts gender and gender relations at the very center of military operations.

From the very beginning, Enloe argues, women were near the battlefield, serving in a variety of support tasks that often put them in as much danger as the soldiers. Yet despite this reality, a gendered distinction between home front and battlefield placed women in the former and men in the latter. The purpose of such a distinction was to make women's contribution to the war invisible, controlling their labor power in a variety of reproductive tasks and defining any participation in wartime production as "temporary"—until the men came back. The image of a woman sitting by the fire waiting for her man, needing to be defended from danger, weak where men are strong, served as a powerful bond among males that helped to control soldiers and keep them fighting, despite danger and despite divisions by rank, class, ethnicity, and race.[10]

In spite of the popular and community-oriented nature of guerrilla warfare in the Puebla highlands, the definition of women as "outside" combat had similar implications. It kept their gendered labor for the war effort invisible and facilitated their marginality from the status and rewards that came from war and political struggle. This marginalization of women increased the size of the promised piece of the pie—in the form of land and political participation—for male combatants, the only "real" contributors to the war. And in a very direct way, the exclusion of women helped to extend and reproduce support for the resistance among the male population of the villages and across potentially divisive class or ethnic lines.

Contrary to the prevailing ideology, however, the gendered labor of women was crucial to the daily conduct of war. The local guerrilla force in the Puebla highlands, based in a core area of five villages, needed about 150 to 200 rations of tortillas daily from each town. According to the military requisition documents I have found, a ration consisted of 12 tortillas. This meant that the women in these towns, in addition to their other tasks, made between 1,800 and 2,400 tortillas every day. When one takes into account all the related tasks—husking, degraining, and soaking the corn; hauling the wood and water; building the fire; grinding the corn; and making and cooking the tortillas themselves—the amount of additional work women had to perform is staggering.

As a point of comparison, Oscar Lewis says that in twentieth-century Tepoztlán before the existence of a mechanized corn mill, the women in the Martínez family were forced to rise at two o'clock in the morning during the heaviest points in the agricultural cycle in order to prepare rations for the three to four men headed for the fields. Even if many of the combatants in the Puebla highlands were from the same villages that were providing the rations, it is doubtful that any family provided a majority of its male members to active combat duty at any given moment. Thus, women's work was multiplied significantly by the war effort, belying the assumption that "women had to do this work anyway."[11]

The ideological separation of women from the battlefield, and their consequent invisibility as laborers and participants, also delegitimized any right they might have to independent reward on the other side of the conflict. This was especially clear in the privatization of communal land by individual title. In Tetela de Ocampo, for example, an important guerrilla town, sixty-one separate municipal plots were parceled out between 1867 and 1871 to individual townspeople, most of whom had participated in the resistance. Not one of the sixty-one plots went to a woman. In neighboring Xochiapulco ten years later, land was given to guerrilla fighters according to their rank in the guerrilla army. Women obtained access only as wives, mothers, or other family members.[12]

Men's sense of entitlement to the rewards of conflict was also intensified by women's marginalization in the area of political participation after the war. The first confrontations in the region during the Restored Republic revolved around the 1867 election for state governor and the manipulation of the popular vote. After nearly two decades of violence and war, highland villagers nevertheless felt that democracy and political accountability were sufficiently important issues to cause them to take up their arms again and confront the Mexican federal army. At this point, however, "popular democracy" meant universal *male* suffrage.[13]

Even before the mid-nineteenth-century wars, villages in highland Puebla had not been paradises of solidarity. Quite the contrary. Access to land and markets varied widely, as did education and political influence. Within municipalities, *sujeto* (politically dependent) villages often had more Indian inhabitants when their *cabeceras* (district or municipal capitals) were mestizo- or white-dominated. The sujetos were often Totonac, a more oppressed indigenous group, when the cabecera was Nahua. In this context, the general sense of male entitlement made possible by the marginalization of women helped paper over any ethnic, generational, or class divisions that might otherwise have separated male combatants. Men with less prestige or resources could claim patriarchal privileges because of their participation in combat and their service to the nation. Such was the case with Domingo Ramos, an Indian soldier from the village of Tzicuilan. After the conflict was over, Ramos decided that he had a better right to the daughter of his fallen son than the child's mother did. The local judge refused his claim, arguing that Ramos had not contributed anything to the support of his grandchild in the two years since she had been born. Ramos then used his contacts in the local battalion of the guerrilla army to enter the house of the mother and try to take the child by force.[14]

War is not only battles, Nancy Huston argues; it is also discourse. Victory in war involves not only physical conflict and the gaining of spoils but also the right to control how the story is told. In the long run, it is the story, the narrative of war, that endures. And this narrative is defined not only by those who tell it but also by those who listen: by those who witness and cry. In Huston's view, women serve as mirrors and symbols; they define the ideological arena where war's victories are decided. Women are the outsiders against whom the war experience is defined. They are motive, pretext, booty, reward. Along with the nation, they are valuable objects to be defended or claimed. They care for the troops, mother the soldiers, cry for the dead, suffer rape by the enemy. "If women were not 'present in their absence' on the battlefield," Huston concludes, "*nothing would happen there worth writing home about.*"[15]

In the Puebla highlands, the ideological separation of women from the battlefield is clear in two distinct ways. First, in the oral traditions that have survived in Xochiapulco, women are presented as witnesses and outsiders to the war experience. In one account Pascuala Martínez, a ten-year-old girl, returns from a cave where she has been hiding and encounters piles of enemy corpses—the remains of an ambush by the guerrillas of Xochiapulco—being thrown into a mass grave. Wives and mothers, in two other accounts, also hide in caves until they are "rescued" by male soldiers.[16]

Second, women's discursive separation from battle allowed them to become symbols of men's revenge. The victors could rape women as part of their booty, or to punish their enemies. Thus, during the 1858–61 civil war, one Mexican troop detachment entered the town of Tlatlauqui repeatedly over a two-week period, purposefully singling out the indigenous neighborhoods and systematically raping the women as well as pillaging the houses. As a local official pointed out, there seemed to be no reason for this, since the town gave them everything they demanded. The reason for the attack becomes clear only when the different liberal detachments involved are identified. The invaders were allied with Miguel Cástulo de Alatriste, while the indigenous soldiers in the area had been collaborating with forces under the command of Juan Nepomuceno Méndez and Ramón Márquez Galindo, who were defending the region's Nahua and Totonac villages from Alatriste's land-greedy allies in neighboring Teziutlán. Punishment for insubordination thus took the form of systematic rape; and the message was clear to the Indian men of Tlatlauqui. Forming a group, they followed the troops on their first visit and attempted to protect "their" women.[17]

In both economic and ideological terms, then, the invisibility of women in the guerrilla war that raged in the Puebla highlands between 1855 and 1874 served to motivate male soldiers. Economically and politically, the definition of combat as "men's work" limited the conflict's rewards to men; ideologically, war was fought, at least in part, to defend women. In an important sense, of course, this is no different from most wars, and it ties in nicely with the work of Enloe and Huston on the economic, political, and ideological functions of women's marginalization from combat. The added wrinkle here is the relationship of women's subordination to the development and power of democratic patriarchal ideology, and the power of that ideology to motivate both women and men.

Patriarchal Democracy in the Sierra de Puebla

The guerrilla forces in the Puebla highlands nurtured and were nurtured by a democratic vision of how society should be organized, a vision that was patriarchal to its very core. It rested on three interconnected pillars: first, the indigenous community, which the guerrillas saw as the model for all forms of political organization and interaction; second, the identification of justice with the vision of the "good patriarch"; and third, the obligation of all community members to struggle for these common principles. Let us examine each in turn.

As the indigenous guerrillas and their adversaries knew, the success of the local forces depended on maintaining a good relationship with the community. Through two decades of active combat, guerrilla leaders were always careful to consult community leaders and to legitimize their decisions to enter combat by holding community assemblies. Aside from the clear ideological and political benefits, community support was also crucial at the material level, since only through local communal networks could soldiers maintain the constant flow of goods and intelligence they required. The importance of this communal connection was not lost on the guerrillas' adversaries. At one point during the 1868–70 civil war General Ignacio Alatorre, veteran of the resistance against the French and leader of the repression against his ex-comrades, found that he could not overcome the guerrillas, even with an entire division of the regular army and 1,200 national guard troops from Puebla City. He suggested that the only way to break the resistance would be to establish a military colony in the area to take charge of maintaining the peace.[18]

What is perhaps less obvious is that the community solidarity upon which the success of the resistance rested was a political and social construct. Communal consensus, when arrived at, was the product of complex articulations of interests, discourses, and perspectives within village society. Alliances across age, gender, ethnicity, and wealth differences were difficult to achieve because each represented a choice that excluded—as well as included—the visions and needs of different factions. The practice of alliance, moreover, often played with shifting boundaries between inside and outside, sometimes setting the bounds around the community as a whole, sometimes around sectors of the village. Where the boundary was set—the very definition of "outside"—depended on the particular issue or conflict at hand.

In this sense, the word *hegemony,* as defined by Ernesto Laclau and Chantal Mouffe to denote the practice of political articulation among different discourses, is most relevant here. Communal consensus was achieved through the construction of a communal hegemony in which a multiplicity of perspectives or discourses were articulated together along lines of equivalence or shared purpose, while boundaries were set along lines of antagonism that defined "inside" and "outside." Defining equivalences and antagonisms was a constant practice of inclusion and exclusion, and the line dividing them could shift at any time.[19]

Yet communal hegemony did emerge out of these struggles: ongoing negotiation and mediation of conflict created vital, changing institutions through which people constructed and modified communal political culture. What had emerged by the mid-nineteenth century in the Sierra de Puebla, combining the disruptions and changes set into motion by colonialism with the new experiments in municipal government brought about by independence, was a new form of communal hegemony. Organized around a civil-religious hierarchy of officeholding that unified municipal and *cofradía* (lay religious brotherhood) posts into a single cargo system, this new form of politics was a negotiated solution among communal factions—especially between younger and older men, or spatially organized lineages and neighborhoods—of how to redefine and control power at the local level.[20]

Though not all men were equally successful within it, the cargo system did provide a sequential, age-defined path along which men could pass in their progressive attainment of communal authority and prestige. Indeed, most males participated in some way in the *mayordomías* (sponsorships) responsible for the upkeep and veneration of the saints associated with the larger villages and the cabecera. Expenditures in goods, labor, and money involved whole families, with wives of *mayordomos* supervising the other women in food preparation, dressing the saint, and other tasks. Thus men with the largest labor pool within their families had the easiest time fulfilling their obligations. As Lourdes Arizpe observed for the twentieth century, "the strength and preservation of the Indian cargo system . . . was related directly to the maintenance of the norms of patrilocality and gerontocracy within the household group."[21]

It was on this cargo system, itself based on the patriarchal control of labor and other resources according to gender and age, that the system of communal politics rested. By the mid-nineteenth century, the various ritual obligations associated with the mayordomías were interlaced with a series of civil posts tied to the municipal administrations of the *sujetos* and cabeceras. Though the religious cargos carried the greatest prestige, the men who proved able to hold all the posts in the civil-religious hierarchy evidenced the deepest commitment to community service as well as the capacity to marshal the necessary human and monetary resources to earn the respect of their fellow villagers. These men became the *pasados*, or elders, the most important and revered members of the community, who met in *juntas* to make all the important decisions: they nominated people to fill posts, decided on a course of action in moments of crisis, mediated internal or external conflicts, and supervised all the officials who represented the community in its dealings with the larger society. By combining political and religious offices and making all positions subject to surveillance by the pasados, the cargo system also provided for communal supervision over the new institution of the *municipalidad* (municipal government)—a different, and potentially divisive, source of local power and mediator with the emerging postcolonial state.[22]

The relationship of elders to the community as a whole represented both the limitations and the strengths of communal democracy. Although, by definition, women and young men could not be pasados, the attainment of this status did not rest exclusively on economic or ethnic prestige. On the contrary, the prestige associated with being an elder was constructed by proving one's willingness to work for the benefit of the community. Local offices were not filled only on the basis of ethnic or linguistic criteria, either. In fact, judges and local officials often did not speak Spanish well and sometimes could not read or write.[23]

It was the combination of kinship networks and the cargo system that gave the community its identity and legitimacy: "Our community, composed of its families and pasados," was a customary way of opening a petition or other document.[24] The relationship between family and community was a reciprocal one. The authority of elder males, as well as their responsibility to look after the common welfare, was clearly understood in both institutions; and the maintenance of this authority in one institution reinforced its maintenance in the other. In the community, pasados had an obligation to earn their authority and prestige continuously by advising, representing, and risking themselves for the common good. Only in this way can we explain, for example, the confusion of the Mexican Defense Ministry in 1869 when officials were trying to decide what to do with the captured guerrilla leaders from the indigenous town of Cuetzalan. Military sources insisted that these leaders were dangerous and should be sent into internal exile, but officials in Mexico City had a hard time believing this judgment because the average age of the prisoners was ninety-two![25]

Patriarchs within families had parallel responsibilities. Just as los pasados had to protect the community as a whole, male elders in families had an obligation to look after and protect their dependents. Given the interdependence of the two institutions, moreover, community authorities could legitimately intervene to preserve the mutuality of family reciprocal relations. An abusive patriarch threatened not only his own dependents but also the collective fabric of the community; thus he had to be subject to community authority.

An excellent example of the interconnectedness of gender and community relations is provided by the case of Gabino Mora in the village of Los Reyes. In May and June 1868, the community of Los Reyes attempted to exile Mora. The documentation provided by the Juez Constitucional of the town to the relevant authorities indicates that among the various offenses committed by Mora (which included public drunkenness, debt, and lack of respect to local authorities) was his mistreatment of the Indian woman he lived with. He slapped and punched her, sometimes chasing her with a knife. The juez goes into detail on Mora's treatment of his companion, concluding that "there are few occasions when this poor woman [*infeliz*] does not have her face bruised, due to the constant torment [*mala vida*] that he gives her." Interestingly, and in this context key to our understanding of the role played by a gendered ideology of reciprocity in structuring local relations more generally, Mora's mistreatment of his partner was given the most detailed treatment of any of the charges. One can speculate that this was the case not only because of the actual damage done to the woman but also because Mora's unwillingness to accept his patriarchal responsibility dovetailed, in a cultural and symbolic way, with his lack of respect for the patriarchal authority of local officials.[26]

In the reinforcing relationship between family and community, and in the mutual obligations that tied different community and family members to each other, lay the basis for identifying justice with the reciprocal relations maintained by the "good" patriarch. Pasados were just if they protected their community and sacrificed themselves in the common interest. Municipal officials were just if they mediated equally between citizens and assured everyone's access to subsistence, as a good father would. State officials were just if they were responsive to the needs of all their "children." In this context, it is especially interesting that Juan Francisco Lucas, the most famous and prestigious leader of the guerrilla resistance, became known in his later years as *el patriarca de la sierra* (the patriarch of the highlands). He took seriously his obligation to watch over the common good, even as he grew older, wealthier, and more powerful. At one point, for example, he petitioned local municipal officials to carry out a *deslinde* (legal fixing of boundaries) between his estate and the neighboring village. As he explained in the document, it was not a question of existing conflicts but rather of preventing future strife; he wanted to make sure that everyone was happy with the boundary and that good relations were maintained. The role of the good patriarch was to guard the peace by acting justly.[27]

The guerrilla war was predicated, then, on its identification with the community and on the mutual and reciprocal obligations that tied community and family members to one another. When the good patriarch functioned properly, everyone benefited. Thus, everyone had the obligation to continue struggling for common principles, because the best insurance of justice was to ensure the survival and viability of "las familias y los pasados." The strong attraction of this discourse became especially clear in 1868 when the reconstituted Mexican state sent troops to the Puebla highlands to repress renewed political conflict. The commander of the federal army refused to negotiate; the guerrillas were ordered to lay down their arms unconditionally. In several of the guerrilla strongholds, soldiers met in community council to consider the situation. Even though they knew it meant the renewal of a bloody and unequal war, the people declined the terms of the offer.[28] A document drafted in Tetela de Ocampo gives the following justification for their refusal:

> The citizens of our District conquered with their blood the fame of the land where they were born [against the French invasion] and . . . various fathers mourn the loss of their sons, many widows weep over the absence of their husbands, and many more orphans suffer from lack of the nurture their parents' physical labor used to provide them. With this in mind, how can the fathers, brothers, and friends of these victims abandon the weapons that the dead hallowed with their blood, having carried them until the end of their days?[29]

This is a compelling image. A compelling ideology bound all in a common fight for the good of the collectivity. Women as well as men, young people as well as old, found solace and meaning in it. But at the same time it was a patriarchal ideology. While it allowed for the benefit and participation of all, it was predicated on the continued subordination of women within the collectivity. In a sense, subordination was all the more effective because it occurred in the context of mutual obligation and reciprocity. But wasn't that better than no reciprocity at all?

Democracy, Patriarchy, and the Peasant Community

Unraveling the interconnected threads of democracy and patriarchy in the peasant guerrilla movement of highland Puebla allows us to postulate why Donna Rivera, an intelligent and independent woman, might decide to become its spokesperson. The exclusion of women from combat and the exploitation of their gendered labor were embedded within an ideological and political construct that promised women mutuality and reciprocity. In this context, the promise of solidarity, of family responsibility and collective identity, fired the imaginations of both women and men. At the same time, however, this broad, collectively organized vision of community contained a variety of potential cracks. Two of these, I have argued—ethnicity and class— were partially resolved through the marginalization of women from combat, since this served to unify male combatants in the common defense of "their" women and in their exclusive entitlement to the political and material rewards of the struggle. But one might speculate that gender divisions existed as well—that women's definitions of *collective* and *community* were different from men's, and that women participated in the conflict with the purpose of tilting the result more toward their side.

My speculation here is based on the social, economic, and political changes that were occurring in the Puebla highlands immediately before the Liberal Revolution and the different impacts these had on men and women. Since the 1840s, the Sierra de Puebla had been undergoing a process of economic expansion in which new possibilities for commercial exchange and production had reached fairly deeply into some of the peasant villages. Given existing sexual divisions of labor—women did not participate in the broader economy, or even in much of the agricultural labor—men were in a much better position to take advantage of the new opportunities. Indeed, much of the political conflict during the Liberal Revolution concerned access to land, labor, and commercial routes in the economic expansion then under way.[30] From this perspective, the promises contained in liberal individualism and equality might actually have quite different connotations for men and women within the communities. For men, the tempering of individualist ideology with community reciprocity might be about extending the promise of equality to all males, regardless of ethnic or class origin. For women, confronting liberal individualism with communal mutuality might entail reestablishing the legitimacy and centrality of their labor and prestige, within the family and the village, by limiting the effects of commercialization and differentiation.

The potential contradictions among these different meanings for communalism were worked out in the specific realities of nineteenth-century Mexico, where the indigenous peasants in the coalition of central sierra villages were united in their grass-roots criticism of subordination to a foreign emperor, and later against the abusive power of the central state. Even as different sectors of the peasantry struggled to change the meaning or emphasis of patriarchal democracy, therefore, they also experienced the need to unify in the face of powerful common enemies. On this complex and dynamic historical stage, where powerful and powerless each played important roles, local democratic politics and patriarchal relations were socially constructed and reconstructed—never as the less powerful would have wished, but neither as the more powerful had envisioned.

Basing a popular guerrilla movement on existing communal and familial networks reproduced the subordination of women and put limits on the development of alternative democratic institutions. At the same time, the intense communal controls and village participatory politics that emerged during guerrilla warfare limited private patriarchal power and individual accumulation, conditioning the form of gender hierarchy and relegitimizing the communal base of women's status and prestige. In the Puebla highlands, then, the interaction between communal democracy and patriarchal or generational power fashioned a powerful yet contradictory discourse of democratic patriarchy: a communally based, inclusive form of mobilization that rested ultimately on the continued subordination of half of that community. This discourse provided a language of reciprocity and mutual obligation that inspired people to action; it provided as well a yardstick with which to gauge the accountability and responsibility of leaders to followers, and of all individuals to one another. Yet it also continued to reproduce lines of authority and submission that prevented a more purely egalitarian political culture from emerging.

In effect, the unwritten condition for access to community benefits and protection was an acceptance of the existing division of patriarchal power. From a gender-centered perspective, this helps explain how women, as conscious actors who chose among existing, imperfect alternatives, could ultimately help to reproduce their own subordination. A democratic patriarchy—resting as it did on a reciprocal definition of patriarchal responsibility and privilege, and giving the community ultimate sanction over the behavior of abusive private patriarchs—was better than unbridled private power. Community tradition legitimized the scrutiny of both public and private relations that helped to uphold the rights of the weak against the abuses of the strong. In addition, upholding community practice and ideology in the face of commercialization and differentiation might allow women to shore up the eroding importance of their subsistence tasks and domestic work.

Access to support from the community was predicated, however, on the acceptance of the basic patriarchal order. Scoring partial victories, either as women or as members of a class or ethnic group, meant reinforcing the overall structures of gender hierarchy. Under existing conditions, it seems that accepting the hierarchies embedded in communal hegemony was a precondition to preserving communal cohesion. The strength of popular liberalism, as represented in the negotiations between pasados and national guardsmen, rested paradoxically on this hierarchical solidarity.

Conclusions: Gender and Political Struggle

Despite the specificity of the Puebla case, I think it provides interesting perspectives that can be applied to more recent cases of women's participation in guerrilla movements and other forms of political struggle, not only in the Mexican Revolution of 1910 but also in other Third World revolutions. In the past several decades, women's dramatic participation in revolutionary movements in developing countries has provided inspiration for the abundant literature on women, war, and revolution. Beginning with Vietnam and ending with Nicaragua, women increased their military participation in revolution to the point that, at the time of the final offensive against Somoza's dictatorship in 1979, around a third of the Sandinista army was composed of female soldiers. In Cuba and other revolutionary societies, the passage of legislation designed to further women's equality, both within the family and in the larger society, has also increased the political visibility of women.[31]

Yet, again and again, women's very visibility has generated debates over the long-term fate of women in revolutionary societies. Why has it been so hard for women to maintain or consolidate their gains, even after their important participation in revolutionary warfare and in the initial revolutionary reforms? Why has it been so difficult for women to reach parity with men in positions of political power?[32]

Scholars writing on women and war have postulated that because women have been so consistently defined as outsiders to combat, the times when women do participate militarily can easily be dismissed as unusual, as emergencies. Once things return to "normal" after a revolution, women are expected to go back to their customary prerevolutionary tasks. Thus, scholars have concluded, participation in a revolution—even in combat—does not guarantee equality when the war is over. Despite their egalitarian pretensions, modern revolutionary movements do not have a good record when it comes to consolidating and advancing women's gains on the other side of the victory. Once the military is reconsolidated as a traditional state institution during the postrevolutionary period, there are strong pressures for women to return to their traditional gender roles.[33] Yet, in two distinct ways, this conclusion seems incomplete and unsatisfying.

First, it is important to see the military as one of many state institutions, as a historically changing and internally contradictory institution with many different kinds of spaces within it. In guerrilla warfare, Cynthia Enloe argues, the distinction between battlefield and home front tends to be blurred, and it is easier for women to participate.[34] Periods of intense conflict or social change may also blur existing boundaries, making it possible for women or other dominated groups to take on new roles and define themselves in new ways. Rather than being a structural given, then, the marginalization of women during revolutionary consolidation is a historical process that can vary a great deal according to specific conditions.

Second, and perhaps more important, to attribute the difficulties of women in postrevolutionary situations simply to their structural position as outsiders to war relegates them to the status of helpless victims of the historical process. Yet, as much of the literature on women shows, they have usually been active and creative participants rather than victims.[35] So why the almost universal failure to achieve parity with men, even after major military participation? The challenge is to find an explanation that credits women with the agency they have had, yet at the same time accounts for their ongoing inequality.

If we examine recent popular movements in historical perspective, the concept of democratic patriarchy may prove particularly useful. The communal ideologies that have empowered twentieth-century peasant revolutions may indeed have been anchored in local patriarchal forms. To what extent has the image of the "good patriarch" reappeared in the building of the revolutionary state? To what extent have ideas of collective justice based on concepts of mutuality and reciprocity had their origins in the patriarchal democracy of peasant villages?[36] My analysis of the Puebla highlands suggests that women negotiated and contested the concepts of mutuality and community contained in democratic patriarchy. In so doing they nurtured, from within the very folds of gender hierarchy, the kernels of an alternative. While ultimately helping to reproduce relations that subordinated them, they also strengthened the elements of reciprocal obligation and community responsibility contained within the image of the "good patriarch." At least in part, it was these negotiations from within that connected the "good patriarch" to the "good society," inspiring both women and men. This double-edged quality of democratic patriarchy, product of internal negotiations between women and men, has probably been its greatest strength.

With the questions above in mind, we might do well to study the various historical manifestations of democratic patriarchy. During the Mexican Revolution of 1910, for example, the twin promises of a return to communal democracy and familial solidarity (which often meant only that men would have authority over "their" women) fired the popular imagination. Village-based militias once again attempted generational and ethnic negotiations with communal leaders and defined power sharing in gendered ways. *Soldaderas*, despite their multiple roles on the battlefield, were defined as outside combat; *coronelas* were the exception rather than the rule. And, predictably, in the aftermath of violence and during postrevolutionary institutionalization, women were once again marginalized from political participation.[37] What happened in this case?

Ilene O'Malley explores an answer by examining the process through which images of male revolutionaries emerged in official revolutionary culture. Bourgeois class domination, she suggests, was articulated through the construction of distinct masculinities for different revolutionary heroes. State control was made effective through the discourse of patriarchy, which was used against all women, but also, perhaps even more importantly, against male lower-class rebels, who emerged in this new system as perpetual adolescents confronting the benevolent yet firm authority of the bourgeois father.[38]

It is useful to remember that the metaphor of adolescent rebellion is not simply a trope used by the postrevolutionary state, nor is it only a bourgeois strategy of manipulation. In the Puebla highlands, as we have seen, generational conflicts stood at the very center of the negotiations that constructed communal political cultures and helped to negotiate the contours of democratic patriarchy. The brilliance of the postrevolutionary state, therefore, lay not just in its use of images and discourses of masculinity, but also in its ability to connect to generational conflict, as metaphor and practice, in popular culture.

In this context, the institutionalized revolution of the 1930s and beyond is in part the institutionalization of democratic patriarchy. A massive state-sponsored agrarian reform, the spread of commercial agriculture and increasing opportunities for labor migration, the erosion of communally based forms of access to land—all these trends helped loosen the ties of the gerontocracy, generating new options for women and younger men in the labor force and market economy. As older patriarchs no longer dominated economic choices and mothers-in-law no longer controlled the labor of their sons' wives, the more extreme public-private dichotomy that stood at the center of the Nahua gender hierarchy began to break down. In the twentieth century, women labored in the fields, plied the markets, and migrated to the cities in larger and larger numbers. The importance of mediators and local intellectuals, most often younger men with more years of education, also increased under the hegemony of the Partido Revolucionario Institucional.[39]

Yet, in the long run, using the metaphors and practices of democratic patriarchy for the purpose of social control has ensured that the patriarchal side of the dyad continues to dominate the democratic side in Mexican politics. I hope I have shown, through my analysis of democratic patriarchy in nineteenth-century Puebla, that this is a legacy of the ongoing articulation of communal hegemonic processes to the construction of a national politics. In Mexican political culture, enduring authoritarianisms coexist uneasily with recurring, stubborn democratic counterhegemonies. Both have their roots in the dynamic and contradictory constructions of communal and national hegemonic politics.

NOTES

A different version of this essay appears as Chapter 3 in Florencia E. Mallon, *Peasant and Nation: The Making of Post Colonial Mexico and Peru* (Berkeley: University of California Press, 1994).

This essay is based on research carried out in Mexico between 1984 and 1985 under the auspices of a Fulbright Faculty Research Abroad Fellowship, with additional support from the Graduate School at the University of Wisconsin-Madison. The Institute for Research in the Humanities at the University of Wisconsin financed a semester's leave during the fall of 1987 during which I organized my data and conceptualized some of the issues. My ideas were further refined in presentations at a colloquium at the University of Iowa in February 1988, where I benefited from the support and comments of Florence Babb, Linda Kerber, and Margery Wolf; at Marquette University in March 1988, at the invitation of Carla Hay; to the Social Science History Association in Chicago in the fall of 1988, where I benefited from the comments of Susan Carol Rogers; and at Middlebury College in April 1989. The present version was discussed at the Seminar on Cross-Cultural Feminisms at the University of Chicago in October 1989. Sarah Chambers helped locate the sources on women and war. I also thank Marisol de la Cadena, Steven Feierman, Eileen Findlay, Stanlie James, Nancy MacLean, Leslie Reagan, and Steve Stern for conversations and suggestions.

1. My first visit to Xochiapulco occurred on April 17, 1985, and I made a two-day follow-up visit a month later. The problems involved with militarily occupying Xochiapulco are clear from a variety of documents dating from the Intervention period (1862–67) and the subsequent civil war (1868–72) located in the Archivo General de la Nación, Mexico [AGNM], and the Archivo Histórico de la Defensa Nacional [AHDN], and from the newspapers of the day. See especially AGNM, II Imperio: Caja 78, Report by Austrian Commander Thun to the French Mariscal Bazaine, Las Lomas, Aug. 5, 1865; and Caja 89, Report by Thun to Bazaine from Zacapoaxtla, Aug. 11, 1865; and "Extracto del Parte Oficial sobre el Combate del 2 y 3 de diciembre entre el 6° Batallón de Cazadores y los de Xochiapulco," *El Monitor Republicano,* Dec. 17, 1869.

2. The summary of the guerrilla movement contained in the previous two paragraphs relies on a variety of documents, most of them in the following Mexican archives: Archivo del Congreso del Estado de Puebla [ACEP]; AGNM; Archivo General de Notarías del Estado de Puebla [AGNEP]; AHDN; Archivo Histórico Municipal de Tetela de Ocampo [AHMTO]; Archivo Histórico Municipal de Zacapoaxtla [AHMZ]; Archivo Juárez, Biblioteca Nacional; and Archivo, Secretaría de Relaciones Exteriores.

3. My tour of the trenches was in May 1985; the rest of the events described in this paragraph occurred during my first visit on April 17, 1985.

4. The bulk of my interaction with Donna Rivera Moreno occurred during my second visit, in May 1985. Her manuscript was recently published as *Xochiapulco: Una gloria olvidada* (Puebla: Dirección de Culturas Populares, 1991).

5. Ibid., *passim.*

6. Judith Stacey, *Patriarchy and Socialist Revolution in China* (Berkeley: University of California Press, 1983), especially 116–17.

7. For a more extensive historical discussion of the period and of the struggles within the community, see Mallon, *Peasant and Nation,* especially chaps. 2–4. For an excellent analysis of the national guard, see Guy P. C. Thomson, "Bulwarks of Patriotic Liberalism: The National Guard, Philharmonic Corps and Patriotic Juntas in Mexico, 1847–1888," *Journal of Latin American Studies* 22.1 (1990):31–68.

8. For further elaborations of the concept of nation as constructed by peasants in the Sierra de Puebla, see Mallon, *Peasant and Nation, passim.*

9. Ibid., chap. 3.

10. Cynthia Enloe, *Does Khaki Become You? The Militarization of Women's Lives* (London: Pluto Press, 1983), especially 4–7, 15, 23–24, 211–12.

11. On assigning tortilla rations and on their composition, see AHMZ, Paquete 1869, Expediente [Exp.] 42, July 9–11, 1868, "Productos suministrados a la fuerza en Apulco"; also AHMTO, Gobierno, Caja S/N 1868: Exp. 64, "El Juez de Paz de Huitzilan al Jefe Político de Tetela de Ocampo," July 26, 1868; and Exp. 65, "Oficio del Juez de Jonotla al Jefe Político de Tetela de Ocampo," July 27, 1868. On the tasks involved in making tortillas, and on modern-day calculations, see Oscar Lewis, *Five Families: Mexican Case Studies in the Culture of Poverty* (New York: Basic Books, 1959), 25.

12. On adjudications in Tetela, see AHMTO, Gobierno: Caja 8, Exp. 9; Caja 9, Exps. 3, 6, 10. On the distribution of land in Xochiapulco, David LaFrance and G. P. C. Thomson, "Juan Francisco Lucas: Patriarch of the Sierra Norte de Puebla," in *The Human Tradition in Latin America: The Twentieth Century,* ed. William H. Beezley and Judith Ewell (Wilmington, Del.: Scholarly Resources, 1987), 1–13. I also gained information about this distribution during my visit with Donna Rivera Moreno in Xochiapulco, May 1985.

13. In Mexico, elections after the Liberal Revolution of 1855—all the way through the Restored Republic (1867–76) and the Porfiriato (1876–1910)—were held, on principle, according to the election law of February 12, 1857, which instituted universal male suffrage; see Laurens Ballard Perry, *Juárez and Díaz: Machine Politics in Mexico* (DeKalb: Northern Illinois University Press, 1978). On the 1867 rebellion in the Sierra de Puebla, see Mallon, *Peasant and Nation,* chaps. 4 and 8.

14. AHMZ, Paquete 1869, Exp. 115: "Oficio del Juez Constitucional de Tzicuilan al Jefe Político de Zacapoaxtla," June 23, 1868. On differences within the villages, see Mallon, *Peasant and Nation,* chaps. 2 and 3. ·

15. Nancy Huston, "Tales of War and Tears of Women," *Women's Studies International Forum* 5.3–4 (1982):271–82. The quote is on p. 275; emphasis in the original.

16. "De la tradición hecha de padres a hijos," notes on oral history recovered by Donna Rivera Moreno and included in her *Xochiapulco,* 101–2.

17. AHDN, Exp. XI/481.3/8025: "Oficio del Subprefecto y Comandante Militar de Tlatlauqui al Comandante General del Estado de Puebla," April 5, 1860; "Oficio del Comandante Militar de Tlatlauqui al Comandante General del Estado de Puebla," April 10, 1860. In another document in the same expediente, the commander of the federal army in the state of Puebla explains to the minister of defense that similar abuses were being committed by the same troops in other local Indian villages, and that sections of the local national guard had refused to participate; see "Oficio de Ramón Márquez Galindo al Ministro de Guerra y Marina," Zacapoaxtla, April 13, 1860.

18. The local political process underlying guerrilla warfare is especially clear in the documents preserved in the AHMTO and the AHMZ; see, e.g., AHMTO, Gobierno: Caja S/N 1866, Exp. 7, "Acta levantada en el pueblo de S. Martin Tuzamapan," Aug. 25 1866; "Acta de la Guardia Nacional en Tetela de Ocampo," July 22, 1868; Exp. 90, "Carta de Juan Francisco Lucas al Jefe Político de Tetela," Xochiapulco, June 21, 1868; Caja S/N 1868, Exp. 65, "Oficio del Juez/Alcalde de Jonotla sobre el acta levantada en Tetela," June 6, 1868; Exp. 64, "Oficio del Alcalde de Huitzilan al Jefe Político de Tetela," June 8, 1868; "Oficio del Juez de Huitzilan al Jefe Político de Tetela de Ocampo," July 26, 1868; and AHMZ, Paquete 1869, Exp. 118: "Elección de oficiales por

la Guardia Nacional de Xochiapulco," June 14–15, 1869. For Alatorre's plan, see ACEP, Exps., vol. 15: "Oficio del Gobernador de Puebla al Ministro de Guerra y Marina," June 4, 1870.

19. Ernesto Laclau and Chantal Mouffe, *Hegemony and Socialist Strategy: Towards a Radical Democratic Politics* (London: Verso, 1985). My use of Laclau and Mouffe's concept of hegemony to analyze communal politics, however, does run counter to their method as defined in this book, since they see noncapitalist politics as transparent and therefore not in need of hegemonizing.

20. Mallon, *Peasant and Nation*, chap. 3. For earlier discussions of the historical emergence of cargo systems, see John K. Chance and William B. Taylor, "Cofradías and Cargos: An Historical Perspective on the Mesoamerican Civil-Religious Hierarchy," *American Ethnologist* 12.1 (1985):1–26; and Jan Rus and Robert Wasserstrom, "Civil-Religious Hierarchies in Central Chiapas: A Critical Perspective," *American Ethnologist* 7.3 (1980):466–78.

21. On *mayordomías*, see Lourdes Arizpe, *Parentezco y economía en una Sociedad Nahua: Nican Pehua Zacatipan* (Mexico City: Instituto Nacional Indigenista/Secretaría de Educación Pública, 1973), quote on p. 205; and James W. Dow, *Santos y Supervivencias: Funciones de la Religión en una comunidad Otomí, México* (Mexico City: Instituto Nacional Indigenista/Secretaría de Educación Pública, 1974), 145–47, 176–211; also James M. Taggart, *Estructura de los grupos domésticos en una comunidad Nahuat de Puebla* (Mexico City: Instituto Nacional Indigenista/Secretaría de Educación Pública, 1975), 177–78. Using twentieth-century ethnographies to describe a nineteenth-century reality is always risky, but Arizpe makes it slightly less so by identifying her informants by age and gender. Her oldest informants gave information relevant for the first decades of the twentieth century, and the contextual evidence in the documents I use and the similarity of descriptions across the ethnographies make me confident that these general communal practices also occurred in the second half of the nineteenth century.

22. On prestige gained through holding religious and political posts and the relationship of these to kinship and community, see, e.g., Chance and Taylor, "Cofradías and Cargos"; Rus and Wasserstrom, "Civil-Religious Hierarchies"; Pedro Carrasco, "The Civil-Religious Hierarchy in Mesoamerican Communities: Pre-Spanish Background and Colonial Development," *American Anthropologist* 63.3 (1961):483–97; Frank Cancian, *Economics and Prestige in a Maya Community: The Religious Cargo System in Zinacantan* (Stanford: Stanford University Press, 1965); Hugo G. Nutini, Pedro Carrasco, and James M. Taggart, eds., *Essays on Mexican Kinship* (Pittsburgh: University of Pittsburgh Press, 1975). On Puebla and Tlaxcala, see Arizpe, *Parentesco y economía*; Hugo G. Nutini and Barry L. Isaac, *Los pueblos de habla Náhuatl de la región de Tlaxcala y Puebla*, trans. Antonieta S. M. de Hope (Mexico City: Instituto Nacional Indigenista/Secretaría de Educación Pública, 1974); Hugo G. Nutini and Betty Bell, *Ritual Kinship: The Structure and Historical Development of the Compadrazgo System in Rural Tlaxcala*, vol. 1 (Princeton: Princeton University Press, 1980, 1984); and Hugo G. Nutini, *Ritual Kinship: Ideological and Structural Integration of the Compadrazgo System in Rural Tlaxcala*, vol. 2 (Princeton: Princeton University Press, 1984). On the complex formal and informal roles played

by pasados in village politics, see Dow, *Santos y supervivencias*, 145–47, 153–57, 171–73, 178, 180, 226.

23. In addition to the sources in the previous note, see also María Teresa Sierra Camacho, *El ejercicio discursivo de la autoridad en asambleas comunales (metodología y análisis del discurso oral)* (Mexico City: Casa Chata, 1987), 8, 11–12, 14–18, 25, 109. On ethnic negotiations over positions of power at the local level, see AHMTO, Gobierno, Caja S/N 1866, Exp. 71: "Acta del Pueblo de S. Martin Tuzamapan," Aug. 25, 1866; "Acta del Pueblo de Jonotla," Aug. 24, 1866; "Acta del Pueblo de Zapotitlan," Sept. 3, 1866; Caja S/N 1868, Exp. 66: "Oficio del Juez de Tuzamapan al Jefe Político de Tetela," Sept. 24, 1868; "Oficio del Nuevo Juez de Tuzamapan al Jefe Político de Tetela," Oct. 20, 1868; and AGNEP, Huauchinango, Caja 2 (1861–70), Libro 1863, "Arrendamiento de algunos solares comunales," Nov. 23, 1863.

24. For the use of familial language when referring to the community, see AHMZ, Paquete 1863-65-64, Exp. 222, "Oficio del Juez de Paz de Taitic al Comandante Militar y Jefe Político de Zacapoaxtla," Aug. 2, 1863; Legajo 37: "Carta de Francisco Cortes al Capitán D. Juan Francisco Lucas," Cuetzalan, March 23, 1863; and AHMTO, Gobierno, Caja S/N 1866, Exp. 71, "Acta de la Guardia Nacional de Tetela de Ocampo." For the political role of los pasados, see Exp. 7: "Acta del pueblo de San Francisco Zoquiapan," March 11, 1867; and "Acta del pueblo de Tenampulco," March 16, 1867; AHMZ, Paquete 1869, Exp. 111, "Copia del acta de los vecinos de Santiago Yancuitlalpan," Jan. 17, 1869. On the role of collective pressure in the historical rise of the closed corporate community, see Steve J. Stern, "The Struggle for Solidarity: Class, Culture, and Community in Highland Indian America," *Radical History Review* 27 (1983):21–45.

25. AHDN, Exp. XI/481.4/9893: "Correspondencia entre el Comandante Militar de Veracruz y el Ministerio de Guerra y Marina," Sept. 19–Oct. 1, 1868, ff. 211–14v; "Oficio de Rafael J. García al Ministerio de Guerra y Marina," Oct. 12, 1868, ff. 218–19.

26. The description of Mora's abuse of his companion is in AHMTO, Gobierno, Caja S/N, 1868, Exp. 68, "Oficio del Juez Constitucional de los Reyes al Alcalde Municipal de Tuzamapan," May 20, 1868; see also Exp. 66, "Informe del Juzgado Constitucional de San Miguel Tzinacapan, sobre la conducta de Gavino Mora," May 20, 1860; and "Oficio del Alcalde de los Reyes al Juez de Tuzamapan," June 1, 1860. Steve J. Stern (pers. comm., 1991) has confirmed a similar role of community authorities as checks against abusive patriarchs in Oaxaca in the late colonial and early national periods.

27. AHMTO, Gobierno, Caja 11: "Solicitud de Juan Francisco Lucas al P. Ayuntamiento de Tetela de Ocampo," Dec. 1, 1868. For the general importance of Lucas in the sierra during the last decades of the nineteenth century, see La France and Thomson, "Juan Francisco Lucas," 4–9.

28. For a particularly passionate explanation of the decision to decline Alatorre's terms, see AHMTO, Gobierno, Caja S/N 1866, Exp. 70, "Carta del General Juan Francisco Lucas al General Alatorre," Xochiapulco, July 25, 1868.

29. AHMTO, Gobierno, Caja S/N, 1866, Exp. 71, "Acta de la Guardia Nacional en Tetela de Ocampo rechazando las condiciones impuestas por el General Ignacio R. Alatorre," July 22, 1868.

30. Mallon, *Peasant and Nation,* chap. 2, describes economic expansion in the Puebla highlands.

31. On legislation, see Maxine Molyneux, "Family Reform in Socialist States: The Hidden Agenda," *Feminist Review* 21 (1985):47–64; and "The Cuban Family Code," *Granma Weekly Review* March 18, 1975, 7–9. On Cuba, see Isabel Larguía and John Dumoulin, "Women's Equality and the Cuban Revolution," in *Women and Change in Latin America,* ed. June Nash and Helen Safá (South Hadley, Mass.: Bergin and Garvey, 1986), 344–68; Muriel Nazzari, "The 'Woman Question' in Cuba: An Analysis of Material Constraints on Its Solution," *Signs: Journal of Women in Culture and Society* 9.2 (1983):246–63; and Margaret Randall, *Women in Cuba: Twenty Years Later* (New York: Smyrna Press, 1981). On Nicaragua, see Jane Deighton et al., *Sweet Ramparts: Women in Revolutionary Nicaragua* (London: War on Want and the Nicaraguan Solidarity Campaign, 1983); Susan Ramirez-Horton, "The Role of Women in the Nicaraguan Revolution," in *Nicaragua in Revolution,* ed. Thomas W. Walker (New York: Praeger, 1982), 147–59; and Margaret Randall, *Sandino's Daughters* (Vancouver, B.C.: New Star Books, 1981).

32. On the debates, in addition to the sources in note 31, see Maxine Molyneux, "Socialist Societies Old and New: Progress Toward Women's Emancipation?" *Monthly Review* (July–August 1982):56–100; Molyneux, "Mobilization Without Emancipation? Women's Interests, the State, and Revolution in Nicaragua," *Feminist Studies* 11.2 (1985):227–54; and Nicola Murray, "Socialism and Feminism: Women and the Cuban Revolution," parts 1 and 2, *Feminist Review* 2 (1979):57–73, 3 (1979): 99–108.

33. Enloe, *Does Khaki Become You?,* 160–72; Carole R. Berkin and Clare M. Lovett, eds., *Women, War and Revolution* (New York: Holmes and Meier, 1980); Delia Davin, *Woman-Work: Women and the Party in Revolutionary China* (Oxford: Clarendon Press, 1976), 22–45; and Nancy Loring Goldman, ed., *Female Soldiers—Combatants or Noncombatants? Historical and Contemporary Perspectives* (Westport, Conn.: Greenwood Press, 1982).

34. Enloe, *Does Khaki Become You?,* 160.

35. This is an especially strong theme in Berkin and Lovett's *Women, War and Revolution.* Perhaps the most powerful recent statement about the importance of women's agency throughout history is Gerda Lerner, *The Creation of Patriarchy* (New York: Oxford University Press, 1986), from which I have derived much inspiration.

36. Judith Stacey argues convincingly that the Chinese revolution involved negotiations between party cadre and peasant men over the reorganization—rather than the abolition—of patriarchy; see *Patriarchy and Revolution, passim.*

37. John Reed, *Insurgent Mexico* (New York: International Publishers, 1969), discusses the patriarchal underpinnings of the popular Villista movement; the underlying gender implications of communal democracy in the Zapatista movement are discussed in John Womack, *Zapata and the Mexican Revolution* (New York: Knopf, 1968). Additional analyses of women in the Mexican Revolution of 1910 can be found in Anna Macías, *Against All Odds: The Feminist Movement in Mexico to 1940* (Westport, Conn.: Greenwood Press, 1982); and Elizabeth Salas, *Soldaderas in the Mexican Military: Myth and History* (Austin: University of Texas Press, 1990); and in other essays in this volume.

38. Ilene V. O'Malley, *The Myth of the Revolution: Hero Cults and the Institutionalization of the Mexican State, 1920–1940* (Westport, Conn.: Greenwood Press, 1986).

39. An analogous, though differently timed, process seems to have gone on in Chiapas during the Cardenista period (1930s). See Jan Rus, "The 'Comunidad Revolucionaria Institucional': Indian Resistance and Indian Policy in Highland Chiapas, 1936–1990" (Paper presented at the U.S.-Mexican Studies Center, University of California–San Diego, La Jolla, February 1991).

2

"Cheaper Than Machines": Women and Agriculture in Porfirian Oaxaca, 1880–1911

FRANCIE R. CHASSEN-LÓPEZ

*I*t is the custom among the Chatino Indians of Juquila, in the southern Mexican state of Oaxaca, that at birth, newborn boys are given a machete by their fathers, and girls receive a *metate* and *malacate* (the stone base and stone instrument used to grind maize) from their mothers, representing their future economic roles. Yet the myth of women as "passive, powerless beings, absorbed in familial duties, confined to the home, and totally subordinated to men,"[1] is fast being destroyed. In this essay I challenge the cultural assumption, prevalent at all social levels, that women historically have been confined to the domestic sphere.

In late nineteenth- and early twentieth-century Oaxaca, women of all social classes were engaged in agricultural pursuits. They were not only elite *hacendadas* (large estate owners) but also owners of medium-sized and small tracts of land. In the wave of land speculation that hit the state during the presidency of Porfirio Díaz (1876–1911, known as the Porfiriato), women were among the buyers of the newly privatized lands. As communal landholders, they received parcels when village lands were privatized. Women's names appear on petitions of *terrazgueros* (sharecroppers) protesting abuses by landlords. Women and children as well as men were transported to work as slaves on the infamous tobacco plantations of Valle Nacional.[2]

Nevertheless, historically, women's role in agriculture has been underestimated. The already controversial Porfirian statistics become even more unreliable with regard to women. According to the 1895 census, for example, only 1.3 percent of economically active females in Mexico worked in agriculture, compared with 72 percent of males. In other words, women accounted for only 0.4 percent of the total population dedicated to agriculture. The 1910 figures indicate that 62,000 women worked in agriculture—8 percent of all economically active females (versus 73 percent of males), and 2 percent of the total population working in agriculture. These figures are grossly inaccurate, and they fail to portray the true extent of women's contribution. The 1900 census is even less accurate: it lists no women as agricultural wage earners in the districts of Oaxaca, when, as I will prove below, they did exist.[3] In fact, women were a significant force in agriculture in Porfirian Mexico.

Recent scholarship strives to make rural women's work more visible, in both quantitative and qualitative terms, reevaluating women's participation in a more comprehensive analysis of agricultural activities.[4] It is impossible to understand the situation of Latin American women today without examining the changing role of women in land tenure, agricultural production, and agrarian protest in historical perspective.[5] Similarly, the historical development of agriculture in general cannot be comprehended without incorporating women's contributions.

Women have been involved in agriculture since pre-Columbian times; *cacicas* (women nobles) of the Mixtec civilization owned sizable tracts of land, and women of the elite owned haciendas under Spanish rule. After independence, women undoubtedly maintained their presence in agriculture (although research is almost nonexistent for the nineteenth century), certainly as hacendadas and *minifundistas* (owners of small plots dedicated to subsistence agriculture). This essay, based on an exploratory study, seeks to chart the impact of capitalist agriculture on women during the Porfiriato, mapping out changes and continuities. It attempts to make women more visible by focusing on land tenure and labor conditions viewed from the regional perspective of Oaxacan agriculture.

The study of rural women requires an analysis of their position in the evolving social structure. Rural women's participation in agriculture and in rural wage labor markets differs according to their social class. Women at the middle and lower economic levels—*finqueros* (producers of cash crops), peasants, and agricultural wage earners—tend to be most active.[6]

Lourdes Arizpe and Carlota Botey state that Mexican women became part of the rural proletariat as a result of postrevolutionary agricultural policies and the solidification of capitalist relations of production. The findings presented here challenge this assertion. The growth of women's role in the agricultural proletariat was clearly prerevolutionary. The earlier transition to capitalism required the inclusion of working-class women as part of the rural labor force. This is not surprising; to a certain extent it follows what

Towner and Ramos affirm with respect to women being integrated into the industrial proletariat as cheap labor during the late nineteenth century.[7]

Carmen Diana Deere and Magdalena León, pioneers in this field, have attempted to evaluate how rural women fared in the process of agrarian capitalist development: whether the subordination of women increased or decreased with the advance of capitalist agriculture. Both negative and positive results are evident in Oaxaca. The rise of capitalism in Porfirian Mexico, while it provided new opportunities for elite and middle-class women to own land and become active in agriculture, necessitated the direct exploitation of working-class women, the cheapest rural wage labor available.

Women and the Legalities of Landholding

The Spanish legal system permitted women in colonial Mexico to buy, sell, rent, inherit, administer, and bequeath property. Women also had the right to enter into business partnerships. Widows and emancipated single women could manage their own affairs independently, although wives and daughters needed their husband's or father's consent to act. This situation continued after independence. The legal codes of 1870 and 1884 recognized women as legal heads of households when widows were finally given the *patria potestad* (the powers inherent in legal guardianship) over children and wards. These codes also freed single women from patria potestad when they reached the age of twenty-one.[8]

Although a woman maintained legal ownership of her inheritance, dowry, or *arras* (property given to the bride by the groom on marriage), her husband generally could do anything he wished with her property short of selling it. Wives could challenge poor administration in court, but this was rarely done. Property acquired during marriage was jointly owned, and only *bienes parafernales* (clothes, jewels, or property received during the marriage through inheritance or donation) were under the wife's sole control.[9]

Undoubtedly widows, especially elite widows, enjoyed the best position to administer property and develop economic holdings. Widows and wives with the necessary *licencia marital* (marital consent) were the most visible women in agriculture. It is far more difficult to document the participation of single women.

Hacendadas and Minifundistas

Elite women were historically an economic power in Oaxaca. What little we know about women in agriculture tends to center on elite women as landowners because documentation of their situation is more available. During the late Porfiriato, the largest hacienda in the state belonged to Matilde

Castellanos, the widow of Esteban Maqueo, a wealthy Italian entrepreneur in Oaxaca. On her husband's death, she inherited the Haciendas Marquesanas, sugar estates that originally formed part of the Marquesado del Valle belonging to Cortés. As the owner of the Hacienda and Sugar Mill of Santo Domingo (77,500 hectares) and of the Hacienda La Venta (41,000 hectares), both in Ixtaltepec, district of Juchitán, she was the largest landowner in the state in the early twentieth century.[10]

When she died in 1904, Elena Casalduero de Larrañaga left her wealth to her husband, José Larrañaga. The estate consisted of the Hacienda of San Miguel (430 hectares in San Antonio de la Cal, Centro district), one house on Hidalgo Street and another on Benito Juárez Street, the La Cubana cigarette factory, and the Ciudad de Londres store, all in the city of Oaxaca.

The Trápaga brothers immigrated to Oaxaca from Spain in the middle of the nineteenth century and built up a fortune, including one of the three textile factories in the state. They and their children married well, among others into the family of the wealthiest miner and landowner in Oaxaca, Juan Baigts. By 1912, María Trápaga owned the cereal-producing Hacienda Blanca in Etla (840 hectares), and Margarita Trápaga owned San Pedrillo Hacienda (75 hectares) in the Tlacolula district and continued to expand her holdings. Guadalupe Baigts controlled the 8,780-hectare Hacienda of San Isidro Catano in Etla, which produced cereals and livestock.[11]

Women sometimes donated land for public use. In 1892, Tranquilina de Aparicio was particularly generous in donating a parcel of land for the *fundo legal* (town municipal center) of the new town of Rancho of Rosario Nuevo in the district of Huajuapan.[12]

The widow Juliana Ruiz de Pérez owned the Hacienda of Yogana (more than 3,500 hectares) in the district of Ejutla and the Hacienda of San Nicolás (800 hectares) in the neighboring Miahuatlán district. An examination of a conflict between Señora Pérez and her terrazgueros in 1899–1900 reveals that women in agriculture sometimes confronted one another from opposite ends of the social spectrum. After unsuccessfully attempting to settle differences with the widow on their own, the terrazgueros of the Hacienda of San Nicolás protested to the state government that she was abjuring the *usos y costumbres de tiempos immemoriales* (traditional custom and usage) when she tried to prohibit their livestock from grazing on the hacienda's pasturelands.

Señora Pérez did not bother to attend the meeting set up by government officials to deal with the case, and she received a stiff fine of three hundred pesos. This was later, extraofficially, rescinded, and thereafter she refrained from bothering her tenants. In 1907, her son Roberto, who had inherited San Nicolás on her death, attempted to remove the terrazgueros' livestock from hacienda lands once again, aided by the *jefe político* (prefect) of the district and the mayor of the town. The terrazgueros once again mobilized to defend themselves, hiring lawyer Constantino Chapital, who lodged a complaint against the jefe político for meddling in affairs beyond his jurisdiction. Chapital successfully defended the tenants and got the government to re-affirm their grazing rights. The complaint he submitted lists the names of the 109 terrazgueros; 15 were women.[13]

This legal document is one of the rare proofs that female sharecroppers existed in Oaxaca. It also demonstrates how women acted in accordance with their class position. Señora Pérez moved to strengthen her interests while the terrazgueras struggled to defend their historic rights and customs. Though women might suffer universal subordination to men and the in-stitution of patriarchy, this fact did not create solidarity among them which might cross class lines in agricultural pursuits.

Women were also among the small landowners producing for local mar-kets and the minifundistas struggling to subsist. In 1888 in the town of San Sebastián Teitipac in Tlacolula, there were 393 parcels of land belonging to 152 men and 50 women (probably widows, but this is not specified). Most of the owners had a parcel for growing maize and another for growing wheat. The one hacienda in the village, Santa Rosa Los Negritos, evidently con-tracted the villagers to work as laborers on a seasonal basis, but we do not know if the women landowners also worked as laborers. It is probable that some of them did, because the village listed 225 male and 50 female wage laborers for 1907.[14]

Women were minifundistas in several villages in the Mixteca region. In 1888, in Santa Catarina Adéquez in Nochixtlán district, there were 8 women landowners out of a total of 73, but their holdings seemed to be limited to small parcels. In Santiago Patlanalá in Silacayoapan district, there were 11 female and 127 male landowners in the village, and once again women generally owned the smaller parcels. In Michapa, a particularly fertile village located on a riverbank in the same district, there were no women land-owners at all.[15] All the available evidence indicates that most of the women landowners were widows who had inherited the land or received it by law when the land was privatized, obtaining just enough so as not to become a burden to the municipal government.

Division and Privatization of Communal Lands

One of the key tenets of the liberal reform (1854–67) captained by Benito Juárez, the president from Oaxaca, was the belief in the sanctity of private property. Nevertheless, in 1854 most Mexican lands were corporate holdings, divided between the extensive real estate of the Catholic church (held in mortmain) and the communal lands of the Indian villages. In order to achieve a capitalist economy under liberal principles, the regime of private property had to be made universal so that land could circulate as a commodity. The Lerdo Law of June 25, 1856, later incorporated into the 1857 Constitution, became the cornerstone of this new economic policy: it decreed the disentailment of church real estate and the privatization of communal lands. The latter lands were to be distributed as private parcels among the *comuneros* (communal landholders), with any land remaining to be sold at public auction to private interests.[16] The process was slow, and it was delayed by the Wars of the Reform and the French Intervention (1857–67), but essentially by the beginning of the Porfiriato (1876) the church was no longer a landed power. The alienation of communal lands, however, faced continued resistance.[17]

In Oaxaca, church lands were disentailed, and some communal lands, mainly in the Central Valleys region, were privatized after 1856, a process analyzed by Charles Berry. But the distribution of communal lands in the rest of the state was more problematic. Oaxaca was populated by at least sixteen tightly knit indigenous ethnic groups; in 1878, 76 percent of the population spoke an Indian dialect, although by the 1910 census this figure had decreased to 49 percent. The communal heritage of Indian societies such as the Zapotecs and Mixtecs was the antithesis of economic liberalism, and they staunchly defended their historic right to communal landholdings.[18]

In 1878, Governor Francisco Meixueiro admitted that the villages of Oaxaca had not obeyed the Lerdo Law and initiated a new battle against communal landholding in the state. A series of decrees followed, but the results were discouraging for the liberal authorities.[19] The decrees and circulars reveal a state government concerned about transforming the Indian comuneros into private owners. At least on paper, the authorities tried to ensure that the Indians would not be stripped of their livelihood by speculators.

Although the economy of Oaxaca stagnated throughout most of the nineteenth century, the Porfiriato ushered in a period of economic prosperity. In 1910, Oaxaca was sixth in the nation in size (92,443 square kilometers) and fifth in population (1,040,398 inhabitants). The new growth was based on the exploitation of mineral wealth, mainly the gold and silver mines of the Sierra Juárez and Central Valleys regions, and the expansion of commercial agriculture (coffee, tobacco, sugarcane, cotton, rubber, indigo, and citrus fruits) in the tropical and subtropical areas of the state.[20] The city of Oaxaca became the center of a mining boom after 1892, hosting a considerable Anglo-American community.

Porfirian economics had a major impact on the agriculture and land tenure systems in the peripheral regions of Oaxaca, which had lower population densities and less tightly knit indigenous cultures (excepting Juchitán and Tehuantepec).[21] The construction of railroads and ports provided much-needed cheap transportation, which in turn permitted the development of mining and commercial agriculture.[22] The areas that benefited most were the regions of the state that bordered on neighboring states: the Tuxtepec-Choapan region (Veracruz), the Isthmus (Veracruz, Chiapas, and the Pacific), the Cañada (Puebla), and the Costa (on the Pacific Ocean). The two interior regions of the state, the Sierra Juárez and the Central Valleys, with the exception of the capital city of Oaxaca, generally stayed with the traditional economy based on the local consumption of maize and wheat. The mining boom centered here did not lead to a transformation of land tenure or agricultural production because most of the land had already been privatized. The Mixteca region, about which the least is known for this period, also maintained a traditional economy, although certain districts began to show signs of transformation.

One of the major trends that my investigations on Oaxaca revealed was the rise of what I call the Porfirian *finca*, an agricultural enterprise integrated into the capitalist market. Increasing in significance after 1880, this type of holding was of medium (30–300 hectares) to large (more than 300 hectares) size and dedicated to commercial, often export, agriculture. Frequently, fincas were situated on land originally owned by indigenous communities. I use the term *finca* (which at the time generally referred to a *cafetal*, a coffee holding) to distinguish this type of holding from the more traditional haciendas of the state, which usually cultivated the main staples of the Mexican diet (maize, beans, chile, squash, agave), with little capital input.[23]

William B. Taylor and Thomas Cassidy both agree that the salient characteristics of the hacienda in Oaxaca were its instability of ownership and its nonprofitability as a business venture.[24] *Finca* thus refers to a different phenomenon: the rise of profitable cash crop agriculture in Oaxaca during the Porfiriato, which prospered mainly in the peripheral regions of the state where capitalism was making the greatest inroads.

Aspiring capitalists and an onslaught of speculators forced the division of communal lands, by both legal and illegal means. According to my research, the number of large private holdings more than doubled between 1880 and 1912. Manuel Esparza's "superficial count" of more than one thousand files in the state archives indicates that most privatization took place in Oaxaca between 1880 and 1910, with the decade of 1890 experiencing the highest number of land transactions. Between 1889 and 1903, 37,533 property owners received 5,060,085 hectares; 4,208,218 hectares were privatized in the peripheral regions.[25] The land tenure system of Oaxaca underwent an important transformation: comuneros became private owners of small plots (worth not more than one or two hundred pesos, depending on the region), and private interests established fincas on larger tracts.

Women were active on different levels of this agrarian transformation. In

1895, the population of Oaxaca was 884,909, of which 287,713 males and 68,472 females were listed as economically active. The circulars and decrees referring to the alienation process made clear that communal lands were to be distributed to widows with children and all other heads of families. The remaining land could be parceled out to single men over twenty-one or those younger who lacked legal guardians. The parcels were to be equal and valued at not more than a hundred pesos each. Leftover land could then be sold to heads of families from the village, and after that, publicly auctioned to anyone.[26]

Each village had to carry out a census of its population in order to establish those eligible to receive lands. The number of widows with children who received parcels of communal lands is surprising. The 1895 census conducted in the district capital of Juquila, in the heart of the coastal coffee country, indicated that 182 men and 58 women were eligible. Given the fact that the value of the parcels was not to exceed two hundred pesos, and based on the cost of land in that region, each person was to receive ninety-six hectares, a sizable parcel.[27]

In the village of Chilchotla, in the coffee-producing district of Teotitlán near the border with Puebla, the townspeople solicited the distribution of communal lands in 1890. The eligible population was divided into 112 married men, 31 single men, and 50 widows. According to the map included in the archive file, each person received equal parcels of ten hectares of farmland and six hectares of forest in December 1893. Interestingly, the map shows that all the women's parcels were in one section devoted only to women. No reason is given, but many of the women worked their own land, and it might have been considered unseemly for them to work alongside married men.[28]

Many towns reluctantly solicited the distribution of their communal lands into private property because they feared losing the land to capitalists and speculators. This was probably the situation in Chilchotla and Juquila, both of which were located in prosperous coffee regions. It was definitely the case for the Indians of Ozumacín in the rich tropical district of Tuxtepec, who feared a takeover by Eugenio Chuetz in 1887. In this district, 90,000 varas in equal lots were distributed among 153 recipients: 78 married men, 35 single men, 5 widowers, 34 widows, and 1 single woman named Manuela Santiago. The women received the first parcels on the list, but they also were segregated into an all-female sector.[29]

The subject of widows as landowners is a vein of inquiry yet to be mined. Theirs was not an easy lot; lacking males to defend them, they became easy targets for despoilers. Such was the case in 1903 with the widow Soledad García of Usila, who complained to the governor about abuses by the local authorities. Federico Ocampo, the local teacher and acting municipal secretary, had convinced another widow, Dolores Miguel, whose husband had legally sold land to Señora García, to deny the validity of this sale. Information on Ocampo's relationship with the widow Miguel is not available, but he evidently saw the possibility of gain if she were to repossess the land. Señora García was forced to travel to the district seat of Tuxtepec, abandoning her home, her animals, and her *milpa* (cornfield), "her sole patrimony and sustenance," to plead her case before the higher authorities, who reaffirmed her right to the property and ordered Ocampo removed as municipal secretary.[30]

In the three cases discussed above, approximately one widow received land for every three men. The number of widows seems inordinately high: approximately 25 percent of the recipients in Juquila and Chilchotla and almost 23 percent in Ozumacín. This does not correspond at all to the available statistics and general picture of women as landowners during the Porfiriato. In 1882, 52.83 percent of the deaths in Oaxaca were males and 47.17 percent were females.[31] Although women's mortality rate was substantially lower than men's, it still does not explain the number of widows in these villages. Certainly, men married to much younger women were likely to predecease their wives; or perhaps widows were less likely to remarry than widowers. Nevertheless, one could speculate that not all of them were really widows. Might not single women with children but no husbands be acknowledged as widows so as not to be a burden to the municipal authorities? This is a question that requires further research.

Women and Land Speculation

Study of the Fondo de Adjudicaciones y Conflictos of the State Archives of Oaxaca indicates that women with capital took advantage of the privatization of communal holdings to acquire tracts of land. Archival research further shows that women were most active as land buyers in the peripheral districts of Juchitán, Cuicatlán, Teotitlán, and Jamiltepec, although they were considerably less visible in Tuxtepec, Choapan, and Pochutla.

In fact, women were ready to take advantage of the new land laws from the very beginning. Within months of the publication of the Lerdo Law, Brígida Mendoza of Juquila asked for privatization of a plot of municipal land that she had been renting (for five pesos a year) and which was her sole source of income in her widowhood. Unfortunately, she ran up against Don Miguel Calleja, who had already applied for the same lands as well as tracts belonging to other towns nearby. This conflict of interest forced the authorities to investigate the situation. Although Señora Mendoza was unable to sign her name on her petition, she was smart enough to get her bid in early not only for the lands she rented but also for those of her neighbors, at whose expense she hoped to expand her own holdings. Her ambitions collided with Calleja's even more audacious petition. Due to his influence with the local authorities, he eventually won out, although the tract of land he applied for was considerably reduced. Calleja did get the widow's parcel, though, because she lacked the papers to prove that she had been renting the land all along.[32] This was a common misfortune. Rent contracts were often verbal, and illiterate people were not always aware of the documentation needed for administrative purposes.

The state government was certainly aware of land speculation in the 1890s. In an official communication dated November 1, 1893, the governor warned the jefes políticos of Etla, Teotitlán, Villa Alta, and Pochutla against "conscienceless speculators who have denounced as *baldíos* [vacant state lands] the communal lands of the villages." The jefes políticos were required to report on this situation and at the same time to assure any threatened villages that "the government would go to any length to see they would not be despoiled."[33]

Nevertheless, the speculation brought on by privatization continued apace. After the ex-comuneros of Chilchotla received 10 hectares of farmland and 6 hectares of forest each, the remaining lands were auctioned off to private owners. In 1893 alone, fifty tracts of land were sold (fifteen of them 1,000 hectares each or more) to forty-one persons, three of them women. Both Rafaela Gómez and María de Jesús Gómez bought 508 hectares each at a cost of $550. Angela Olivares bought 1,001 hectares for $1,100 in Chilchotla and the following year acquired another 1,000 hectares in Teponaxtla, in the neighboring district of Cuicatlán. Manuela Muñoz and her partners picked up 3,000 hectares in Teponaxtla for $3,300 in June 1894.[34]

Women also bought up land in the prosperous coastal district of Jamiltepec. The largest of thirteen tracts of land alienated in Pinotepa Nacional in 1856 went to Marcelina Melo, five leagues for $500. In 1873, of nine tracts of land privatized in Tlacamama, Bárbara Díaz bought one league for $333, and the eight other tracts (of the same or smaller dimensions) were sold to men. María Eulogia Guzmán picked up three leagues in Yxcapa for $1,000 in 1856.[35]

Not surprisingly, the region in which women were most active in land acquisition was Juchitán in the Isthmus of Tehuantepec. The women of the isthmian districts of Juchitán and Tehuantepec were famous for their industriousness and independence; historically they controlled local commerce in the markets and were fond of wearing heavy gold jewelry to advertise their wealth.[36]

As the site of coffee, sugar, rubber, indigo, citrus fruit, and livestock production, Juchitán, and to a lesser degree Tehuantepec, became prime targets for capitalists, women included. As early as 1856, women were taking advantage of privatization there; for example, Genoveva de la Rosa bought seven leagues of land in Zanatepec for $1,533. In Niltepec, out of thirty-two tracts privatized, nine went to women. In Tapanatepec, three of the seven available tracts were acquired by women. It is significant that most of the land bought by women consisted of middle-sized tracts costing between $50 and $100. In cattle-raising Juchitán, women became ranchers. By 1912, Josefa Toledo and Saveida Nieto each owned ranches larger than 1,000 hectares in Ixhuatán.[37]

Probably the most famous woman of the Isthmus in Porfirian times was Doña Catalina Romero (known affectionately in Oaxaca as Juana Cata), a cacica and the benefactress of the town of Tehuantepec. Never married, she is purported to have been the one enduring love of President Porfirio Díaz. They met about 1860 when Díaz was the young prefect of Tehuantepec. The story goes that when the Tehuantepec National Railway was built in the 1890s, the tracks were routed to pass directly in front of Juana Cata's house for the president's convenience.

But Juana Cata did not become a cacica or gain respect because of her paramour. In fact, this relationship hurt her, because Tehuantepec tradition-ally supported the Conservative party and Díaz was a radical liberal. She was wealthy in her own right as a merchant and owner of the Santa Teresa sugar estate, whose products won international competitions, including awards at the Crystal Palace in London and the St. Louis World's Fair. She was respon-sible for the reconstruction of the town cathedral, convent, and cemetery; and she founded two Catholic schools, one for boys and one for girls.[38]

In order for a married woman to take advantage of the sale of municipal lands, she needed her husband's formal permission. In 1903, Señora Jesús Sandoval de Ziga bought 1,342 hectares from the village of Tonameca in the rich coffee district of Pochutla. But she and her husband first had to present themselves before the mayor and secretary of the village so that she could obtain her licencia marital. Señor Sandoval verbally declared that he freely granted his wife the marital license that the law required in order for her to complete the purchase, the judge validated the license, and the bill of sale was signed.

A similar legal act was needed for a women to delegate power to her sons. In the same town of Tonameca, in 1902, Luisa Merlín de Gómes, a widow, appeared before the village authorities with her son, Estanislao Gómez, to transfer her power of attorney to him so that he could administer her holdings. This act also required both parties to appear in person.[39]

Women and Agrarian Protest

Women had been major participants in agrarian protests since colonial times, and they continued to be active during the Porfiriato.[40] The advance of capitalist agriculture in the peripheral regions of the state on lands originally owned by the villages often met with steadfast resistance from the Indian communities. Other communities, as we have seen, saw the writing on the wall and solicited the division of their lands in private parcels to avoid losing them to outsiders. Sometimes, even this was not enough.

The ongoing struggle of the villagers of Usila, in the district of Tuxtepec, is revealed in their pleas to the state government for assistance. In 1882, the village lands had been duly distributed among the comuneros as private property, with each paying five pesos for a land title. The villagers established their homes on these parcels and planted coffee trees, a little tobacco, maize, and beans. In 1897, in league with the municipal authorities, the firm of Vives and Nouvelares obtained a large tract of land in Usila that included the parcels of some of the villagers and threatened others. The villagers protested to the jefe político, who informed them that their titles were not legal after all. Fourteen of them, including two women, were forced to accept an arrangement with the foreign capitalists that in effect left the latter in control of the land (the document implies that the villagers ended up as laborers on their own land).[41]

In 1903, the Usileños again protested, this time to the newly appointed jefe político, but to no avail. In 1908, adding insult to injury, they were being pressured by the mayor of Usila to pay taxes on the land to which they supposedly held title but did not control. The state authorities turned a deaf ear to their plight, claiming the case was outside their jurisdiction. In 1909, seventeen Usileños, only three of whom had been party to the first petition, protested the foreign company's expansion into their lands with the collusion of local authorities.[42] Although the villagers were represented in Oaxaca by the well-known opposition lawyer Juan Sánchez, their case does not seem to have been resolved.

One of the longest battles waged in defense of communal lands was the struggle of the comuneros of Benito Juárez, a colony of residents of San Mateo Piñas in the coastal district of Pochutla, against the expanding interests of German coffee producer Leo von Brandestein. Much as it had happened in Usila, Brandestein protested that he had legally purchased the Cafetal San Pablo (almost 3,000 hs); the comuneros of Benito Juárez insisted that part of his holdings were their communal lands. On occasion, they defended their lands with arms. Brandestein finally sold the property to Rosing Brothers, an English company that took over various individual fincas in the area. Widow comuneras joined with their neighbors in these protests too.[43]

Women as Wage Laborers

One of the most enlightening files in the state archives includes a series of 1907 agricultural statistics gathered by the jefes políticos for the governor's

Table 2.1
Wage Labor in Oaxaca, 1907

District	Wage laborers		Daily wages (centavos)	
	Men	Women	Men	Women
Centro	5,372	496	50	25
Cuicatlán	3,000	1,500	62	30
Choapan	3,489	44	25–50	12–25
Ejutla	5,791	45	25–50	25
Etla	1,134	359	25–50	6–19
Huajuapan	1,600	—	31	—
Ixtlán	2,995	811	38	18
Jamiltepec	8,000	500	31	18
Juchitán	12,818	—	75	—
Juquila	4,414	581	37–50	25–30
Miahuatlán	10,101	3,977	31	18
Nochixtlán	455	—	25	—
Ocotlán	859	—	31–50	—
Pochutla	814	223	25–50	12–25
Putla	1,927	108	25–100	37
Silacayoapan	45	4	25–37	—
Tehuantepec	2,151	700	20–75	9–25
Teotitlán	3,173	581	50	31
Teposcolula	955	—	15–25	—
Tlacolula	4,755	925	25–44	15–25
Tuxtepec	9,810	1,570	75	44
Villa Alta	6,387	5,350	25–37	12
Yautepec	3,388	509	37	25
Zimatlán	10,409	—	38	—
Total	103,842	18,283		
Total Workers		122,125		

Source: AGEO, Sec. de Gobierno, 1908, Varios Districtos, Datos y Estadísticas para la Memoria Administrativa.
Note: All districts of the state are included except Coixtlahuaca (no information available) and Tlaxiaco (data evidently in error; e.g., gave a total of 224,575 workers for a district with a population of 68,000).

annual report. In addition to production figures, the number of *jornaleros* (wage laborers), both male and female, and their daily wages are listed by district and municipality (see Table 2.1). The total number of wage laborers in the state in 1907 (with only two districts missing) was 122,125, of which 18,283, nearly 15 percent, were women. This is an extraordinary increase compared with the 1900 census, which lists no female laborers at all in Oaxaca.[44]

The numbers in Table 2.1 support the hypothesis that women were more active in agriculture in peripheral regions. Many of the districts that retained traditional agriculture in the form of haciendas, minifundios, or communal lands either listed no women wage laborers at all or showed very few: Ejutla, Ocotlán, and Zimatlán in the Central Valleys districts, and Huajuapan, Nochixtlán, Silacayoapan, and Teposcolula in the Mixteca districts.

The peripheral districts of Pochutla, Juquila, Jamiltepec, Putla, Tuxtepec, Tehuantepec, and Teotitlán, on the other hand, had quite a few women laborers. Nearly one-third of the wage laborers listed for Cuicatlán were women. The one anomaly in this group is Juchitán, which had the largest number of wage laborers in the state but listed no women laborers at all. This is hard to believe, especially considering the women of Juchitán's reputation for economic independence.[45]

The question would seem to turn on how the different jefes políticos defined *jornalero,* and this we do not know. The district of Villa Alta, which in large part maintained its communal lands, listed 5,350, the highest number of female laborers; Juchitán listed none. Although some of the villages of Villa Alta did cultivate coffee, this number of women workers seems incredibly high because the district registered no fincas or haciendas at all. The number of women laborers listed for Tlacolula, Miahuatlán, and Yautepec (the latter two did have some coffee fincas) is also inexplicably high. Given the myriad problems attached to collecting statistics in Porfirian Mexico, these data serve only as a guide to historical trends.

Apparently, the lower a woman's social class, the more difficult her situation. The female minifundistas in Mixteca had smaller parcels than the men, although this was not always the case. The wages of female jornaleros were far inferior to men's, usually half or less for the same work. Some women received only six or more centavos while men in the same district received twenty-five to fifty centavos a day, as was the case in Etla and Tehuantepec. Men received up to a peso in the inflationary port of Salina Cruz, but women earned only twenty-five centavos a day. Men's wages tended to be higher in commercial agriculture in the peripheral districts; women's salaries followed suit, but they still earned only half of what men did.

Table 2.1 lists wages for male laborers in the Tuxtepec district at seventy-five centavos, while female laborers received forty-four centavos a day, the highest of all the women's salaries on the list. But there is reason to doubt these figures. Tuxtepec was notorious in the Porfiriato for its deplorable working conditions, and Valle Nacional was also known as the Valley of Tears.[46]

Isolated in the tropics, where labor was scarce, this district became a major producer of a very high quality tobacco in the late nineteenth century. Land speculation and illegal takeovers of Indian lands were common, as we saw in Usila. Spaniards, Cubans, and Canary Islanders came first to exploit the tobacco trade, followed by a plethora of United States, English, French, and Italian firms, which also produced coffee, cotton, and rubber. When the region could not provide the necessary labor, workers were brought in from all over the nation. A 1907 list of thirty-three *contratas* (as jornaleros were called in Tuxtepec) included four women from four different states: Michoacán, San Luis Potosí, Querétaro, and México. Lured by promises of high wages, men and women workers arrived to find horrendous living conditions. Workers were policed by an army of overseers wielding whips, and rewards were offered for returned runaways. John Kenneth Turner, who visited the area in 1908, calculated the life span of workers arriving in Tuxtepec at seven to eight months.[47]

Political dissidents were often exiled to Valle Nacional. Drunks who had fallen asleep on the streets of any Mexican city might awaken to find themselves on a train headed for Tuxtepec. The plantation owners had to pay agents or politicians for each potential worker: men cost sixty pesos before the 1907 crisis and forty-five pesos afterward, women and children half of that. Turner calculated that women formed one-fifth of the labor force, a figure higher than the approximately 14 percent calculated from the figures in Table 2.1. Women not only labored in the fields, they also did all the cooking, sewing, and cleaning. When Turner asked the mayor of Valle Nacional why the planters did not install cheap mills to grind corn, he replied, "Women are cheaper than machines."[48]

Many contratas of Valle Nacional had been *enganchado* (hooked) by an advance, which they were supposed to pay off with their labor (making this a form of debt peonage). But they were paid in scrip that could be used only at the company store, where prices were inflated. Constantly in debt, they could never hope to work off the debt; most died first. While in many respects the workers were treated like slaves, it was not the same type of slavery that had existed in the United States, since the laborers did receive a salary in scrip. Labor relations in Tuxtepec combined the Mexican enganche/debt peonage system with aspects of slavery.[49]

Living conditions on the tobacco plantations of Tuxtepec were intolerable. Every night workers were herded into dirt-floor dormitories. Depending on the size of the plantation, there could be from seventy to four hundred men, women, and children in these barnlike jails with barred windows. Turner's account, from which I quote, is appalling.

> And on not a single ranch did I find a separate dormitory for the women or the children. Women of modesty and virtue are sent to Valle Nacional every week and are shoved into a sleeping room with scores and even hundreds of others, most of them men, the door is locked on them and

they are left to the mercy of the men. Honest, hard-working Mexicans are taken into Valle Nacional with their wives and children. If the wife is attractive in appearance she goes to the planter or to one or more of the bosses. The children see their mother being taken away and they know what is to become of her. The husband knows it, but if he makes objection he is answered with a club. Time and time again I have been told that this was so, by masters, by slaves, by officials. And the women who are thrust into the sardine box must take care of themselves.[50]

Conclusions

Whether as large landowners, hacendadas, cash-crop finqueras, livestock ranchers, minifundistas, comuneras, sharecroppers, wage laborers, or contratas of Tuxtepec, women of all social classes were engaged in agricultural pursuits. No economic level in Oaxacan agriculture was devoid of female participation during the Porfiriato; however, the quantity, quality, and level of participation varied according to women's position in the social structure. Elite women owned haciendas and fincas and speculated in privatized communal lands. They were few in number, but their economic power was significant.

It is impossible to look into the heart of the rural Oaxacan family of a hundred years ago to assess exactly how involved women were in the day-to-day affairs of agricultural management. Did Señora Jesús Sandoval de Ziga take a direct interest in the lands she acquired in Pochutla, or did she use her wealth to increase her family's holdings while her husband, who owned other estates in the area, managed her lands as well? Did the female landholders in Teotitlán, Cuicatlán, and Jamiltepec actually set up capitalist fincas themselves, or did they also use their personal wealth based on a husband's or son's advice? We do know that Juliana Ruiz de Pérez was directly involved in a dispute with her terrazgueros, as was Margarita Trápaga. More information must be culled from other sources (notarial, judicial, and private archives) in order to understand how active elite women were in agriculture.[51]

The lower her economic level, the more directly involved the woman was likely to be, both quantitatively and qualitatively. Percentages calculated for female agriculturalists per village at the peasant level (minifundistas and ex-comuneras) are astonishing if compared with state or national statistics. This is even more true for the number of female wage laborers. The women of the village of San Sebastian Teitipac made up 25 percent of the small-holders in 1888 and almost 15 percent of the wage laborers in 1907 (although some of the peasants may have also worked as seasonal laborers). In Santa Catarina Adéquez and Santiago Patlanalá, women formed 11 percent and 8 percent of peasant holders, respectively. In the privatization process in Juquila, Chilchotla, and Ozumacín, between 23 and 26 percent of those receiving land were widows. In fact, according to archival documents, female wage laborers made up almost 15 percent of the salaried agricultural workers in the state of Oaxaca (see Table 2.1). While these data are no substitute for state or nationwide statistics, they seriously challenge the prevailing view of women's role in agriculture in Porfirian Mexico.[52]

On the lower economic levels, women were more directly engaged in the day-to-day business of agriculture, especially widows, whose parcels formed their main source of income. Both Brígida Mendoza and Soledad García insisted that their land was their sole support; García decried having to leave her animals and milpa to complain to the authorities in Tuxtepec. The plots owned by most of the peasant women were too small to produce sufficient income to hire day laborers.

The lower her social class, the more the woman was subjugated by the double yoke of economic inequality and patriarchy. The female peasants of Mixteca held the smaller parcels. Widows given communal lands were cordoned off into a particular area (it is not known if these lands were of the same quality as those given to men). As wage laborers, they earned half or less of what men earned for the same work. On the tobacco plantations, women lived the worst nightmare of Porfirian Mexico. Forced to work as day laborers, they were responsible as well for grinding maize, making tortillas, and sewing and washing the clothes of the male population, and they were sexually exploited by the male administrators and laborers.

We have seen that women were active in agriculture before capitalism became the dominant mode of production, but capitalist agriculture demanded their further integration into the rural workforce.[53] The transition to capitalism in Latin America brought with it extremely exploitative working conditions, especially for women. The mayor of Valle Nacional told the truth: women *were* cheaper than machines, and they were much cheaper than men. In fact, women formed a far more important part of the cheap agricultural workforce needed in the transition to capitalism than historians previously recognized.

Women tended to be more active in agriculture in the peripheral regions of the state, reinforcing the thesis that their role increased with the growth of commercial agriculture. This seems to hold true for females in almost all the categories discussed here: hacendadas, finqueras, rancheras, speculators, comuneras, and wage laborers.[54] (The exception is female sharecroppers, but these have been documented only in the Central Valley region.)

The invisibility of women in agriculture is sadly but aptly symbolized by the segregation of the widow campesinas working their land in a female ghetto. But these ghettos eventually disappeared as the land passed from the widows to their sons and as new widows and daughters inherited parcels of land elsewhere in the community's holdings. Women also continued to join forces with their male neighbors in agrarian protest: either to defend their right to communal lands or to prevent their own privatized lands from being taken away by expanding capitalist interests.

Various factors have not been addressed here, including the ethnic composition of women in land tenure, although this is an important issue. The documentation I used does not usually indicate the ethnic or racial background of the subjects. Comparative production statistics for men and women are also lacking.

There is a pressing need to analyze the role of widows in the economic system. Depending on the woman's social class, widowhood could be emancipating (for the elite and middle class)[55] or debilitating. Certainly it often led lower-class women into worse hardships than before. An educated guess, derived from the documentation presented here, is that widows were the women most active in agriculture in Porfirian Oaxaca.

As Florencia Mallon emphasizes, women's economic participation must be established in order to "avoid attributing their subordination simply to their exclusion from the public sphere or from 'productive' labor." But this participation, measured quantitatively (as here), does not tell the whole story of gender relations in these societies. Mallon suggests that qualitative analyses will document a "high degree of patriarchal control over women, exercised within the household and reinforced through legal and political institutions."[56] We have had only glimpses of this reality here. But it is true that women who received parcels within the community did not receive political parity as well: economic power did not bring concomitant political power. The patriarchal structure of society was maintained.

NOTES

I thank the following people for comments or source materials for this article: Héctor G. Martínez, Anselmo Arellanes, Francisco José Ruiz Cervantes, Ronald Spores, Víctor de la Cruz, Hayward Wilkirson, Kathi Kern, Margaret Brown, Heather Fowler-Salamini, Mary Kay Vaughan, Piedad Peniche, Carmen Ramos, and two anonymous reviewers.

1. Jorge Hernández Díaz, "Mujeres chatinas, matrimonio y trabajo," in *Las mujeres en el campo,* comp. Josefina Aranda (Oaxaca: Instituto de Investigaciones Sociológicas de la Universidad Autónoma Benito Juárez, 1988), 291–92; Silvia Marina Arrom, *The Women of Mexico City, 1790–1857* (Stanford: Stanford University Press, 1985), 1, 154ff.; Margaret Towner, "Monopoly Capitalism and Women's Work During the Porfiriato," *Latin American Perspectives* 4.1–2, issues 12–13 (1977):90–105; Carmen Ramos, "Señoritas Porfirianas: Mujer e ideología en el México progresista, 1880–

1910," in *Presencia y Transparencia: La mujer en la historia de México,* ed. Carmen Ramos et al. (Mexico City: El Colegio de México, 1987). In Oaxaca, women's role in commerce was probably even more significant than their participation in agriculture.

2. The one historical study of women in agriculture in Oaxaca is Kate Young's discussion of rural women in the Sierra Juárez, which contains mostly speculation and Marxist theory; see "Modes of Appropriation and the Sexual Division of Labour: A Case Study from Oaxaca, Mexico," in *Feminism and Materialism: Women and Modes of Production,* ed. Annette Kuhn and AnnMarie Wolpe (London: Routledge and Kegan Paul, 1978), 123–54.

3. See, e.g., John Coatsworth, "Anotaciones sobre la producción de alimentos en el porfiriato," *Historia Mexicana* 25.2 (1976). Margaret Towner used the statistics from *Estadísticas Económicas del Porfiriato* compiled by the Colegio de México in "Monopoly Capitalism," 99–100. See *Censo General de Población 1900 Estado de Oaxaca,* 3 vols. (Mexico City: Direccion General de Estadística).

4. Carmen Diana Deere and Magdalena León characterize Latin American peasant agriculture as a "family farming system," in which women, children, and men are involved in numerous activities beyond fieldwork such as animal husbandry, natural resource management, and marketing. Rural women also "carry the burden of reproductive tasks"; see Deere and León, eds., *Rural Women and State Policy: Feminist Perspectives on Latin American Agricultural Development* (Boulder: Westview Press, 1987), 1–6; Verena Stolcke, "The Exploitation of Family Morality: Labor Systems and Family Structure on São Paulo Coffee Plantations, 1850–1979," in *Kinship Ideology and Practice in Latin America,* ed. Raymond T. Smith (Chapel Hill: University of North Carolina Press, 1984), 264ff.; and Stolcke, *Coffee Planters, Workers and Wives: Class Conflict and Gender Relations on São Paulo Plantations, 1850–1980* (New York: St. Martin's Press, 1988).

The use of the term *farms* or *farming systems* is controversial for the historical period treated in this essay because Latin America did not follow the farmer road to capitalism.

5. Asunción Lavrín points this out in "Some Final Considerations on Trends and Issues in Latin American Women's History," in *Latin American Women: Historical Perspectives* (Westport, Conn.: Greenwood Press, 1978), 313. K. Lynn Stoner emphasizes the need for more historical studies in "Directions in Latin American Women's History, 1977–1984," *Latin American Research Review* 22.2 (1987):101–3. The historical perspective is examined by Stolcke in "Exploitation" and *Coffee Planters;* and Florencia Mallon, "Gender and Class in the Transition to Capitalism Household and Mode of Production in Central Peru," *Latin American Perspectives* 13.1 (1986):147–74. On elite women, see Fiona Wilson, "Marriage, Property, and the Position of Women in the Peruvian Central Andes," in R. Smith, *Kinship.* On Oaxaca and Mexico, see the articles in Aranda, *Las mujeres.*

6. Deere and León underscore the necessity of investigating "what work women actually did and how this changed over time and . . . how women's economic participation was related to their class position and social status" (*Rural Women,* 2–6). I use *finca* to refer to new agricultural properties whose cash crop production was inte-

grated into the capitalist market. This was the common term used in Oaxaca at the time. Nevertheless, the precise size of fincas is indefinite; they ranged from 30 hectares to more than 1,000. The owner of a finca is a *finquera* or *finquero*.

7. Lourdes Arizpe and Carlota Botey, "Mexican Agricultural Development Policy and Its Impact on Rural Women," in Deere and León, *Rural Women*, 67ff. See Towner, "Monopoly Capitalism"; and Carmen Ramos, "Señoritas Porfirianas."

8. Single women could be emancipated by their fathers voluntarily or by court order if the father were guilty of abuse. "They were automatically emancipated if he was incapacitated by illness, committed incest or was banished from the realm" (Arrom, *The Women*, 58); see Arrom, "Changes in Mexican Family Law in the Nineteenth Century: The Civil Codes of 1870 and 1884," *Journal of Family History* 10.3 (1985):305–17.

9. See Arrom, *The Women*, 68–75; for women's legal status in Peru, consult Wilson, "Marriage, Property."

10. Charles Brasseur, *Viaje por el istmo de Tehuantepec* (Mexico City: Fondo de Cultura Económica, 1984), 131. Santo Domingo also produced cotton, indigo, beans, and maize. In 1910 it had a population of 220 inhabitants, divided equally between women and men; see *División territorial de los Estados Unidos Mexicanos correspondiente al Censo de 1910. Estado de Oaxaca* (Mexico City: Oficina Impresora de la Secretaría de Hacienda, 1918). La Venta was dedicated to sugarcane and maize production (Archivo General del Estado de Oaxaca [AGEO], Secretaría [Sec.] de Gobierno, Fomento, February 1912, Varios Districtos, Estadísticas).

11. See AGEO, Conflictos, Leg. 49, Exp. 30, 1904; and P. G. Holms, *The Directory of Agencies, Mines & Haciendas* (Mexico City: American Book and Printing, 1905–6), 311. It is not clear in this case whether Guadalupe Baigts was male or female (Guadalupe can be used for either sex), but the San Isidro hacienda had originally been owned by Trápaga and Company (AGEO, Sec. de Gobierno, Fomento, February 1912, Varios Districtos, Estadísticas). Margarita Trápaga de Díaz was owner of the Hacienda de Aguayo in the 1920s. See Anselmo Arellanes, "Del Camarazo al Cardenismo," in *Historia de la cuestión agraria mexicana: Estado de Oaxaca*, coord. Leticia Reina (Mexico City: Juan Pablos Editors, Universidad Autónoma Benito Juárez, Centro de Estudios Históricos del Agrarismo en México, 1988), 2:97.

12. In the documents her name appears as Doña Tranquilina, the doña denoting a high socioeconomic status (AGEO, Adjudicaciones, Leg. 12, Exp. 16, 1892).

13. AGEO, Sec. de Gobierno, Sept. 1907, Cuestiones Laborales, Miahuatlán; see Holms, *Directory*, 309; J. R. Southworth, *The Official Directory of Mines and Estates of Mexico* (Mexico City, 1910), 220; and AGEO, Sec. de Gobierno, Fomento, February 1912, Varios Districtos, Estadísticas.

14. AGEO, Sec. de Gobierno: 1888, Leg. 96, Exp. 17, Estadísticas; 1908, Varios Districtos, Datos y Estadísticas para la Memoria Administrativa.

15. The Mixteca includes northwestern Oaxaca and parts of southern Puebla, the area of residence of the Mixtec Indians. It is divided into the Mixteca Alta (Nochixtlán, Teposcolula, Coixtlahuaca, and Tlaxiaco), and the Mixteca Baja (Huajuapan, Silacayoapan, Juxtlahuaca, and Putla). Jamiltepec is considered the Mixteca Costa. AGEO, Sec. de Gobierno, 1888, Estadísticas, Leg. 96, Exps. 4, 10 and 11.

16. See T. G. Powell, "Los liberales, el campesinado indígena y los problemas agrarios durante la Reforma"; and Donald J. Fraser, "La política de desamortización en las comunidades indígenas, 1856–1872," both in *Historia Mexicana* 21.4 (1972).

17. For example, John Tutino, *From Insurrection to Revolution in Mexico: Social Bases of Agrarian Violence, 1750–1940* (Princeton: Princeton University Press, 1986); Friedrich Katz, ed., *Riot, Rebellion, and Revolution: Rural Social Conflict in Mexico* (Princeton: Princeton University Press, 1988); and Leticia Reina, *Las rebeliones campesinas en México, 1819–1906* (Mexico City: Siglo XXI Editores, 1980).

18. Charles F. Berry, *The Reform in Oaxaca, 1856–1876: A Microhistory of the Liberal Revolution* (Lincoln: University of Nebraska Press, 1981); Moisés González Navarro, "Indio y propiedad en Oaxaca," *Historia Mexicana* 8.2 (1958):176–78.

19. *Periódico Oficial del Estado Libre y Soberano de Oaxaca,* June 26, 1890, and Feb. 24, 1893; and Manuel Esparza, "Los proyectos de los liberales en Oaxaca (1856–1910)," in Reina, *Historia de la cuestión agraria,* 1:288.

20. *Estadísticas sociales del Porfiriato, 1877–1910* (Mexico City: Secretaría de Economía, 1956), 7–9. See Francie R. Chassen and Héctor G. Martínez, "El desarrollo económico de Oaxaca a finales del porfiriato," *Revista Mexicana de Sociología* 48.1 (1986):285–305; and Chassen, "Oaxaca: Del Porfiriato a la Revolución, 1902–1911" (Ph.D. diss., National Autonomous University of Mexico, 1986).

21. The peripheral regions included Tuxtepec and Choapan; the isthmian districts of Juchitán and Tehuantepec; and the coastal districts of Pochutla, Juquila, and Jamiltepec (I include Putla, which was formed in 1906 from parts of Tlaxiaco and Juxtlahuaca, because of its growing sugar production and shared characteristics with Jamiltepec). The Cañada region is considered peripheral (Teotitlán and Cuicatlán) because the arrival of the Mexican Southern Railway acted as the stimulus to this region's commercial agriculture. The regions that maintained basically traditional agriculture for local consumption were the Central Valleys (Centro, Ocotlán, Zimatlán, Tlacolula, Yautepec, Miahuatlán, Ejutla, and Etla districts), the Sierra Juárez (Ixtlán and Villa Alta districts), and the Mixteca.

22. Chassen, "Oaxaca"; Chassen and Martínez, "Desarrollo económico"; Carlos Sánchez Silva, "Estructura de las propiedades agrarias de Oaxaca," in *Lecturas históricas del estado de Oaxaca,* vol. 4: *1877–1930,* comp. María de los Angeles Romero Frizzi (Mexico City: Instituto Nacional de Antropología e Historia and Gobierno del Estado de Oaxaca, 1990), 107ff. On the growth of infrastructure, see Francie R. Chassen, *Regiones y ferrocarriles en la Oaxaca porfirista* (Oaxaca: Carteles Editores, 1990).

23. See Chassen, "Oaxaca," 84ff. No size distinction is made here between fincas and haciendas.

24. See William B. Taylor, *Landlord and Peasant in Colonial Oaxaca* (Stanford: Stanford University Press, 1972); and John Thomas Cassidy, "Haciendas and Pueblos in Nineteenth Century Oaxaca" (Ph.D. diss., Cambridge University, 1981). Although haciendas were profitable economic ventures in other parts of Mexico, these authors found this not to be the case in Oaxaca. Information on fincas is available in the Fondo de Adjudicaciones y Conflictos at the AGEO.

25. Chassen, "Oaxaca," 85; Esparza, "Los proyectos," 288ff. Esparza refers to the peripheral regions as the Cañada-Tuxtepec and the Isthmus-coastal regions.

26. Census of 1895, cited in *Estadísticas Históricas de México* (Mexico City: Instituto Nacional de Estadísticas Geografía e Informática, 1985), 1:256. If the village did not have sufficient land to give each recipient a parcel worth one hundred pesos, the value could be reduced, as long as everyone received an equal parcel. "Reglamento," June 26, 1890; *Periódico Oficial,* June 26, 1890, 2. The 1862 law decreed that the equal parcels could be worth up to two hundred pesos, but there seemed to be some confusion in the 1890s over whether this meant one hundred or two hundred pesos per person; see Esparza, "Los proyectos," 294–95.

27. Esparza, "Los proyectos," 294–95.

28. AGEO, Adjudicaciones, Leg. 27, Exp. 1, Teotitlán, Chilchotla, 1890. See Arrom's discussion of the importance of propriety and tradition as a basis for legal restrictions pertaining to women, in *The Women,* 59.

29. The lands of Teotitlán became attractive because they were near the Mexican Southern Railway, which was under construction by 1890 and completed in 1892. Juquila had its outlets in the nearby coffee port of Puerto Angel on the Pacific Ocean and later the improvised port of Minizo on the same coast.

A vara is 83 centimeters. Ozumacín's list is one of the rare ones that shows an unmarried women receiving land (AGEO, Adjudicaciones, Leg. 37, Exp. 15, Tuxtepec, Ozumacín).

30. The subject of widows is discussed by Arrom in *The Women,* 185–86; and by Edith Couturier, "Women and the Family in Eighteenth Century Mexico: Law and Practice," *Journal of Family History* 10.3 (1985):298–99. On elite widows in Peru, consult Wilson, "Marriage, Property." AGEO, Conflictos por Tierras, Leg. 85, Exp. 22, Tuxtepec, Usila.

31. *Estadísticas sociales del Porfiriato,* 159.

32. AGEO, Adjudicaciones, Leg. 17, Exp. 3, Santa Catarina Juquila.

33. AGEO, Adjudicaciones, Leg. 2, Exp. 3, Centro. Baldíos were vacant federal lands. They could be acquired by private interests through the process of *denuncio,* soliciting them openly from local authorities. Huge speculation in baldíos went on during the Porfiriato. Lands belonging to communities could be subject to denuncios if communal titles were questionable or lost. Lands were also illegally taken over in this manner when local authorities acted in collusion with private interests.

34. The dollar sign ($) refers to pesos throughout this essay. No relationship between the two Gómezes has been established. AGEO, Adjudicaciones, Leg. 9, Exp. 32, Etla, Cuicatlán, Teotitlán, etc., 1895. On Manuela Muñoz and her partners, see AGEO, Adjudicaciones, Leg. 6, Exp. 26, Cuicatlán, Teponaxtla, 1894.

35. AGEO, Adjudicaciones, Leg. 9, Exp. 32, 1895.

36. See, e.g., Miguel Covarrubias, *El Sur de México* (Mexico City: Instituto Nacional Indigenista, 1980); Beverly Newbold de Chiñas, *Mujeres de San Juan: La mujer zapoteca del Istmo en la economía* (Mexico City: SepSetentas, 1975); Anya Peterson Royce, *Prestigio y afiliación en una comunidad urbana: Juchitán, Oax.* (Mexico City: Instituto Nacional Indigenista, 1975).

37. AGEO, Adjudicaciones, Leg. 9, Exp. 32, 1895; AGEO, Sec. de Gobierno, Fomento, February 1912, Varios Districtos, Estadísticas.

38. Ibid. See Enrique Krauze, *Místico de la autoridad Porfirio Díaz* (Mexico City:

Fondo de Cultura Económica, 1987), 109–110; "Doña Juana C. Romero, Benefactora de Tehuantepec. Discurso del Dr. Samuel Villalobos" *Ex-Alumnos,* April 30, 1954, 2. See the description of the beautiful and strange young Indian woman, said to be the young Juana Cata, in Brasseur, *Viaje,* 159–60.

39. AGEO, Adjudicaciones, Leg. 24, Exps. 23 and 24, 1902, Tonameca, Pochutla.

40. William B. Taylor, *Drinking, Homicide and Rebellion in Colonial Mexican Villages* (Stanford: Stanford University Press, 1979), 155ff.; Leticia Reina, "De las Reformas Borbónicas a las Leyes de Reforma," in Reina, *Historia de la cuestión agraria,* 1:205ff.

41. AGEO, Adjudicaciones: Leg. 43, Exp. 25, 1908; and Leg. 43, Exp. 27, 1909, Tuxtepec, Usila.

42. Ibid.

43. See Holms, *Directory,* 309; AGEO, Sec. de Gobierno: Fomento, February, 1912, Varios Districtos, Estadísticas; January 1912, Pochutla, Quejas Particulares; AGEO, Adjudicaciones, Leg. 22, Exp. 26, Pochutla, Huatulco, 1913. The land under question was also disputed by the villagers of Huatulco as their property. The foreign interests kept this dispute alive in order to divide and conquer the comuneros. Women were also present in defense of Huatulco's interests.

44. AGEO, Sec. de Gobierno, 1908, Varios Districtos, Datos y Estadísticas para la Memoria Administrativa; see sources in note 3 above.

45. See sources in note 36 above. There are other questions here—for instance, the high number of female laborers in certain districts of the more traditional Central Valleys.

46. See Chassen, "Oaxaca," 103ff.; and John Kenneth Turner, *Barbarous Mexico* (Austin: University of Texas Press, 1969), 54ff.

47. AGEO, Sec. de Gobierno, February 1907, Cuestiones Laborales, Tuxtepec; Turner, *Barbarous Mexico,* 54.

48. Turner, *Barbarous Mexico,* 66; AGEO, Sec. de Gobierno, 1908, Varios Districtos, Estadísticas.

49. When the Maderistas liberated the contratas at the hacienda of Málzaga in Tuxtepec in 1911, they executed Angel Sustaeta, the notorious Spanish overseer, and distributed the food from the hacienda company store to the starving Yaqui families working there. See Pedro Chávez, "Episodio de la Revolución en la Hacienda de Málzaga," *Novedades,* April 7, 1968.

50. Turner, *Barbarous Mexico,* 65. This description contrasts sharply with that of the situation of the slave laborers on the Yucatecan henequen plantations. According to Piedad Peniche's essay in this volume, women were considered part of the reproduction of capital, and even their dowries were paid for by plantation owners to ensure that workers would have wives.

51. See the suggestive analysis and interpretation of women's roles and gender relations within the family by Carmen Diana Deere in "What Difference Does Gender Make? Rethinking Peasant Studies," in *Women and Agriculture in the Third World,* ed. Simi Afonja (London: Macmillan, 1994).

52. One must take into account the specific characteristics of Oaxaca to appreciate these data. Not only was agriculture dominant there, Oaxaca probably had more

communal lands remaining in 1910 than any other state in Mexico. Therefore, this information on landholding could not be used to explain national patterns.

53. Heather Fowler-Salamini's findings coincide closely with these conclusions: the expansion of capitalism and the coffee economy demanded the integration of cheap female labor into the workforce; see her essay in this volume.

54. This is a preliminary conclusion. I have not yet finished reading all the material available in the state archive on this subject. Nonetheless, the majority of the files in the Fondo of Adjudicaciones y Conflictos deal with the peripheral regions.

55. Angeles Mastretta's magnificent novel, *Arráncame la vida* (Mexico City: Cal y Arena, 1989), ends on the note of just how emancipating widowhood could be for women of the twentieth century, who now might be able to do as they please.

56. Mallon, "Gender and Class," 153.

3

Gender, Work, and Coffee in Córdoba, Veracruz, 1850–1910

Heather Fowler-Salamini

*S*tudies of haciendas, rancheros, and communities in nineteenth-century Mexico have painstakingly unveiled the complexity of land tenure and rural labor systems and their interrelationships with regional economies, family elites, class conflict, ethnicity, and capitalist development, but too often these studies fail to consider issues of gender. The rural family has generally been viewed as a patriarchy in which the male head of the household is the principal provider of income as well as the major decision maker. Landownership has been considered almost exclusively a male domain. In general, rural labor has been studied in terms of individual male wage earners supporting their rural households, and other members of the family have been envisioned as invisible bystanders or dependents whose primary attribute is their need to be supported.[1]

This perspective overlooks two facts: (1) nineteenth-century Mexican rural family members shared diverse agricultural activities in a complex household in which multiple income earners, including women, contributed to family income; and (2) female-headed households were actually quite common. Assumptions to the contrary have largely been dispelled by the pioneering work of Lourdes Arizpe, John Tutino, Carmen Diana Deere, and others, and the nineteenth- and early twentieth-century rural family is now viewed as a heterogeneous family farming unit in which multiple producers, male and female, contributed to the family's income.[2]

The gender division of family labor is related to multiple interrelated socioeconomic factors and conditions, including the nature of the economy, land tenure, regional variations in population, crop production, social organization, size of the family, family life cycle, rural class structure, ethnicity, and the social construction of the concept of gender.[3] This essay examines these factors to explore gender dynamics among rural cultivators and laborers in Córdoba, Veracruz, in the second half of the nineteenth century. I will argue, first, that the gender division of labor in coffee cultivation and processing was already well established in Cordoban ranchero households by 1850, well before the coffee boom occurred. Second, the ensuing boom in coffee production brought on by international demand led to more concentration of land and capital in the hands of a non-Cordoban oligarchy, the parcelization of smaller properties, the growing impoverishment of poorer rural households, and an influx of migrants from the sierra states during the second half of the Porfiriato. Third, state and municipal census data reveal that increasing numbers of women became engaged in coffee production during this period. Fourth, the commercialization of coffee accompanied by an ever-increasing demand for rural labor opened up new agricultural activities and occupations to both men and women; yet the vast majority of these new jobs were temporary, labor-intensive, gender-segregated, and low paying. Finally, the consequences of this new dynamic in the gender division of labor were somewhat contradictory. Although women did find new labor opportunities in the expanding labor market, they were relegated to poorly paid, low-prestige positions.

Any discussion of the relationship between gender and the division of labor must take into account the impact of economic development. Gender analysis has revealed that Porfirian economic development affected men and women both negatively and positively, but in quite different ways. Certainly, new "spaces" were opened for many urban women, but these new economic opportunities seem to have been limited in the sense that they legitimized inferior gender-segregated positions. In rural society, the commercialization of agriculture over the long term led, on the one hand, to the elimination of some traditional female occupations.[4] On the other hand, great numbers of women entered the agricultural labor force to supplement the shrinking rural household income. In the canton of Tenango del Valle, México, for example, capitalist penetration led to a significant increase in the number of women entering the labor force as rural wage earners.[5] It is within this context of economic expansion that the dynamics of gender division of labor in coffee production must be examined.

Coffee Production in the Canton of Córdoba Before 1873

Córdoba, once described as the place Adam and Eve lived before they were cast out of the Garden of Eden, lies on the eastern slopes of the Sierra Oriental in a valley that descends and opens out into the Veracruz coastal plain. Situated at an elevation of 843 meters, its subtropical climate and plentiful rainfall, which support an abundance of vegetation, make it a paradise for farmers as well as naturalists. Although the canton of Córdoba encompasses only 1,755 square kilometers, its fertile soil has attracted a multitude of commercial producers to the region. When its capital became a major transport and communication center on the Mexico City–Puebla-Veracruz route during the colonial period, Córdoba was clearly destined to develop into a major agrocommercial center.[6] The Spanish colonists invested heavily in sugar and tobacco in the Córdoba-Orizaba region because its proximity to the port of Veracruz and close links to the sierra cities made crops easy to market. Sugar planters realized huge profits on their estates, which ranged in size from 128 to 2,130 hectares, in the second half of the eighteenth century, for they enjoyed the benefits of a monopoly in New Spain's market. The Córdoba-Orizaba region gained the exclusive right to cultivate tobacco for the colony after 1765. Tobacco production increased dramatically thereafter, and it emerged to become the second most important crop in the region.[7]

The outbreak of the Wars of Independence brought the collapse of the Cordoban sugar hacienda economy, as slave rebellions broke out between 1813 and 1818 and landowners resorted to military force to reclaim their properties. Most of the thirty-two major haciendas in the region were ravaged by fire—the buildings destroyed and the machinery and animals lost. According to contemporary accounts, the region was so devastated that abandoned hacienda lands began to return to forest. The regional economy was not to reemerge from the economic recession until the 1840s, for landowners were reluctant to invest when sugar prices remained low and transportation costs were prohibitively high. In addition, expensive Cordoban tobacco could not compete with the cheap Virginian and Cuban imports now flooding into the Mexican market. Agricultural production was also hampered by the United States and French invasions and the Wars of Reform, which racked the region from the 1840s through the 1860s.[8]

The introduction of coffee as a commercial crop at mid-century was a major factor in the economic revival of Córdoba. Although the coffee plant had been introduced as early as the 1790s, commercial production dates from 1817 when the Spaniard Juan Antonio Gómez de Guevara imported plants from Cuba to produce coffee for export. High export costs, primarily due to the terrible roads, and relatively low international prices kept coffee second to tobacco until the 1870s. This situation changed dramatically when the market opened up in the United States and the Veracruz–Mexico City railroad was completed. By 1880 Córdoba was exporting 2.5 million kilograms of coffee annually, primarily to New Orleans buyers.[9]

Beginning in the mid-1850s, a dozen or so Cordoban landowners initiated major renovations of their old sugar haciendas for the expressed purpose of cultivating sugar, coffee, and tobacco. Granted, coffee is not generally grown on sugar lands, but the Cordoban terrain offered enough gently sloping fields to warrant these entrepreneurial investments. One of the entrepreneurs was Hugo Finck, a U.S. naturalist who purchased a fifty-hectare hacienda for 3,500 pesos and proceeded to plant coffee alongside his orchids. Medium-sized haciendas were not the only landholding unit in the region by this time. A growing number of modest *ranchos,* small family farms a *caballería* (42.8 hectares) or less in size, began to appear on the lands leased in perpetuity by town councils beginning in the 1840s. The subsequent privatization of communal lands also encouraged the creation of ranchos in central Veracruz. The poor rancheros, who raised most of their own food and sold small surpluses of coffee, tobacco, and cattle to local merchants, probably had more in common with the peasant smallholders than with the wealthier cattle rancheros. In his excellent study of credit practices in the Córdoba-Orizaba region between the 1840s and 1860s, Eugene Wiemers discovered that one-half of the borrowers were rancheros requesting credit to finance the planting, cultivation, and harvesting of tobacco and coffee.[10]

What information is available on the gender division of labor in coffee production at mid-century? Carl Sartorius, a German naturalist and Huatusco hacienda owner, left behind an accurate account of coffee cultivation on the central Veracruz rancho. To begin with, coffee was still a relatively new export crop in central Veracruz in 1850. In Córdoba alone, he wrote, rancheros regularly cultivated coffee in garden lots shaded by orange, banana, and mango trees. It was the perfect crop for the small family producer, Sartorius believed, for one could easily grow a few thousand trees next to his cottage to supplement the family's income. Even though it takes coffee trees six or seven years to reach full maturity, subsistence crops could be raised within the coffee groves in the meantime. "One man can attend to 5,000 trees (the harvest not included); it is therefore evidently an advantageous investment for a small planter."[11]

Agricultural activities on the ranchos were clearly divided along gender lines and varied according to the time of year. During the rainy months the ranchero devoted his time to sowing corn, beans, tomatoes, chiles, and bananas on his half-hectare cultivated plot, which then needed little or no attention. The rest of the year he tended his cattle. The ranchero's wife concerned herself with household and reproduction activities in the main, but when the three or four months of labor-intensive coffee harvesting and processing came around, she contributed her fair share to the rural household income. Sartorius obviously considered the harvesting and processing of the coffee beans to be women's work: "Picking the ripe berries, cleaning, and drying them, is the work of women and children, and is all the easier, as they continue to ripen from November till March and the harvest can therefore be got in most leisurely."[12]

Sartorius's remarks make it quite clear that women were active contributors to the ranchero economy. The ranchero household was *not* supported by a single male worker but by multiple workers, male and female, all contributing to the shared or pooled family production. There is also evidence that women contributed to the harvesting of other commercial crops, such as sugar and tobacco, in nineteenth-century Veracruz.[13] On the other hand, Sartorius's words imply that women's work in the ranchero household was secondary to that of their spouses; that picking coffee, a "leisurely" task, could be easily sandwiched between a woman's other chores. Coffee harvesting, like many other forms of temporary labor-intensive work, was thus conceptualized as "women's work." The gender division of labor in ranchero coffee production seems to have been linked to several critical factors, including small-scale agriculture, the nature of coffee cultivation, low household income, and a patriarchal ideology. Women's agricultural activities outside the house were a part of family production, a logical extension of their household duties in a poor household economy. Their work was conceptualized by Sartorius as temporary and expendable, and thus supplementary. Patricia Arias sustains essentially the same argument elsewhere in this volume.

The Coffee Boom

Four interrelated factors dramatically changed Córdoba's economy during the Porfiriato. First, its economy became integrated into the international market with the development of the Porfirian transportation and communication systems. In 1873 Córdoba was linked to the railroad line just recently completed between Mexico City and Veracruz. Two decades later the Ferrocarril Veracruz al Istmo began to be constructed from Córdoba south through the Valle Nacional to meet the Tehuantepec line. Roads and telegraph services were also extended during the same decade, giving Córdoba cheap and fast access to both the port of Veracruz for the export of commercial crops and to the interior of the republic.[14]

Second, the Cordoban economy began to feel the impact of the world market more directly. The dramatic decline in demand for tobacco in the

1870s coupled with the simultaneous growth in demand for coffee resulted in rapid changes in crop production throughout Mexico. In Veracruz alone, coffee production increased between 1895 and 1907 from 5 million to 32 million kilograms, representing approximately half the coffee cultivated in the entire republic. Although speculation in coffee growing occurred primarily in virgin land in the Coatepec, Huatusco, and sierra regions, Cordoban production increased from 3 million to 5.6 million kilograms. A dramatic shift from sugar to coffee production occurred throughout the canton in the 1880s as major hacienda owners such as Ramón Garay converted their sugar haciendas into coffee fincas. Coffee became the predominant crop cultivated on medium-sized fincas, ranchos, and smallholdings, and sugar dropped to second place.[15]

The third factor explaining the coffee boom was President Porfirio Díaz's economic policies, founded on the principle of "development from without." His initiatives to woo North American and European entrepreneurs and corporations to invest in large-scale coffee production had less impact in Córdoba than in Chiapas, yet foreign investment increased considerably in coffee fincas, coffee processing, and the wholesale business within the region. Outside capital was also attracted by the developmentalist policies of Governor Teodoro Dehesa, who gave tax exemptions to producers growing export crops such as coffee, tobacco, sugar, and fruit trees.[16] The expansion of commercial coffee production did not occur until the largest producers had accumulated enough finance capital to invest in the machinery for coffee processing. Until 1882 the entire state had only four old-fashioned *beneficios húmedos* (wet processors) to depulp and wash the coffee berries. Most of the small coffee producers depulped the coffee of its outer shell manually in mortars and then spread it out on large cement terraces to dry. Unable to proceed further, these producers then sold their coffee as *café corriente* (ordinary coffee) to middlemen at very low prices. By 1889 Córdoba boasted numerous sophisticated processors that mechanically depulped and washed the coffee berries, after which they dried, skinned, polished, and separated the beans. The owners of these new coffee processors were often local coffee producers or buyers. Coffee processors Ramón Garay, Juan A. Foster, and Emilio Pardo and Son owned four of Córdoba's largest fincas: Tapia, Zacatepec, La Luz, and San Miguelito. By 1907, foreign capital had made inroads into the region and had established a flourishing banking community alongside the coffee-processing industry. Córdoba's four new steam and electrically powered processors were no longer owned by municipal landowners but by new outside entrepreneurs (see Table 3.1).[17]

Fourth, President Díaz and Governor Dehesa, his close friend, had created a climate of political stability in Veracruz that fostered the rapid expansion of coffee production. His ability to tie political moderation to develop-

Table 3.1
Coffee-Processing Plants in the Municipality of Córdoba, 1907

Owner	Year	Kilograms coffee processed	Workers		Wages (centovos)	
			Male	Female	Male	Female
Vda. Pedro Díaz	1903	1,400,000	2	—	50	—
B. L. Tomblin	1895	690,000	70	200	100	50
Menendez	1907	644,000	50	180	100	50
P. Candandass	1902	920,000	10	40	100	50

Source: Municipal Archive of Córdoba, 1908, vol. 310, Exp. "Fomento, Geografía, y Estadística."

mentalist economic strategies made Dehesa the darling of the landowning classes, who profited from his fiscal and land policies during his tenure (1892–1911). The only exception to the favorable treatment granted to commercial farmers was the high tariffs levied on agricultural exports, which were used to finance the state's educational system. The coffee landowners exercised unquestioned hegemony over the canton's political affairs.[18]

The coffee boom contributed to a demographic increase in the canton of Córdoba during the Porfiriato. Population growth did contribute to the rapid increase, but internal migration played a more important role. In 1877 Córdoba's largely mestizo population numbered only 26,000. Two decades later it had soared to 79,000, and by 1910 it had expanded to 91,000. Much like the neighboring canton of Orizaba, Córdoba's booming economy attracted impoverished rural sierra families searching for employment. *Poblanos* (inhabitants of the state of Puebla) made up the most important contingent of migrants between 1895 and 1910, roughly 10 percent of the Cordoban population. The gender ratio of the out-of-state population in 1910 was roughly equal, leading to the inference that entire families rather than individuals were migrating down from the sierra to rural communities and urban settlements within the canton.[19] These demographic developments were to significantly change the landholding patterns and rural labor systems.

By the turn of the century the Cordoban land tenure system was quite complex. The coffee finca had emerged out of the colonial sugar haciendas, although the landholdings remained essentially intact.[20] Three noticeable changes affected these medium-sized landholdings, which averaged 550 hectares in size, in the last two decades of the nineteenth century: their numbers had been somewhat reduced, and some fincas had undergone consolidation, but the most significant transformation was a change in ownership. Adrianna Naveda's excellent study of Cordoban colonial sugar haciendas reveals that several families continued to monopolize most of the land resources after the Wars of Independence: Zevallos, de la Llave, Jaurequi, Morgado y

Table 3.2
Landholdings and Rural Laborers in the Municipality of Córdoba, 1897, 1907, 1910

	Landholding			Hectares		Rural laborers		Daily wage (centavos)	
Year	Haciendas	Ranchos	Others	Cultivated	Uncultivated	Male	Female	Male	Female
1897	14	151	660*	—	—	—	—	50	25
1907	15	13	713	3,541	34,982	2,175	430	50–75	25
1910	15	25	749	4,520	34,002	2,380	545	50–75	25

Source: Municipal Archive of Córdoba, 1898, vol. 258, Exp. "Estadística"; 1908, vol. 310; 1911, vol. 325.
*Estimate based on number of coffee producers in Table 3.3.

Clavijo, Bringas Manzaneda, Segura, and Gómez. By 1902, however, only one of those names appeared on Southworth's list of canton landowners. Foreign names such as Braniff, Uhink, Lemaistre, Marure, Zaldos, and Adams appeared, and their number continued to grow. Members of the new coffee elite did not spend their time living sedately on remote coffee estates. They preferred to cavort for half the year with the European elite in Paris and thought nothing of spending coffee profits to import French artwork and furniture for their mansions.[21]

In the municipality of Córdoba, one of fourteen municipalities in the canton, ranchos and smallholdings coexisted alongside the medium-sized fincas. The 1897 agricultural census lists only 151 ranchos (see Table 3.2), but evidence suggests that hundreds of smaller holdings, classified here simply as "other," dotted the municipality. An 1897 list of 831 coffee cultivators reveals how high the percentage of small coffee properties actually was (see Table 3.3). When I broke down the cultivators based on the number of *matas* (coffee trees) they cultivated, I was able to distinguish different types of landholdings. These figures do not in any way correlate with the exact size of property holdings, but they do approximate the size of the coffee groves. The list includes the largest fincas as well as the tiniest parcels, described sometimes simply as *solares*.[22] In Veracruz a farmer needed to cultivate a minimum of ten hectares of coffee to support a family. To be classified as a rancho a property would have had to be larger than ten hectares in size to produce any surplus for sale in the outside market. Therefore, I use the term *rancho* in Córdoba to describe a property with a coffee grove approximately eight to thirty-eight hectares in size—the equivalent of a 10,000 to 49,000 coffee tree grove.[23] Of all the coffee producers, 9.7 percent (103) had access to coffee groves of this size. As many as 85.0 percent of the producers (706) cultivated less than eight hectares—that is, fewer than 10,000 trees—and will be referred to as subsistence smallholders.

The classification of coffee groves in Table 3.3 clearly reveals the overparcelization of Cordoban landholdings. Karl Kaerger, an agricultural expert sent by the German government to investigate investment possibilities for German investors, remarked that the coffee fincas in Veracruz were less impressive than the new plantations in Soconusco. With the exception of the few fincas owned by foreigners, Kaerger observed, they were so small that a harvest of three hundred *quintales* (1 quintal = 100 kilograms) was considered large. What is more, growers planted the coffee trees too close together, provided no shade trees over the groves, and weeded so poorly that their yields were only one-fourth to one-half a pound per tree. On the smaller fincas, trees were horribly overpicked. The smaller finqueros, Kaerger lamented, were still depulping the coffee with wooden mortars.[24] Despite his obvious preference for large-scale agriculture and foreign entrepreneurs, Kaerger's comments give the distinct impression that overparcelization and overcultivation hindered production and held down yields on the smallholdings in Córdoba. The diminishing productivity encountered by small-scale producers seems to have resulted in greater land parcelization, underemployment, surplus labor, and falling real incomes.[25]

Economic impoverishment of the peasant household was one of the most important factors behind the growing number of rural women entering coffee production in Córdoba. Lack of access to advanced coffee-processing techniques on the ranchos and smallholdings depressed family income-earning capacity. For the landless peasant family, economic conditions were not much better. Rural wages in Córdoba remained unusually low and did not keep pace with the soaring cost of living that plagued the final years of the Porfiriato. A single male day laborer who had earned fifty centavos in 1899 was still receiving the same wage in 1910, and other members of the family were forced into the labor market just to sustain the family. At the same time, the coffee boom was creating a new demand for wage labor, thus providing women as well as men with new employment opportunities.

Table 3.3
Coffee Producers in the Municipality of Córdoba by Gender, 1897

| Gender | Smallholdings (trees) | | Ranchos[a] | Haciendas[b] | Total |
	1–4,999	5,000–9,999			
Males	493	108	93	19	713
Percent	84.6	87.8	90.3	86.4	
Females	90	15	10	3	118
Percent	15.4	12.2	9.7	13.6	
Total	583	123	103	22	831

Source: Municipal Archive of Córdoba, 1898, vol. 258, Exp. "Fomento, Geografía y Estadística."
[a]10,000–49,999 coffee trees.
[b]50,000–510,000 coffee trees.

Gender Division of Labor and Porfirian Censuses

Mexican census takers during the Porfiriato based their data-collection procedures on a male-dominated farming system, and the category *jefe de familia* always referred to the male head of household. This socially constructed view of the rural family contributed to imprecise definitions of family, work, and occupational categories and encouraged inaccurate data collection up until the 1960s. "Work" comprised activities that were directly or indirectly remunerated. The socially constructed gender roles predisposed women to perceive themselves as primarily housewives and mothers, and they were reluctant to list a primary occupation other than these two categories. Unfortunately, since the census data do not account for all the income-generating activities of family members, the multiplicity and heterogeneity of rural occupations for men and women remain unclear.[26]

The national population censuses of 1900 and 1910 supply data on occupation by gender at the canton or district level, but only the 1900 census includes information for the municipal level. Only three major categories are used to describe rural occupations: farmer (*agricultor*), cattle rancher (*ganadero*), and rural laborer (*peón/jornalero*). A number of difficulties arise from the use of these limited occupational categories. For example, the term *peón/jornalero* was incorrectly used as a catchall for all rural occupations not included in the other two categories; that is, resident peon, day worker, tenant farmer, sharecropper, comunero, and part-time small property owner.[27] Here, I use the term *rural laborer* for the many types of day laborers living and working on the hacienda and/or in an independent community under a variety of labor management arrangements.

Despite these definitional pitfalls, these censuses do reveal more about the gender division of labor than the pre-1940 postrevolutionary censuses. Compared with the 1900 census,[28] the 1910 census reveals a surprisingly high level of female participation in agriculture in certain cantons of Veracruz. In the categories of farmer and rural laborer, three of the eighteen cantons stand out (see Table 3.4).[29] In Córdoba, Orizaba, and Jalacingo, between 21.7 and 34.6 percent of the rural laborers were female. In terms of total numbers, these three cantons had roughly 22,000 of the estimated 25,475 female rural laborers in the entire state. These figures must be taken with a grain of salt, as Francie Chassen-López's essay on Oaxaca in this volume reveals. Despite the underestimations, these figures provide a number of striking revelations with regard to the gender division of labor in agriculture. In the canton of Córdoba, roughly one out of every four wage laborers (23 percent) was female; further, almost one out of every three farmers (29.9 percent) was female.

How can we account for the high percentage of women wage laborers in

Table 3.4
Rural Occupations by Gender in Three Veracruz Cantons, 1910

	Farmers				Wage laborers			
	Male	%	Female	%	Male	%	Female	%
Córdoba	1,638	70.1	697	29.9	22,719	77.0	6,800	23.0
Orizaba	968	96.2	38	3.8	17,725	65.4	9,360	34.6
Jalacingo	351	96.2	14	3.8	18,312	78.3	5,062	21.7
Subtotal	2,957	79.8	749	20.2	58,756	73.5	21,222	26.5
Veracruz	17,086	92.8	1,319	7.2	270,101	91.8	24,155	8.2

Source: Tercer censo de población, 1910, 2:1215–59.

these three cantons in 1910? González Montes argues that the high number of female workers in the state of México was due in large part to impoverishment, concentrated landholdings, the penetration of commercial agriculture, and the migration of male workers in increasing numbers to Morelos to work on sugar plantations, leaving the women at home to perform the agricultural work.[30] The increasing parcelization of landholdings, miserably low wages, rising cost of living, and sizable migration into Córdoba certainly contributed to rural impoverishment and did indeed act as push factors forcing more members of peasant families into income-generating activities. At the same time, however, the rapid growth of coffee as the principal commercial crop in the three cantons created a new demand for rural labor, a pull factor. (The low levels of female wage labor in the coffee-producing cantons of Coatepec and Huatusco are hard to explain; perhaps data collection was uneven.)

If national census data can provide only an outline of female participation in wage labor in these three cantons, municipal data for Córdoba furnishes more clues. The municipal census data, like most microlevel material, are incomplete and regionally variable. For instance, the Cordoban agricultural censuses of 1895, 1907, and 1910 classify rural laborers according to gender, but Orizaban municipal censuses do not.[31]

Local census takers defined women's occupations according to their own socially constructed views of women's roles. The municipal census takers employed numerous male occupational categories (rural laborer, worker, blacksmith, muleteer, tenant farmer, etc.) but only one female occupational category, *doméstica* (housewife). Even more commonly, the local census taker left the space for occupation blank for women. The one exception I found was in the census from the settlement of Monte Blanco, which lists as "jornalero" or "jornalera" every man, woman, and child between the ages of twelve and fifty-five.[32] Whether this reflected laziness on the part of the census taker or a recognition of the economic reality is impossible to determine. Despite these shortcomings, the municipal census data provide sufficient material on gender with regard to agricultural producers, permanent and temporary day laborers, and agroindustrial workers engaged in coffee processing to substantiate the argument that the commercialization of coffee production contributed to a higher level of female participation in coffee production.

Gender and Work in a Coffee Economy

When the 831 coffee cultivators in Table 3.3 are divided on the basis of gender, it becomes clear that women played a substantial role in coffee production (118 out of 831 cultivators). The largest numbers of both male and female cultivators were poor smallholders cultivating less than eight hectares of coffee. In terms of the male-female ratios in the four categories of growers, females made up 10–15 percent of the total.[33]

The list of coffee cultivators often provides the name of the property, so some parcels can be located on or outside the larger coffee fincas according to gender. For instance, fifty-one producers, cultivating on the average 1,000–5,000 trees, listed Monte Blanco as the name of their parcel. The Braniffs, the owners of Monte Blanco finca, gave parcels to *colonos* or sharecroppers, to tie them to the estate. Since coffee finca owners did not have sufficient work all year round to support a large resident population, they arranged for the peasants to pay some percentage of their harvest in cash or in kind for the use of the parcel. Only two of the fifty-one coffee producers on Monte Blanco were women, and both were single and over the age of fifty-five.[34] This one example suggests that finca owners preferred to dole out small parcels to male heads of families rather than to females. On the other hand, many of the remaining female cultivators on the list probably were independent smallholders.

The list also hints at the marital status of the female cultivators and the type of family unit to which they may have belonged. The majority of the 118 females in Table 3.3 seem to have been unmarried or widowed women. This observation is based on the fact that 62 of the women's names had no family member listed on either side of their name. The other 56 names had either male or female relatives listed beside theirs, which might mean that they were members of a heterogeneous family. In these cases, females generally cultivated the same amount of land as males with the same last name, suggesting that gender was not such an important factor in land inheritance.[35]

The gender division of day laborers was tightly linked to the nature of coffee production. Coffee is a labor-intensive crop that does not lend itself to economies of scale. In Córdoba, coffee trees were usually planted close together in hilly regions underneath shade trees, making mechanization of production difficult. As a consequence, few labor-saving devices were available for coffee production, and producers could economize only by trying to impose forms of work organization that reduced wages and monetary costs.[36]

Cordoban finqueros used a variety of labor systems to obtain a stable labor supply and reduce labor costs. They usually engaged in mixed agriculture, so resident peons harvested different crops at varying times of the year. We also know that finqueros rented out small parcels to tenant farmers on the fringes of their estates to retain a reserve labor pool at little or no cost. Third, they gave parcels to resident sharecroppers to tie them to the hacienda. Sharecroppers lived permanently on the hacienda, and their main source of income was the land the hacienda put at their disposal. At harvest time planters obliged them to work as temporary forced laborers. Fourth, finqueros hired poor peasants from the surrounding communities as well as migrant families as supplemental temporary workers for harvesting. Finally, they contracted all available female relatives of the above groups as permanent or temporary day workers.

The labor needs of coffee fincas varied enormously according to the growth cycle of the coffee trees and the time of the year. Once the initial capital and labor investment had been made to clear the land, plant the seedlings, and transplant them in carefully laid out rows, a relatively large labor supply was needed for only three critical tasks: monthly weeding, the harvest, and processing. The largest landowners—Thomas Braniff, Ignacio Vivanco, José Lama and his successors, and the Escandón sisters, who owned Monte Blanco, Las Animas, Zapoapita, and San Francisco, respectively— employed between one and three hundred permanent wage laborers on their estates in 1910. Even though the coffee harvesting usually required only one-fifth more laborers than that, Cordoban planters would contract three to four times as many temporary workers, a good many of whom migrated down from the sierra to harvest coffee. Furthermore, the many impoverished rancheros, tenant farmers, sharecroppers, and smallholders from the surrounding area who needed supplemental income also hired themselves out as temporary workers.

Labor conditions for temporary workers on wealthy fincas were dismal. Usually they lived in rows of sheds in which each family was allotted one room; a shelf along the wall served as a bed. The workers were continually in debt to the landowner, and flogging was not uncommon. Foreign observers were wont to describe this labor system as a form of disguised slavery.[37]

Cordoban rancheros and subsistence cultivators either farmed their small coffee groves directly or rented them out. They cultivated a variety of crops, including tobacco, corn, and other subsistence crops, underneath the coffee trees. Smallholders sold their coffee and tobacco to the large processors. Very often they also earned additional income by working as day laborers.[38] Gender did not play a significant role in the subsistence coffee economy, where economic priorities took precedence over patriarchal family values. Once the coffee trees had been planted, the cleaning, harvesting, and drying of the beans could be handled by any member of the peasant family. Thus women could be actively engaged in coffee cultivation as either rancheras or subsistence cultivators.

The Córdoba municipal census provides good data on the gender division of labor for permanent rural workers (peones/jornaleros). Table 3.2 shows that women made up 16.5 percent of the rural workers in 1907 and 18.6 percent in 1910. In other words, roughly one out of every six wage laborers was a women. The number of women engaged in coffee production seems to have increased more rapidly than the number of men during the last decade of the Porfiriato. The percentage of women wage laborers in the municipality of Córdoba was lower than the percentage for the canton as a whole (see Table 3.4), probably because urban women living in the city of Córdoba did not need (because of their higher income level) or desire to engage in supplementary agricultural work. They more often listed their principal occupation as housewife.[39] In the other more rural municipalities, there were few employment opportunities other than coffee production.

Unfortunately, the Cordoban data do not provide information on the gender division of temporary workers. We know only that the eighteen largest landowners hired 3,615 temporary workers in 1910.[40] The standard practice was to contract entire families by the day to fulfill a particular task or to harvest a specified number of coffee trees.

John Southworth, Karl Kaerger, Matías Romero, and Charles Macomb Flandrau all distinguished between male tasks and female tasks in coffee production. Preparing the land for the coffee trees, including burning the forest, sowing corn during the first year, preparation of the rows, care of the seedlings, and their transplanting, were male tasks. Men pruned the coffee trees each year. Weeding and harvesting, on the other hand, were female tasks. With regard to the monthly weeding, Southworth thought that "the best and cheapest labor for this purpose is . . . women and children."[41]

In the case of coffee harvesting, Romero was of the opinion that "women and children perform the labor of picking the fruit better than men." The implication here is that women were more meticulous and patient in performing such boring work. Another indication that the labor-intensive task of coffee picking was in fact a predominantly female occupation can be gleaned from Southworth's photographs of coffee harvesters in Veracruz, which portray only women and children.[42]

Gender division in coffee processing was clearly established before the 1850s. Men were in charge of the depulping and cleaning and the drying on the large cement terraces; the women and children picked over the coffee by hand and classified it into different classes before it was sacked. The steam and electric processors constructed in the 1890s created new jobs. The skilled positions—operating the machines to depulp, wash, skin, and polish the coffee beans—went to men. The manual, labor-intensive occupation—the sorting of the dry coffee into five to seven categories—was left entirely to women and children. Thus, the new agroindustrial positions perpetuated the already established gender segregation. By 1907, roughly 500 women and 150 men were employed by the four processors of Córdoba (see Table 3.1). Even though women represented 75 percent of the workforce, they held the lowest-paying, lowest-prestige, most labor-intensive positions.

"The famous coffee sorters of Córdoba," as they were euphemistically referred to, might have been famous for their contribution to the region's coffee production, but in no way was their work glorious. Coffee growers contracted only rural or urban women and their children to work as sorters because they could pay them lower wages and make them work long hours in miserable working conditions for four to six months each year. Hundreds of women spent twelve hours a day in one room, hunched over a table in their wooden clogs, sorting the beans and depositing them into different chutes to be sent to adjoining rooms for packaging. Despite these inhumane conditions, women still preferred factory jobs to working in the fields. Women sorters interviewed by Cecilia Sheridan considered themselves in a more favorable occupational position than rural workers in the 1920s, for the pay was higher and the working day was shorter.[43]

Thus, the commercialization of coffee in Córdoba seems to have increased the employment opportunities and the variety of agricultural work open to women. A sizable number of both coffee producers and permanent and temporary rural laborers before 1910 were women. Yet commercialized agriculture was at the same time exploiting women as a cheap, readily available labor force, relegating them to temporary, low-paying occupations.

Gender, Wages, and Families

The interrelationship between gender and rural wages is a complex one; it must be examined in terms of all forms of monetary and nonmonetary family income. Although my information on nonmonetary sources of income, including rations, sizes of residents' plots, and family expenditures, is incomplete, the information available on wages does highlight the gender differences in rural wages.

In new regions of coffee production, where labor was scarce, the common practice was to hire and exploit entire sierra families, including the children. In Chiapas, according to Kaerger's report, the colono system was used to keep families on the fincas. Each colono family was given a parcel to grow subsistence crops, and in return, male and female able-bodied workers were obliged to work all year on the estate. Their salary depended on whether the family was in debt. Rural workers without debts earned 62.5 centavos a day; those with debts were paid only 50 centavos. Kaerger did not record wages according to gender.[44]

The wage system was more complex in central Veracruz because of the multiplicity of landholding units, the denser population, and the interlocking labor systems. Day laborers were paid at a task rate for clearing, preparing the ground for coffee cultivation, and planting. In 1886, for example, a worker was paid 37 centavos per day for digging one hundred holes one *vara* (1 vara = .838 meters in depth). Wages for harvesting were based on either a task rate or a piece rate. On the Sartorius finca, a (male) worker was compensated 37.5 centavos for picking 0.25 *carga* (1 carga = 1.25 bushels) or 900 square varas. Wages did not keep up with the rise in the cost of living by the end of the Porfiriato. In 1900 Kaerger reported that permanent coffee finca workers in Córdoba were still being paid 37.5 centavos, and only rarely did they receive a plot of land to cultivate. Temporary harvesters who migrated from the altiplano were paid a daily wage based on a specified amount of piecework. Unfortunately, the data do not reveal how much of this wage was paid in cash. On Ignacio Vivanco's estate in Fortín, wages were very often paid in food and in kind rather than cash. The rural laborers observed by Hendrik Muller were not given plots to grow subsistence crops and were obliged to buy their food supplies from the hacienda owners. Many of them had been advanced monies for alcohol, medicine, and the fees for marriage ceremonies (usually about 50 pesos), which kept the laborers continually in debt. The landowners allowed laborers to pay off their debts only through additional labor service.[45]

Table 3.2 shows that permanent female rural laborers were paid one-third to one-half of what men earned, and this ratio did not change between 1897 and 1910. While women's wages remained constant at 25 centavos per task per day, men's rose slightly from 50 to 75 centavos. Both socioeconomic factors and gender ideology could be called on to explain this unequal treatment. The surplus of inactive, accessible female laborers living on or near the fincas made it possible for planters to hire them for lower wages. Yet there can be no doubt that patriarchal values discouraged women from working for wages outside the peasant household unit unless the household was in dire economic circumstances. Since women's income was viewed by rural society as supplemental and temporary, women could be offered—and would accept—a lower wage. It was the general belief that women could complete only 50–60 percent as much work as men, so why should they be paid more?[46]

It is interesting that temporary workers hired for the harvest season regardless of gender were often paid as well as or better than the permanent laborers in Córdoba. Cordoban female harvesters earned 50 to 62 centavos in 1897, the equivalent of a permanent male laborer's wage. When the demand for labor was high, wage differentiation based on gender seems to have disappeared. At harvest time, coffee producers ceased treating peasant families as patriarchal peasant household units and instead paid family members as individual wage earners.[47]

In the processing plants, female coffee sorters earned double what they would have earned as day laborers in the coffee groves of Córdoba: 50 centavos as opposed to 25. Yet a gender gap certainly existed in the factory wage scale. Women were confined to unskilled work, while the men worked in skilled jobs that paid twice as much (see Table 3.1).[48] The increased gender differentiation in the division of labor brought on by the expansion of commercial agriculture was institutionalized into a two-tiered wage scale. When Lourdes Arizpe and Josefina Aranda observed the same phenomenon in the Zamora strawberry industry in the 1960s, they aptly called this strategy "comparative advantage."[49] Coffee processors in Córdoba used the same practices sixty years earlier to lower production costs by employing abundant, cheap female labor.

Conclusions

This essay has explored the gender division of labor in coffee cultivation and how it was modified by the onset of coffee commercialization. As early as the first half of the nineteenth century, long before capitalist penetration into the ranchero coffee economy, the gender division of labor was already clearly delineated. With the commercialization of coffee production in the last half of the nineteenth century, medium-sized hacienda owners shifted to growing coffee and began to employ interlocking labor systems to retain a stable labor supply and minimize labor costs. The continued concentration of coffee fincas in the hands of a small rural oligarchy and the burgeoning population contributed to the parcelization of ranchos and smallholdings. Struggling peasant households sent more family members out to work as wage laborers. The coffee boom contributed to an increase in employment opportunities and resulted in a diversification of specialized occupations. The net effect of these long-term socioeconomic processes was greater involvement of women in coffee production. Yet the diversification of economic roles had a negative effect on gender segregation. Patriarchal values seemed to have reinforced a two-tiered system of work and wages, relegating many women to lower-paying, less skilled, temporary manual work.

What were the implications of the greater participation of women in coffee production by the end of the Porfiriato? We cannot discount the adverse effects of capital development on female rural workers. The view of "women's work" as temporary, seasonal, lower-paying work was certainly reinforced by the traditional gender ideology, and women suffered for it. But we should not ignore the positive effects. One out of seven cultivators, one out of six permanent day workers, as many as half of the temporary workers, and four out of five processing workers were female: women were now contributing to the rural family income in a significant way. A female day worker in a nuclear household with only two wage earners could have earned as much as one-third of the family's income.

This increase in women's economic contribution to family income must have affected their social status within and outside the family. The multitude of ownership, rental, and labor systems permitted women to work outside the confines of the rural household in many different agricultural occupations; this gave them greater economic and social autonomy. In his study of the increased role of women in the Colombian coffee economy during the same period, Michael Jiménez suggests that it was more difficult for families to supervise working women, thus giving them greater freedom of action. In addition, with men spending more time outside the home as hired day laborers, women were gaining more responsibility in the household.[50] Women's enhanced status and decision-making power might well have begun to influence gender ideology.

I will do no more here than suggest the implications of these findings, for these same issues are taken up in greater detail by Gail Mummert and Soledad González Montes later in this volume. What is clear, however, is that the rural family economy of the nineteenth century must be studied as a heterogeneous family economy, with multiple income generators, in which women played significant economic as well as social roles.

NOTES

I gratefully acknowledge the financial assistance of a National Endowment for the Humanities Research Fellowship for College Teachers, which allowed me to conduct part of the research for this essay during the fall of 1991. I also thank Francie Chassen-López, Soledad González Montes, Carmen Ramos-Escandón, Mary Kay Vaughan, and two anonymous reviewers for their comments on an earlier version of this chapter.

1. See, e.g., Jan Bazant, "Landlord, Labourer, and Tenant in San Luis Potosí Northern Mexico, 1821–1910," in *Land and Labor in Latin America,* ed. K. Duncan and I. Routledge (Cambridge: Cambridge University Press, 1977), 59–81; Friedrich Katz, "Labor Conditions on Haciendas in Porfirian Mexico: Some Trends and Tendencies," *Hispanic American Historical Review* 54.1 (1974):1–47; Franz Schryer, *The*

Rancheros of Pisaflores. The History of a Peasant Bourgeoisie in Twentieth Century Mexico (Toronto: University of Toronto Press, 1980), 26–29, 53–4; Charles A. Harris, *A Mexican Family Empire: The Latifundio of the Sánchez Navarro Family, 1765–1867* (Austin: University of Texas Press, 1975).

2. Lourdes Arizpe, "Mujer campesina, mujer indígena," *América Indígena* 35.3 (1975):575–86; Arizpe, *Parentesco y economía en una sociedad nahua* (Mexico City: Instituto Nacional Indigenista, 1973). John Tutino discusses multiple wage earners and the economic contributions of women in "Family Economics in Agrarian Mexico, 1750–1910," *Journal of Family History* 10.3 (1985):259–62. For a discussion of the heterogeneous family farming system, see Carmen Diana Deere, *Household and Class Relations. Peasants and Landlords in Northern Peru* (Berkeley: University of California Press, 1992), especially 95–147.

3. Carmen Diana Deere, "What Difference Does Gender Make? Rethinking Peasant Studies," in *Women and Agriculture in the Third World*, ed. Simi Afonja (London: Macmillan, forthcoming).

4. Carmen Ramos-Escandón, "Mujeres trabajadoras en el México porfiriano: Género e ideología del trabajo femenino, 1876–1911," *European Review of Latin American and Caribbean Studies* 48 (June 1990):27–44.

5. Soledad González Montes, "Trabajo feminino y expansión de las relaciones capitalistas en el México rural a fines del Porfiriato: El Distrito de Tenango del Valle, Estado de México, 1900–1910," in *Hacienda, pueblos y comunidades. Los valles de México y Toluca entre 1530 y 1910*, ed. Manuel Miño Grijalva (Mexico City: Consejo Nacional para la Cultura y las Artes, 1991), 270–341.

6. Luis González y González, *Historia moderna de México. La república restaurada. La vida social* (Mexico City: Editorial Hermes, 1974), 74; Eugene L. Wiemers, Jr., "Agriculture and Credit in Nineteenth Century Mexico: Córdoba and Orizaba, 1822–71," *Hispanic American Historical Review* 65.3 (1985):522.

7. Adrianna Naveda Chávez-Hita, *Esclavos negros en las haciendas azucareras de Córdoba, Veracruz, 1690–1830* (Jalapa: Universidad Veracruzana, CIH, 1987), 87, 92–4; Wiemers, "Agriculture and Credit," 523.

8. Naveda, *Esclavos negros*, 155–56; Carl Christian Sartorius, *Mexico about 1850* (Stuttgart, 1961), 176; Wiemers, "Agriculture and Credit," 523; Enrique Herrera Moreno, *El Cantón de Córdoba. Apuntes de geografía, estadística, historia, etc.* (Córdoba, 1892), for the political and military history of the region before 1850.

9. Ramón Rodríguez Rivera, *Apuntes históricos, geográficos, estadísticos y descriptivos, tomados de distintas obras para la formación de la historia de Córdoba* (Córdoba: El Porvenir, 1876), 83, 88; Gabriel Gómez, *Cultivo y beneficio del café*, 2d ed. (Mexico City: Oficina Tipográfica de la Secretaría de Fomento, 1899), 23–24; Nelly Josefa León Fuentes, "Conformación de un capital en torno a la caficultura en la region de Xalapa-Coatepec, 1890–1940" (Master's thesis, Universidad Veracruzana, 1983), 24; R. Herrera, "El Café de Córdoba," *Boletín de la Sociedad Agricola Mexicana* 24.4 (1889):64; F. A. Ober, *Travels in Mexico* (San Francisco: J. Dewing, 1884), 205, 209.

10. Wiemers, "Agriculture and Credit," 524, 528–33; Ober, *Travels in Mexico*, 205, 208; José María Naredo, *Estudio, geográfico, histórico, e estadístico del Cantón y de la Ciudad de Orizaba* (Orizaba, 1898), 68–80; Carlos Sartorius, "Memoria sobre el

estado de la agricultura en el Partido de Huatusco," *Boletín de la Sociedad Mexicana de Geografía y Estadística* 2 (1870):165.

11. Sartorius, *Mexico about 1850*, 178–62, and "Huatusco," 162.

12. Sartorius, *Mexico about 1850*, 175.

13. Naveda discovered female slaves participating in sugar harvesting in Córdoba in the early 1800s (*Esclavos negros*, 114). Women and children migrants worked in tobacco production around San Andrés Tuxtla, especially during the curing season. León Medel y Alvarado, *La historia de San Andrés Tuxtla* (Mexico City: Editorial Citlaltépetl, 1963), 1:435.

14. González y González, *La vida social*, 74; Daniel Cosío Villegas, *La historia moderna de México. La República Restaurada. La vida económica.* (Mexico City: Editorial Hermes, 1955), 576, 694; Francie R. Chassen, *Regionales y ferrocarriles en la Oaxaca porfirista* (Oaxaca: Carteles, 1990), 13, 31–2.

15. Ministerio de Fomento, *Anuarios estadísticos de la República Mexicana* (1895, 1907) (Mexico City: Oficina Tip.[ográfica] de la Secretaria de Fomento, 1896, 1912), 824–25, 521, 535; Karl Kaerger, *Agricultura y colonización en México*, trans. Pedro Lewin and Gudrin Dohmann (Mexico City: Universidad Autónoma de Chapingo, 1986), 77; see Daniela Spenser's discussion of the same phenomenon in Chiapas: "Soconusco: The Formation of the Coffee Economy in Chiapas," in *Other Mexicos: Essays on Regional History, 1876–1910*, ed. Thomas Benjamin and William McNellie (Albuquerque: University of New Mexico Press, 1984), 123–43.

16. "Memoria presentada a la H. Legislatura del Estado libre y soberano de Veracruz-Llave el 18 de septiembre de 1890 por el gobernador constitucional, C. General Juan Enríquez," in Veracruz, *Informes de sus gobernadores, 1826–1986* (Xalapa: Estado de Veracruz, 1986), 4100; María Elena Sodi de Pallares, *Teodoro A. Dehesa: Una época y un hombre* (Mexico City: Editorial Citlaltépetl, 1959), 118.

17. R. Herrera, "El Café de Córdoba," 65–66; Cosío Villegas, *Historia moderna. La vida económica*, 222; "Memoria presentada a la H. Legislatura del Estado libre y soberano de Veracruz-Llave el 16 de septiembre de 1892 por el gobernador constitucional C.," in *Informes*, 1455; José María Mena, "El Cantón de Córdoba," *Boletín de la Sociedad Mexicana de Geografía y Estadística* 3 (1908):459; Carmen Blázquez and Soledad García, "Córdoba y la crisis económica de 1906–7" (unpublished MS, 1983); Cecilia Sheridan, *Mujer obrera y organización sindical. El sindicato de obreras desmanchadoras de café, Coatepec, Veracruz.* Cuadernos de la Casa Chata 76 (Mexico City: Centro de Investigaciones y Estudios Superiores en Antropología Social, 1983), 9.

18. Luis Cossio Silva, "La agricultura," in Cosío Villegas, *Historia moderna. La vida económica*, 100; Elena Azaola Garrido, *Rebelión y derrota del magonismo agrario* (Mexico City: SEP/80, 1982), 11–12, 68, 71. The coffee growers controlled the municipio in September 1911 when José Luis Vivanco Estevas was elected mayor; see Archivo Municipal de Córdoba [AMC], 1911, vol. 325, Exp. "Elecciones municipales."

19. Moisés González Navarro, *La historia moderna de México. El Porfiriato. La vida social* (Mexico City: Editorial Hermes, 1970), 124; *Segundo censo de población de los Estados Unidos Mexicanos verificado el 28 de octubre de 1900, Estado de Veracruz*, 131, 160; *Tercer censo de población de los Estados Unidos Mexicanos verificado el 27 de octubre de 1910. Estado de Veracruz*, 1:68, 398–99, 2:146. The city of Córdoba's popula-

tion grew only from 6,000 to 8,000 between 1877 and 1900; see Bernardo Díaz García, *Un pueblo fabril del porfiriato: Santa Rosa, Veracruz* (Mexico City: Fondo de Cultura Económica, 1981), 29, fn. 3.

20. If we discount the largest hacienda, Monte Blanco with 2,500 hectares, the average size of the twenty-one Cordoban haciendas listed by John Southworth in 1902 was 552 hectares; see Southworth, *The Official Directory of Mines and Estates of Mexico* (Mexico, 1910), 243.

21. AMC: 1908, vol. 310, Exp. Estadística, "Censo de Fomento, Colonización e Industria, 1907"; 1910, vol. 322, Exp. Estadística, "Agricultores en Grande." See Naveda, *Esclavos negros,* 56, 70–86; Ricardo Corso, José G. González, and David A. Skerritt, . . . *Nunca un desleal. Cándido Aguilar (1880–1960)* (Mexico City: El Colegio de México y Universidad Veracruzana, 1986), 13; R. Herrera, "El Café de Córdoba," 66. I am indebted to Raymond Th. Buve for recommending and translating Hendrik P. N. Muller's description of his visit to Ignacio Vivanco's coffee estate in Fortín in 1900. Muller, a Dutch geographer, was an expert on South Africa who compared labor conditions in Mexico with those in South Africa; see *Door Hetland van Columbus. Een Reisverhaal Door* (Haarlem: De Erven F. Bohn, 1905), 285.

22. *Solar* is a term generally used for a house lot. Since a solar was often as large as half a hectare, it often included a family garden. See Karl Kaerger, "El Centro," in *La servidumbre agraria en México en la época porfiriana,* ed. Friedrich Katz (Mexico City: SEP, 1976), 166.

23. Ober calculated it was necessary to cultivate a minimum of 25 acres of coffee in 1883 (roughly 10 hectares) to support a family (*Travels in Mexico,* 208). I used John Southworth's estimate that 1,300 trees could be grown on 1 hectare to arrive at my calculations. Therefore, 10,000 trees could be grown on roughly 8 hectares. See Southworth, *El Estado de Veracruz-Llave. Sus historia, agricultura, comercio e industrias* (Jalapa: Gobierno del Estado, 1910), 38–39.

Franz Schryer described the ranchos of Pisaflores, Hidalgo, during the same period as landholdings worth 50 to 999 pesos (roughly 20 to 400 hectares). The rancheros were heads of households owning cattle, paying taxes on commercial production of sugarcane or coffee, owning stores, and slaughtering cattle, and thus were able to accumulate small surpluses (*Rancheros,* 31–33). Much less land was devoted exclusively to coffee production than in Córdoba.

24. Kaerger, "El Centro," 126–28.

25. Corso et al., *Nunca un desleal,* 14. See a discussion of the same minifundization in Colombia in Marcos Palacios, *Coffee in Colombia, 1850–1950* (Cambridge: Cambridge University Press, 1980), 69.

26. Carmen Diana Deere and Magdalena León de Leal, *Women in Andean Agriculture* (Geneva: International Labor Office, 1982), 11–12.

27. Francois-Xavier Guerra, *Le Mexique de l'ancien regime a la Revolution* (Paris: Editions L'Harmattan, 1985), 2:472–89; Jean Meyer, "Haciendas y ranchos, peones y campesinos en el porfiriato, algunas falacias estadísticas," *Historia Mexicana* 35.3 (1986):491–92.

28. I discount this census because I believe the enormous difference between the 1900 and 1910 levels of female participation in agriculture are better explained by

serious underreporting in 1900 rather than by any significant change in women's level of agricultural activity. González Montes makes the same observation with regard to the 1900 census for Tenango in "Trabajo feminino," 280–81, 286–87.

29. *Segundo censo,* 72–73, 162–63, 252–53.

30. González Montes, "Trabajo feminino," 288–97.

31. Two explanations for this inconsistency come to mind. In industrialized Orizaba, few women hired themselves out as rural workers because they could find more lucrative employment in the textile mills. In addition, the major coffee and tobacco fincas in the canton of Orizaba were found in municipalities farther to the east toward Córdoba. Archivo Municipal de Orizaba: 1895, vol. 135, Exp. Estadística; 1908, vol. 208, Exp. Estadística; 1911, vol. 315, Exp. Estadística.

32. AMC, 1900, vol. 269, Exp. Padrones generales.

33. Although the municipal census employs the word *propietario* for these coffee and sugar growers, I prefer the term *cultivator* because I have no way to verify land titles. In the 1950s in the coffee region of the Sierra Norte of Puebla, Lourdes Arizpe found that 38.6 percent of the property owners were women, based on records in the Registro de Causantes de la Propiedad (*Parentesco,* 92).

34. AMC, 1900, vol. 269, Exp. Padron, Monte Blanco.

35. Soledad González Montes and Pilar Iracheta found in Tenango that patriarchal values influenced fathers to bequeath smaller parcels of land to their daughters than to their sons. See "La Violencia en la vida de las mujeres campesinas: El distrito de Tenango, 1880–1910," in *Presencia y transparencia: La mujer en la historia de México,* ed. Carmen Ramos (Mexico City: El Colegio de México, 1987), 123 and fn. 11.

36. Palacios, *Coffee in Colombia,* 95.

37. AMC, 1910, vol. 322, Exp. Estadística, "Agricultura en Grande"; Corso et al., *Nunca un desleal,* 14, fn. 7; Informe de Pedro Cruz, December 1924, Dotation, First Instance, El Barreal, no. 598, Mixed Agrarian Commission, Jalapa, Veracruz. Charles Macomb Flandrau, in *Viva Mexico* (New York: Appleton, 1910), 63, 67, describes the coffee harvest season in Misantla. The relationship between the finca owners and laborers reminded him of pre–Civil War relations between plantation owner and slaves, even though the workers received wages under various kinds of verbal agreements. Some of the smallholders closed up their houses for the picking season and moved to one-room huts on the coffee fincas. All these people were indebted to their employers for loans, medicines, and other assistance. Also see Muller, *Door Hetland van Columbus,* 285–88.

38. For example, Eustaquio Aguilar, the father of Cándido Aguilar, cultivated 18,000 coffee trees on his 44-hectare rancho in Palma de Montes. When he was not working his own land he hired himself out as a day worker. AMC, "Agricultura por Familia: Pequeño propietarios"; Corso et al., *Nunca un desleal,* 13–14; Kaerger, "El Centro," 128; Wiemers, "Agriculture and Credit," 529, 535.

39. Twenty-one thousand women listed their primary occupation as housewife (*Tercer censo de población, Veracruz,* 2:1225).

40. AMC, "Agricultores en Grande."

41. Southworth, *El estado de Veracruz,* 40–41; Matías Romero, "Coffee Culture on the Southern Coast of Chiapas," *Artes de México* 22.192 (1975):128.

42. Romero, "Coffee Culture," 118, 130; Southworth, *El estado de Veracruz*, 40–41; Kaerger, "El Centro," 105, 107; Flandrau, *Viva Mexico*, 86–87.

43. Olivia Domínguez, "Las desmanchadoras de Coatepec" (Paper presented at the Latin American Studies Association meeting, Mexico City, October 1983), 14; Sheridan, *Mujer obrera*, 14, 28–29.

44. Kaerger, "El Centro," 104–5.

45. "State of Agricultural Labor in Mexico," 1886, 562; Kaerger, "El Centro," 128; Verena Stolcke, *Coffee Planters, Workers and Wives. Class Conflict and Gender Relations on Sao Paulo Plantations,1850–1980* (New York: St. Martin's Press, 1988), 270–71, 280–81; Muller, *Door Hetland van Columbus*, 285–88; Flandrau, *Viva Mexico*, 63–67. Also see "State of Agricultural Labor in Mexico," in *Reports from the Consuls of the United States on the Commerce, Manufactures, etc. of Their Consular Districts*, no. 67 (Washington, D.C.: Government Printing Office, 1886).

46. In the 1880s Brazilian planters contracted men to cultivate two to three thousand trees, but women were contracted to cultivate only half that number; see Stolcke, *Coffee Planters*, 18.

47. In Soconusco, landowners paid by the *destajo*, or task; a *cosechero* (or *cosechera*) received fifty centavos for a *cajón* of 100–120 pounds of coffee. It was assumed that a family of six, including women and children, could earn up to three pesos a day if they picked steadily; Kaerger, "El Centro," 105–7.

48. This system of two wage rates had not changed in the coffee-processing plants by the 1920s in Coatepec, where women were paid a piece rate but at a lower rate than the men received. The argument was still used that men were the heads of families and needed to earn more. This was one of the main reasons why women organized a militant union; see Sheridan, *Mujer obrera*, 10, 14, 28–29.

49. Lourdes Arizpe and Josefina Aranda, "The 'Comparative Advantages' of Women's Disadvantages: Women Workers in the Strawberry Export Agribusiness in Mexico," *Signs* 7.2 (1981):453–73; Carmen Diana Deere and Magdalena León de Leal, "Peasant Production, Proletarianization, and the Sexual Division of Labor in the Andes," *Signs* 7.2 (1981):358.

50. Michael Jiménez, "Class, Gender, and Peasant Resistance in Central Colombia, 1900–1930," in *Everyday Forms of Peasant Resistance*, ed. Forrest D. Colburn (Armonk: M. E. Sharpe, 1990), 124–25.

4

Gender, Bridewealth, and Marriage: *Social Reproduction of Peons on Henequen Haciendas in Yucatán, 1870–1901*

Piedad Peniche Rivero

*I*n this essay about social reproduction among hacienda peons in Yucatán, Mexico, I focus on the period of major expansion in the world demand for henequen (*Agave fourcroydes*), the native agave used in the manufacture of industrial and agricultural fibers. This "gilded age" coincided with the dictatorship of Porfirio Díaz. When the demand for labor on henequen plantations increased dramatically at the end of the nineteenth century, the *hacendados* (hacienda owners) came to rely on a system of debt peonage to reproduce their labor force. The hacendados' control over social reproduction in general and marriage in particular was indispensable to the system's functioning.

The Relationship Between Social Reproduction and Marriage

Claude Lévi-Strauss was the first to suggest that kinship is founded upon and through marriage rather than through descent. From a global structural perspective, matrimony is a process based on the exchange of women that commits two or more exogamous groups to a network of *reciprocal* relations; the exchangers are the fathers, brothers, and uncles.[1] Lévi-Strauss limited himself to studying the forms in which women are circulated among groups of men through direct and indirect exchange and to classifying systems of matrimony and kinship. Feminist theorists such as Gayle Rubin have used Lévi-Strauss's concept of the exchange of women to argue that the oppression of women has social rather than natural origins.[2]

Pierre Etienne expanded on the theory of marital exchange, contending that Lévi-Strauss had dexterously hidden the destiny of the offspring of marriages that took place *without* reciprocity. In the Alladian culture that Etienne studied, marriages with strangers, female slaves, or women given as presents or dowry could produce offspring without the same status as children produced in sanctioned unions. Etienne concluded that the rules of circulation of women are not necessarily based on reciprocity; exchange can, in fact, promote capitalization—the accumulation and multiplication of commodities—especially when the exchangers are not fathers, brothers, or uncles but male outsiders or enemies. Etienne challenged Lévi-Strauss's all-inclusive concept of reciprocity and argued for an antiexchange model that would explain marriage without reciprocity.[3]

Based on his studies of African societies, Claude Meillassoux took the anti-exchange model one step further by arguing that it can function precisely at the level of social reproduction. In societies whose production depends on human energy, controlling people's labor becomes critical, and controlling the creation of workers' progeny can ensure the continuity of unequal relations.[4] This theory can be applied to the Yucatán hacienda system in the late nineteenth century, when hacienda owners gained control over matrimonial exchanges and bridewealth and transformed these into forms of domination of social reproduction which propagated an indebted, stable peasant population. This essay briefly discusses the historical background of the Yucatán haciendas and their modernization in response to external market demands; then examines the social organization of work based on gender, marital status, and age; and concludes by describing how hacendados promulgated a system for circulating women and developed a form of bridewealth that allowed them to control social reproduction.

The Rise of the Henequen Hacienda

The transformation of the colonial cattle- and corn-producing haciendas into large-scale commercial henequen plantations at the end of the nineteenth century was driven by commercial, technological, and financial forces operating outside the Yucatán. In the northwest quadrant of the region centered on Mérida, where the soil was often too poor to grow corn more than two years in succession, henequen had been grown on a small scale before the 1850s by Maya peasants and large landowners for local production of fibers, ropes, sacks, and bags. The commercial development of henequen hinged on two technological developments: a process to extract large quantities of fiber from henequen leaves and a mechanism whereby the twine made from these fibers could be used in a grain binder. The development of a rasper in 1856 that could mechanically remove the fibers from the agave leaves and the invention of a knotting device for Cyrus McCormick's grain binder in 1878 contributed directly to the development of a U.S. market for Yucatecan henequen. The arrival of North American capital to finance the expensive process of converting the haciendas from cattle and corn production to henequen production was the third major ingredient in the development of capital-intensive, monopolistic agriculture in Yucatán. Beginning in the 1870s, the production and exportation of henequen soared as the demand for hemp to manufacture binder twine multiplied. With this boom a new type of henequen producer entered on the scene, bent on reaping huge profits from his investments rather than simply farming to maintain his family's estate and preserve his social status.[5]

The export-oriented henequen haciendas had entirely different labor requirements than their predecessors, for they needed a year-round labor supply to weed, cut, and transport the agave leaves to the processors for extraction. The delicate balance that had existed in the pre-1850 labor system between the cattle-producing haciendas around Mérida and the peasants in the free villages that surrounded them was bound to change with the increased demand for labor. The old labor system had been relatively flexible, for the abundance of available labor allowed hacienda owners to hire laborers from the surrounding peasant communities whenever they were needed. Three types of laborers predominated: the resident servant (*peón acasillado*), the renter/sharecropper (*aparcero*), and the *lunero* (Monday man; a renter who paid for his *milpa*, or cornfield, with one day of labor). In the preboom era, resident peons lived much like their brothers in the neighboring independent peasant communities.

The henequen boom changed these labor arrangements, and the peons' lifestyles, dramatically. The entrepreneurial landowners now needed large and stable resident populations on their estates throughout the year. As a consequence, they took measures to systematically reduce the lands held by independent villages. They pressured the state authorities to privatize communal holdings and took steps to ensure their own control over a sizable resident workforce. Although the populations in communal villages stayed relatively stable between 1879 and 1910, a dramatic rise occurred in the hacienda populations (see Figure 4.1). Moreover, the landowners developed a number of practices for tying male peons to the estate through debts.[6]

The increased commercial demand for henequen combined with the invention of a steam-powered rasper that could extract fibers on a very large scale had an enormous impact on social relations of production because the cultivation of the agave did not itself undergo technological improvement. The imbalance between the capital-intensive sector and the labor-intensive

Figure 4.1
Hacienda, Village, and Rancho Populations in the Parish of Umán, 1879–1910

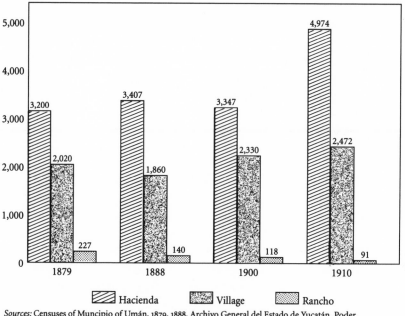

Sources: Censuses of Muncipio of Umán, 1879, 1888, Archivo General del Estado de Yucatán, Poder, Ejecutivo; Censo General de la República Mexicana, 1900 and 1910

sector raised the premium on male labor in henequen cultivation. Although the growers could now process enormous amounts of henequen, the cultivation and harvest proceeded at the same slow rate as always. The tools the workers used for cultivation—the knife and the *coa* (a curved iron blade, set on a wooden shaft about two feet long, used for weeding)—remained the same rudimentary hand tools they had been for centuries. The hard physical labor required for henequen production was tremendous, especially given the very low level of liquid capital on the hacienda.

The Cultivation of Henequen

The cultivation of henequen is a process regulated more by nature than by humans. A henequen plant requires seven years to reach maturity and produce its first harvest. After that, it is necessary to cut *las pencas* (the leaves) almost the entire year. Harvesting involves six distinct operations: (1) cutting the leaf itself, (2) removing the end spine, (3) shearing off the side spines, (4) gathering and (5) tying the leaves into bundles of fifty, and (6) transporting the bundles to the tramway. Besides the harvesting, the weeds that invade the fields all year, most intensively during the rainy season, must be cleared continuously—from the time the agave is in the nursery until it dies twenty-five years later.

The brutal task of removing the fiber from the outside of the leaf requires much less human energy when assisted by the rasper. The arriving bundles of leaves are raised by elevator to the second floor, where two men catch, untie, and spread out the leaves on a conveyor belt which carries the henequen into the rasper. The leaves are rasped, and their raw fibers are extracted. The fibers are then taken to dry in the sun, and in one or two days they are ready to be pressed and sent to market. The waste—the leaf pulp, the juices, and the short fibers, approximately 95 percent of the leaf—flows down to a collection site where it is loaded onto a tram pulled by mules and transported to the refuse heap.

The social organization of the labor force can be pieced together from the *semanarios de trabajo* (weekly labor reports) found among turn-of-the-century judicial documents relating to hacienda commercial affairs. The semanarios show that gender, age, and marital status were the primary criteria determining workers' places in the work organization, which was based on access rights to technical processes and the division of labor according to tasks. Thus the semanarios divide the peons into boys, young single men, and married men.[7] At the highest level were the married men, regular workers who enjoyed full employment and performed the tasks that required the most energy: cutting, rasping, and weeding the fields. None of the workers had specialized occupations, so they could be rotated into and out of the production process at all levels. The single men generally weeded the fields and nursery and transported the refuse, and the boys hung the fibers for drying in the sun and cultivated the seedlings.

The organization of work by marital status was directly linked to remuneration, which thus indirectly supported the institution of marriage. The work books reveal that peons were paid *jornales* (wages) according to their work category, and the married workers earned more than anyone else. The weekly jornales fluctuated between 3.5 and 6.5 pesos, which did not in any way meet the economic needs of the peasant household.[8] Yet the practice of paying married workers more allowed for the circulation of money where it was most needed and provided an incentive for single men to marry quickly. In other ways as well a peon entered a higher economic status upon his marriage on the hacienda. The landlord did not give a *milpa* to a male laborer until he was married. Although it appears that marriage was a beneficial rite of passage for the peon, he did not have as much control over his own marriage as his landlord did, as I will show below.

Women's work was considered supplementary to that of their husbands. They were not directly employed; nor, for that matter, did they become indebted to the hacienda. Within the Mayan household, women's labor was considered part of the unpaid informal household economy,[9] and the hacienda system exploited this practice. When temporary workers were needed to cut leaves in the harvesting process, married cutters often employed their wives and children. Women never went to work in the fields alone, but they did accompany their husbands, and, as one report puts it, "the wife of the cutter . . . [gave] . . . perfectly efficient help to her husband."[10] Women were not paid for their labor, however, and in this sense they were "invisible" workers whose labor was exploited by the hacendados. In addition to these unpaid agricultural chores, women performed unpaid domestic services in the houses of the hacendados.

Marriage Among Peons on Henequen Haciendas

Maya communities placed special emphasis on marriage as an institution that strengthened mutual relations between families and their control over economic resources. The function of marriage was to bring together families or social groups and oblige them to cooperate and share territory and resources. Theoretically the hacienda also functioned as a community, one composed of exogamous families of Maya workers linked through the land and the power of the hacendado. While the function of matrimony in both communities was essentially economic, the hacienda used and promoted the institution for quite distinct ends. Through the fiction that the hacienda population was linked in social kinship to him, the *patrón,* the hacendado was able to exercise control over the marriages of his workers and to develop a system whereby women were circulated in a network of marital exchanges among the haciendas, villages, and ranchos of the region. In this way landowners could avoid charges of incest (intermarriage was prohibited down to the third generation) and also overcome the demographic problem of gender imbalances among the workers, which usually meant a shortage of male workers. Thus the circulation of marriageable women became a mechanism that adapted the rate of growth of the peon population to the hacienda's labor requirements.

The Books of Matrimony of Umán, a parish that included three villages, twenty-five haciendas, and six ranchos, provide considerable information about the circulation of women as prospective wives. The parochial registries give the names of each married couple, their respective residences, and the year they were married. A sample of 2,922 marriages in the parish of Umán between 1860 and 1900 was divisible into three types of marital exchanges: within the hacienda system, within the village system, and between villages and haciendas (see Table 4.1).[11]

My analysis of residence patterns makes it clear that a high percentage of endogamy occurred within the hacienda system—that is, both within as well

Table 4.1
Types of Marital Exchanges on Henequen Haciendas, 1860–1900

Type of exchange	Number of marriages	Percentage
Within the hacienda system	2,083	71.29
Within the villages system (Umán, Bolon, Samahil)	367	12.56
Between villages and haciendas	406	13.89
Unknown	66	2.26
Total	2,922	100

Source: Piedad Peniche Rivero, "Parish of Umán Marriages, 1860–1900," computer files based on Libros de matrimónios de la Parroqũia de Umán, Archivo del Arzobispado, Mérida.

as between haciendas. The evidence suggests that the hacendados encouraged their male peons to select mates from their own haciendas. This is confirmed when the fifty-eight largest haciendas, owned by eighteen families, are singled out for inspection. On these large haciendas between 1880 and 1900, endogamous marriages made up 83.95 percent of the sample.[12] Moreover, the level of endogamy was positively related to the size of the hacienda; that is, the greater the number of inhabitants on the hacienda, the smaller the number of exogamous matrimonial exchanges, and vice versa.

The most obvious explanation for the high level of endogamy is the landowners' desire to exercise control over social reproduction. Since the social reproduction of peons was considered a cost of production, the circulation of women could be regulated within the regional economy. This cost had to be the same at all times for all the hacendados. Thus it follows that marital exchanges—on the largest haciendas, at least—were organized on the principle of endogamy and practiced on a reciprocal basis.

The data also show that the village system yielded up more women than it received (see Figure 4.1).[13] This finding seems to support Pierre Etienne's anti-exchange model, in which the giving of the woman does not require equal compensation. Because they were outside the haciendas' exchange system, the villages' relations with the haciendas did not entail marriages of reciprocity; instead the haciendas accumulated wives.

In a second study of the parochial registers of Umán, I cross-checked the residence of the married couple with demographic information to measure the number of wives switching residence in three different patterns: on and between one hacienda and another, on and between one village and another, and from village to hacienda or vice versa. Checking the marriage register for the period 1860–69, the first decade for which I found complete records, against the municipal population census of 1879, I found 267 cases of circulation (see Table 4.2).

Table 4.2 shows the importance of the circulation of women as a mechanism to enforce marital exchanges in the hacienda system. Of the 212 women for whom residential information is available, 193 moved out of their homes to live with their husbands, confirming the long-standing tradition of virilocality. The majority of these 193 women moved within their hacienda or from one hacienda to another; only 19 men circulated to the residence of their wives; and 20 women switched residence from pueblo to hacienda or vice versa.

There is also abundant evidence to suggest that within the hacienda system women had very little to say in the choice of their mates. A woman from Telchac in the henequen zone confirmed this: "The rich control their workers. You are a young man and they say you must marry. They take you to the master and then they get all the unmarried women, line them up and then say to you, there they are, now choose your wife. You choose the one that you like best and say, 'this one.'"[14]

In summary, the available evidence suggests that three different forms of marriage existed in the henequen region of Yucatán at the turn of the century. A direct, or bilateral, marriage occurred when the exchange of women was an act of immediate reciprocity between two haciendas or two families within an hacienda or a village. An indirect, or multilateral, marriage took place when a bilateral exchange of women was carried out between a large number of haciendas, assuring the fluidity of the transaction. There was reciprocity here, but it was deferred. This was the most common

Table 4.2
Circulation of Women on Haciendas and Villages
in the Parish of Umán, 1860–1879

Type of circulation	Number
Pueblo to hacienda	12
Hacienda to pueblo	8
Subtotal	20
Among pueblos	2
Within pueblos	47
Subtotal	49
Among haciendas	31
Within haciendas	93
Subtotal	124
Did not circulate	19
Unknown	55
Total	267

Source: Piedad Peniche Rivero, "Parish of Umán Marriages 1860–1900," computer files based on Libros de matrimónios, and Municipal Census of Umán, 1879, Poder Ejecutivo, Archivo General del Estado de Yucatán.

form of marital exchange in the sample. Finally, an unequal marriage occurred when the delivery of a woman did not result in reciprocity. This type of marriage came about as a result of the unequal circulation of women between large haciendas and villages, where kinship relations did not coincide with the functioning of the *no hoch cuenta* (discussed below).

Thus it is possible to say that between 1860 and 1900, two principles concerning marriage of the hacienda workers affected the circulation of women. First, the prescription that men should marry women on the hacienda meant that endogamous marriages prevailed in the hacienda system. Second, the colonial preference for virilocal residency benefited the hacienda system more than the villages, for prospective brides were taken from their villages, never to return. Let us now see how marriage was used to place and keep male workers in debt.

The Debt System

The system by which male workers on Mexican haciendas were kept in debt was actually a social form of labor appropriation used to create a forced labor system. In Yucatán debts were considered the primary social instrument behind the creation and sustenance of the peonage system.[15] Unfortunately, information on the debt system that developed on the henequen haciendas in the nineteenth century is scarce and dispersed. It is unlikely that we will ever have all the information needed to completely comprehend this system.

The debts hide the true nature of the social system, in which production of goods was carried out by means of control over the male producer—or, more precisely, over his wife. In this system the hacienda owner appropriated traditional obligations and used them as a mechanism for reproducing his own labor force and accumulating capital. In other words, traditional systems of reciprocity were appropriated for private capital accumulation.

Certainly the debt system was linked to the miserable jornales, wages paid in paper scrip and worthless outside the hacienda. In addition, the peons were forced to perform personal services without pay for the maintenance of the hacienda. Their wives were likewise not remunerated for the services they were obliged to perform as cooks, laundresses, and maids in the planters' mansions. This forced labor system was reinforced by physical abuse, which was widely reported by contemporary observers.[16]

Oral testimony of an ex-hacendado shows that in the world of the hacienda, two types of debt, known by their Mayan names, were clearly differentiated: the *chichán cuenta* (small account) and the *no hoch cuenta* (large account). The small accounts were loans, never more than fifty pesos, which could be repaid slowly. They were no different from the debts one might incur with merchants, and they required only additional work or some other minor hardship to pay off. The large accounts were another thing altogether.

> The large accounts they [the landowners] did not collect on, for they included payments to the workers to cover wedding, purchases, and entertainment during the fiestas of the surrounding villages, family burial and subsequent social gatherings eight days or one year afterward. None of these debts accrued interest and generally they reached 1,000 pesos [sic];[17] but for good workers, especially those who had sons who would eventually become workers, the debts easily rose to two or three thousand pesos.[18]

This testimony is useful in showing the differences between the types of debts. The principal distinction between the chichán cuenta and the no hoch cuenta was their origin: the latter began with matrimony. The repayable versus nonrepayable nature of the chichán cuenta and the no hoch cuenta, respectively, gave these debts contradictory natures. The latter debt took on a social function, as opposed to the economic function of the former.

The no hoch cuenta signified the financing of the social obligations of the peons (much like ecclesiastical fees) for baptisms, marriages, and funerals, and for entertainment—fiestas and fairs on the haciendas and in neighboring villages. The entries registered in the section entitled "Funds" of the weekly workbooks also include social services to protect the well-being of the peons: financial support during illness, old age, and widowhood; payments for caskets, house repair, civil, and religious marriage fees, and so on.

The social function of the no hoch cuenta made it a form of indirect wage that the landowners paid for the social reproduction of their resident peons. In effect, as good capitalists, they saw the necessity of paying for the reproduction of their peons. They divided the remuneration into direct and indirect wages. The direct wage, based on tasks performed, was equivalent to what the peon produced but did not include what his wife or children produced, which was "invisible." The indirect wage represented the amount needed for the maintenance and reproduction of a married man, taking into account all his specific family needs; that is, the social reproduction of the male peon and his family.

To substantiate the theory that hacendados paid an indirect wage to maintain the peon household, consider how they subsidized the price of corn. The maintenance of a fixed price for corn was the primary factor keeping the worker's cost of living stable. The normal price was three pesos for a *carga* (46–48 kilograms). If the price of corn remained at or below this level, the planter did not intervene, but when the price rose above three pesos, he bought provisions of corn at whatever price he could and sold it to his peons for three pesos.[19] The hacendado saw the reproduction of his servants as his obligation, evidence that the social relations of production between the "master" and his "servants" were not regulated by the market but by a social principle of reproduction of the peasant household.

A debate continues over whether the hacienda residents consented to their own exploitation.[20] One look at the fiesta pictures in L. Martínez-Guzmán's photographs shows that peons and hacendados shared gender kinship and religious ideology, which seems to support the theory that peons did consent. This information not only contradicts the view that violence was an intrinsic part of debt enforcement but also makes the debts appear relatively attractive. The Maya traditions of patriarchal authority and kinship were strong forces influencing the peons' compliance with the debt system. Male peons held *patria potestad* (legal guardianship) over their off-spring and considered it their right to receive financial assistance from the landowner to pay the ecclesiastical and civil fees for baptism and marriage. They prolonged this practice through the godparenthood system so as to be ritually related to the hacendado family. Inasmuch as they shared the same Catholic ideology with regard to the sacraments and rituals (including the cult of the patron saint of the hacienda) and participated in processions, dances in the main house, bullfights, markets, and so on, they were support-ing and perpetuating the social and cultural aspects of the hacienda system just as much as the planters themselves did.[21]

On the other hand, the resident population did resist exploitation in many ways. Some fled as far away as the forests of Campeche and Quintana Roo, leaving behind their debts, and sometimes their families. To combat the threat of escape, the laws of indebtedness required the return of runaway peons to their estate. The police stationed on the haciendas were an added deterrent discouraging peons from fleeing.[22]

The contradictory nature of the no hoch cuenta makes it possible to infer quite a bit about the nineteenth-century mentality of the peons and the hacendados. Although the servants and the planters shared a common real-ity, they understood it quite differently. For the hacendados, the no hoch cuenta was a financial obligation that allowed them to maintain a stable workforce, and thus it could be considered a cost of production. For the servants, it was an obligation to the patrón in exchange for their loyalty. In fact, the peons were unable to understand that their exploitation ensured the patrón's riches and at the same time kept them from ever being able to finance their social obligations. Let us now turn to a discussion of how the hacendado class appropriated Maya marital customs for their own advan-tage in this society undergoing capitalist transformation.

Matrimony and the Debt Structure

Matrimony in the Maya culture had the function of strengthening the bonds of families or social groups. Bridewealth was a tangible way this union between two community families was cemented. The *mu'huul*,[23] or bridewealth, consisted of clothes and jewelry for the bride and money and food offered to the bride's family by the groom's family through the good offices of an outside "marriage maker," the *casamentero*.[24] Property was not transferred to the family of the betrothed woman in payment for the rights to her offspring, as in the bridewealth in African societies, nor was it an anticipated inheritance paid to the man by her family, like the dowry (*dote*) in the agricultural societies of Eurasia. When the henequen hacendado in nineteenth-century Yucatán assumed the practice of paying the no hoch cuenta, he usurped the role of the groom's family. He also changed the function of matrimony from one of creating reciprocal rights between two families and groups to one of supplying offspring for the hacienda system.

Planters used the institution of matrimony to alter the function of the no hoch cuenta. No longer based on reciprocity, matrimony now served an antireciprocal function: it put and kept the male peon permanently in debt. Moreover, the landowner had made himself the casamentero by supplying eligible women and by providing financial incentives to his male peons to marry. The German agronomist Karl Kaerger, who visited Yucatán, said it quite clearly: "In general, credit is given when a young worker gets married, or when he is between 18 to 20. The patron gives him 100 to 200 pesos to set up housekeeping. Between the two contracting parties there is a tacit agreement that this sum, as well as all other debts originating after this due to accidents or problems, will not be repaid and the Yucatecan can only recover his liberty for that price."[25]

Numerous documents show that the first one hundred pesos of the no hoch cuenta, which could be considered equivalent to the bridewealth, came to include a number of things on the henequen hacienda. The gifts sent by the groom's family to the family of the bride included clothes, rings, and a long necklace. My calculations indicate that this cost was not less than eight pesos.[26] Second, the civil matrimonial fees were approximately twenty-five pesos (five pesos was set aside for the ceremony and the rest was used to cover the wedding fiesta and gifts). The religious ceremony fees were approximately seventeen pesos.[27]

Once the marriage had taken place, the peon obtained certain benefits from his marital status. He gained usufructuary rights: a milpa to cultivate for his family's needs and a wattle-and-daub house with household goods. The peon also won access to full employment, as described above. The woman won the right to work as a housekeeper. Doña Victoria Catzim, an expeon's wife, perhaps said it best: "On the hacienda there is no such thing as love. . . . The patron arrives and tells you, this man will be your husband. Then they give you your household utensils (your things for maize grinding)."[28]

Conclusions

At the beginning of the twentieth century the traditional henequen hacienda economy was transformed into a capitalist system by the emergence of an international henequen market. The old colonial system of dependent personal relations still prevailed in the sense that money—commercial capital, that is—played a marginal role. Specifically, the social relations of production in the hacienda system were the relations between two social groups, the planters and the peons, united through social reproduction.

The increasing demand for labor on the henequen haciendas obliged large landowners to develop strategies to support peasant households on their estates while at the same time luring additional male laborers and prospective brides from the neighboring Maya communities. In effect, to counter gender inequalities on the hacienda the planters developed the means to control the circulation of women on a regional scale. By exchanging women, the hacienda system tried to stimulate the growth of its peon population to meet the labor needs of the commercial market.

The rules of marriage on the hacienda were adapted from traditional Mayan customs, so in this case one could say that ethnicity actually reinforced oppression. According to chronicler Diego de Landa, the Maya preferred endogamy within the pueblo, strongly upheld the practice of bridewealth, and maintained the patriarchal family structure. The hacendados adapted these communal and patriarchal practices of social control to perpetuate the hacienda system.

It would have served no purpose to force single male peons into debt if the planters had not also encouraged them to marry. A network of endogamous marriages through exchanges on and between haciendas and between the hacienda and pueblo guaranteed a continual supply of marriageable women. The hacendados practiced reciprocity, particularly among the large haciendas, in contrast to their relationship with peasant villages, which lost brides and gained little in return.

The planter's cost of sustaining stable reproduction of the male workforce was equivalent to an indirect salary paid to the male peon upon his marriage, which included his bridewealth payment. In the mind of the peon, the reception of this indirect wage signified that the patrón was acknowledging an obligation to him in return for his loyalty. Thus, the structure of the no hoch cuenta, which consisted principally of the bridewealth, signified a set of conscious and unconscious relations that functioned through the mechanisms of gender, kinship, work, and indebtedness.

To be sure, there was a basic difference between the hacienda system and the slave plantation. The latter operated through physical control of production. On the henequen hacienda, in contrast, control was exerted socially through the reproduction of peons. Yet this was not a simple process. We must remember that the hacendados had to renew their control over each generation of peons through marriage and that they had to continually finance it through the no hoch cuenta.

NOTES

My thanks to Heather Fowler-Salamini, who translated this essay and offered comments and criticisms of an earlier version.

1. Claude Lévi-Strauss, *Les structures elementaires de la parenté* (Paris: Mouton, 1967), 57–60.

2. See Gayle Rubin, "The Traffic of Women. Notes in the 'Political Economy' of Sex," in *Towards an Anthropology of Women*, ed. Rayna Reiner (New York: Monthly Review Press, 1975), 157–210.

3. Pierre Etienne, "Du mariage en Afrique Occidentales: avant propos," *Cahiers OSTROM* 8.2 (1971):133–35.

4. Claude Meillassoux, *Antropologie et économie des Gouro de la Cote d'Ivoire* (Paris: Mouton, 1958), 90–91; and Meillassoux, *Mujeres, graneros, y capitales* (Mexico City: Siglo XXI, 1979), 92–94.

5. Allen Wells traces the origins of the henequen boom in *Yucatán's Gilded Age: Haciendas, Henequen and International Harvester, 1860–1915* (Albuquerque: University of New Mexico Press, 1985), 18–59; Gilbert M. Joseph, *Revolution from Without: Yucatán, Mexico and the United States, 1880–1924* (Cambridge: Cambridge University Press, 1982), 13–32.

6. Allen Wells, "Yucatán: Violence and Social Control on Henequen Plantations," in *Other Mexicos: Essays on Regional Mexican History, 1876–1911*, ed. Thomas Benjamin and William McNellie (Albuquerque: University of New Mexico Press, 1984), 214–23; Joseph, *Revolution from Without*, 20–22, 25–29.

7. Archivo General del Estado de Yucatán [AGEY]: First account of the administration of the hacienda Cuzumal y Anexas presented to Alonso Patrón Espadas, 1909, Justicia 706; Account of the administration of hacienda Tahcibichen y Anexas, 1908, Justicia 706; First account of the administration which gave a depository of the estate Xcanchakán in the mortgage decision which General Francisco Cantón pressed against Mrs. José María Ponce, Avelino López, Miguel Irigoyen Lara, and Mercedes Irigoyen de Herrera, 1908, Justicia 697. Little change in the social division of work took place between 1900 and 1910, so these sources are relevant to the period under discussion.

8. Idem. The workbooks also show that the administrative staff, including the

administrator, overseer, *mayocol* (supervisor in charge of fieldwork), machinist, and herdsmen, were salaried positions; that is, they were not paid by the task as peons were.

9. Robert Redfield and Alfonso Villa Rojas, *Chan Kom, a Maya Village* (Chicago: University of Chicago Press, 1967), 61–71.

10. Gobierno del Estado, *La inmigración de trabajadores del campo a la ciudad* (Mérida: Tipografía Moderna, 1914), ff. 10–11.

11. Piedad Peniche Rivero, "Parish of Umán's Marriages, 1860–1900" (undated MS based on the Libros de Matrimonios, Parroquia de Umán, Archivo del Arzobispado, Mérida).

12. Piedad Peniche Rivero, "Mujeres, matrimonios y esclavitud en la hacienda henequera durante el porfiriato," *Historia* (Instituto nacional de antropologia e historia) 17 (1987):133.

13. Ibid., 131.

14. Esther Iglesias, "Historia de vida de campesinos mayas," *Yucatán: Historia y Economía* (Mérida) 7 (1977):1–16, esp. 11–12. For a discussion of marriage as a rite of passage see Peniche Rivero, *Sacerdotes y Comerciantes. El poder de los mayas y los itzaes en Yucatán en los siglos VII–XVI* (Mexico City: Fondo de Cultura Económica, 1990), 72–75.

15. Frank Tannenbaum, *The Mexican Agrarian Revolution* (New York: Anchor, 1968), 109–10; François Chevalier, *La Formation des Grandes Domaines, au Mexiques. Terre et societé au Mexique* (Paris: Musée de l'Homme, 1952), 368–73; Woodrow Borah, *New Spain's Century of Depression* (Berkeley: University of California Press, 1951); Silvio Zavala, "Orígenes históricos del peonaje en México," *El Trimestre Económico* 10 (1944):711.

16. For oral history testimony, see Iglesias, "Historia de vida de campesinos mayas"; Blanca González Rodríguez, "Henequén y población en Yucatán, Dzemul a manera de ejemplo" (Licenciatura thesis, Universidad de Yucatán, 1980); see also the descriptions of hacienda conditions by journalist John Kenneth Turner, who toured Yucatán in 1907 impersonating a rich investor, in *Barbarous Mexico* (Austin: University of Texas Press, 1969).

17. The "1,000 pesos" must be an error; it is far too high. The sums in this quote should read 100, 200, and 300 pesos, respectively, as other sources attest.

18. Alberto García Cantón, *De mi archivo*, 2 vols. (Mérida, 1973), 2:20–21.

19. Ibid., 20–21.

20. See Wells, "Yucatán: Violence and Social Control," 213–41, for a discussion of this debate. Christopher Gill argues that the patriarchal tradition among Maya peons reinforced their compliance; see "Campesino Patriarchy in the Times of Slavery: The Henequen Plantation Society of Yucatán, 1860–1915" (Master's thesis, University of Texas at Austin, 1991).

21. For discussion of the common practice of godparenthood between master and servants, see Carlos Kirk, *Haciendas en Yucatán* (Mexico City: INI, n.d.), 142–51. See Lourdes Martínez-Guzmán, private stereoscopic photograph collection, Mérida, Yucatán, México, for information on hacienda fiestas. See Gill, "Campesino Patriarchy," 133.

22. For information on the flight of servants, see the Simón Peón Collection in the Special Collections of the Library of the University of Texas at Arlington. For the legislation on debts that began in 1824, see *Las Colecciones de Leyes y Decretos de Yucatán*. The law that invested the hacienda overseers with judicial powers was promulgated August 30, 1881; *Leyes, decretos y ordenes*, comp. Eligio Ancona (Mérida, 1896), 4 (1880–89):191.

23. *Mu'huul* is a Maya word translated as "bridewealth" or "brideprice" in the anthropological literature. According to the *Diccionario de Motul* (sixteenth century) it was "the present which the father of the groom sent to the father of the bride, which in the marriage tradition was called 'dote' or 'arras,' and if he accepted it, it was a signal that he wanted to give away his daughter and that they would marry. But if he rejected it, it was a sign that he did not want to give her away" (see *Diccionario Maya Cordemex* [Mérida: Ediciones Cordemex, 1980], 533).

24. Redfield and Villa Rojas, *Chan Kom*, 193–94.

25. Karl Kaerger visited Yucatán on a mission to study investment prospects for German investors. See his "Yucatán," in *La servidumbre agraria en México*, ed. Friedrich Katz et al. (Mexico City: SepSetentas, 1976), 92.

26. See the marriage of Mateo Cauich, Book of the Hacienda San Simón, 1891–96, Simón Peón Collection.

27. AGEY: Administrative account of the hacienda Xcanchakán, April 10, 1908, Justicia, 708; and workbook included in the Fourth account, April 11–May 20, 1908, Justicia 665. It appears that the 100 pesos was given all at one time, as was the case with Simón Tún, who was then charged 100 pesos for his marriage on the large account; AGEY, workbook, Fourth administrative account, December 15–21, 1908, Justicia 697.

28. González Rodríguez, "Henequén y población en Yucatán," 399–400.

PART TWO

Rural Women and Revolution in Mexico

5

The Soldadera in the Mexican Revolution: *War and Men's Illusions*

Elizabeth Salas

*T*he Spanish writer Vicente Blasco Ibañez described the forces of
the Mexican Revolution of 1910 as armies of "both sexes,"[1] and he
could not tell who was more valuable, the women or the men. Women
foraged, cooked, cared for the wounded, and "fought when they felt like it,"
observed the American journalist Anita Brenner.[2] Yet by the 1930s, women
had been eliminated from the ranks, and the campesino folk armies responsible for initiating the struggle had been transformed into a modern male
military machine. Simultaneous with women's ouster from the ranks, male-
constructed renditions of the soldaderas in Mexican popular culture distorted the women's activities in battle and recast them as prostitutes, self-
abnegating patriots, or Amazons subdued by male romantic prowess.[3] These
depictions are at odds with the real conditions faced by Mexican women
during the war, and they tend to obscure the ways these women's experiences
may have helped them navigate the chaotic events and demographic shifts
that shaped their lives.

Mexican Women in War: Historical Precedent

Warfare was common in nineteenth-century Mexico, beginning with the
struggle for independence in 1810. Between 1821 and 1870, rebellions, civil
strife, and foreign invasions marked a tortuous process of state formation.

Even under the dictatorship of Porfirio Díaz, when the army was consolidated and brought under state control and Mexico supposedly entered a long period of peace, government troops fought Indians on the northern frontier in long and bloody campaigns.

Despite the prevalence of war and the importance of armies, however, no official commissary corps was organized to cook food and provide personal care for soldiers. Armies relied on women for such services. While guerrilla warriors could look to women in their nearby home communities to make their tortillas, other soldiers, forcibly or voluntarily serving far from home, relied on *soldaderas,* women they paid to purchase and prepare food for them.

In the late nineteenth century, as Porfirian and middle-class morality redefined the double standard sanctifying the wife's cloistered domesticity and celebrating the concubine as a playmate, the soldadera was increasingly viewed as a shameless prostitute. New versions of gender construction articulated by elites perceived soldaderas as symbols of primitive backwardness and servility. In a tract of developmentalist thinking written in 1901, the sociologist Julio Guerrero suggests that the soldadera was part of the disorganized, unpredictable, irrational "other" and ought to be eliminated from any military establishment that aspired to "modernity."[4]

A far more serious study than Guerrero's is needed of the nineteenth-century soldaderas—their origins, their motivations, and their experiences—for they were certainly products, and sometimes beneficiaries, of the dislocation and mobility associated with nineteenth-century warfare and modernization. It is fair to say, however, that Guerrero's indictment was as prophetic of postrevolutionary elite thinking as the nineteenth-century army women were of the famous soldaderas of the Mexican Revolution.[5]

The Soldadera in Revolutionary Action, 1910–1917

In the Revolution of 1910, soldaderas functioned as foragers and cooks for large armies and rebel factions alike. True to its nineteenth-century tradition of using women in lieu of an official commissary, the federal army forcibly recruited women as well as men from the south and the north, from rural and urban areas. The rebel armies, supporting the cause of Francisco I. Madero and commanded by such homespun leaders as Pancho Villa in Chihuahua and Emiliano Zapata in Morelos, expressed the spontaneity of popular revolt as their ranks swelled with women as well as men. The historian Friedrich Katz calls Pancho Villa's army, recruited from the towns, mines, and countryside of the northern states, a "folk migration."[6] Rosa E. King, an Englishwoman living in the southern state of Morelos during the Revolution, observed that the peasant villagers taking leadership from

Zapata were a "people in arms."[7] The early rebel armies lacked tight control by an officer corps, and consequently women performed a variety of roles as frontline soldiers and officers, sharpshooters, and spies.

The soldaderas came by and large from the lower classes: rural and urban, mestizo and indigenous. They came from diverse parts of Mexico, reflecting the strength and composition of the rebellion in different areas. Wives and family members were numerous among the federal irregulars and rebels in the early years. Some women joined up looking for survival or opportunity. Many were abducted and kidnapped by individual soldiers or forced by federal press gangs operating in larger cities to become army cooks.

In his classic account, *Insurgent Mexico*, U.S. journalist John Reed asked a soldadera why she was fighting with the armies of Pancho Villa. She pointed toward her man and said, "Because he is." Another had asked her husband why she had to go and fight for "Pancho Madero" when she was pregnant. He had responded, "Shall I starve, then? Who shall make my tortillas but my woman?"[8] In 1914, when federal forces fled Paredón, Coahuila, leaving behind three hundred soldaderas, within twenty-four hours they had all set up new households with "Villa's 'bachelors.'"[9] Still, many women with the Villistas were not willing volunteers. Villista soldiers kidnapped María Villasana López and her sister from their small Chihuahua village.[10] Mollie Gossett, a young woman of U.S.-Mexican background from Monterrey, recalled how her mother covered her head and her sister's with rags so their long hair would not be detected by Villista soldiers. Her father remarked that if "those bandits" boarded the train the family was on, he would have to shoot the girls to save them from the more horrible fate of rape.[11]

Soldaderas and their children made up about one-third of the early folk armies. Enriqueta Longeaux y Vázquez, today a Chicana activist in New Mexico, remembers her mother's story about a Villista army that moved through her Chihuahua town. The men marched continuously for three days while it took a full day for the women's battalion to get through the town.[12] Ordinarily, the male soldiers rode horseback and the women ran on foot behind them.[13] In the early years, trains often served as homes to the folk armies; women and children rode on the roofs, inside the boxcars, and on the break beams underneath.[14]

The soldadera was vital to securing and preparing food. A typical soldadera in 1910 carried a food basket complete with tablecloth, decorative plates, and flowers as she vied with other women to take a soldier's money to purchase food and cook it for him. Villista Major Constantino Caldera Vázquez told of soldaderas stealing "what they could" to feed their fighting husbands.[15] Penniless soldiers appealed to the soldaderas as "madres," pleading for food. Some soldaderas fed the friends of their men for free; others sold food to hungry soldiers.

The reconstruction of a series of encounters experienced by the federal army under the command of General Salvador Mercado in 1913 and 1914 shows how women transferred their traditional roles as wives, cooks, and nurturers to battlefield conditions. Mercado's troops, comprised of regulars and irregulars, faced a fierce challenge in Chihuahua from the army of Pancho Villa. During official lulls in the battle, or siesta times, soldaderas with the Federales brought food and coffee, and sometimes young children, to the trenches, where family groups talked, smoked, ate, and enjoyed each others' company. On January 5, 1914, at Ojinaga, Chihuahua, some soldaderas paid dearly for their visits to the trenches. The corpse of a woman caught there when the action resumed was taken by litter from the trenches, still holding a small infant in her arms. A newspaper reporter noted that "the little one still lived, and sat contently by its mother's side and patted her face as if to waken her."[16] One soldadera gave birth to a boy in the trenches and had to be evacuated to the rear and across the Río Bravo at Presidio, Texas, where a doctor took care of her.[17]

Soldaderas regularly went through the battlefields retrieving useful objects, picking up the wounded, and burying the dead. When a group of women found a dying twenty-one-year-old soldier, badly wounded and still alive despite having received a mercy shot to his head, they carried him by litter to Presidio, where he made a miraculous recovery.[18] After performing burial ceremonies for fallen soldiers, the soldaderas would erect crosses made from stones or cactus thorns.[19]

In 1914, the forces of Pancho Villa forced General Mercado and his army to retreat over the Río Bravo. The U.S. Army on the other side of the border quarantined the Federales in a vast corral. Counting the children of the soldaderas proved to be embarrassing to the Americans. An initial count found only a few. A more accurate account, the Americans complained, would require them to search every woman closely. Most of the 500 or so children finally counted were found nursing or strapped to their mothers' bodies in rebozos. The U.S. officers finally determined that Mercado's army consisted of 4,557 soldiers, 1,256 soldaderas, and 554 children.[20]

In time, an order came to march Mercado's army to Marfa, Texas, and to ship them from there by train to Fort Bliss. Newspaper reporters noted that women were among the best marchers, carrying all manner of things from *metates* (corn-grinding stones), sacred religious and familial bundles, pots, bedding, pets, chickens, and firewood, to breast-feeding infants.[21] When a soldadera gave birth to a baby girl on the march, the news became a topic of lively conversation. After a child was born, the entire company would gather for a baptism ceremony. When night camps were set up, a Red Cross official noted that the army divided into family units, especially the irregulars, who were more likely to comprise intact families. The soldaderas would hollow out small niches in the dirt walls of the arroyo where they camped and put in them religious and family articles, pictures, and lighted candles.[22]

At Fort Bliss, the Americans interned the Mexican forces and made plans to separate the soldaderas from the men. They asked the women to return voluntarily to Mexico, but few went home. In fact, American officials had many requests from Mexican women who wanted to join their men in the camp. A problem arose when the Americans set up mess tents with male cooks to prepare food for the prisoners. Few Mexicans would touch this American food. Finally, it was decided to hand out food rations to heads of families and let the soldaderas do the cooking.[23]

Women did not confine themselves to the roles of foragers and cooks. They were active smugglers of arms and ammunition over the U.S.-Mexican border.[24] Often, when soldaderas brought food and coffee to their men in the trenches, they took up the men's rifles and fired away as the men ate. Many women also had more permanent combat roles.

Women fighters were better incorporated into the command structure of the federal irregulars than the regulars. "Capitana" Clara Ramos was a roving mercenary who did not retreat with Mercado across the Rio Grande. She and other women among the irregulars such as Capitana Carmen Parra y Alanis, Capitana Luisa García, Señora Castillo, and Cimona Gallejos defied orders and remained in Mexico to fight the Villistas. In January 1914, Capitana Ramos evaded U.S. guards at Presidio and convinced seventy men to follow her back into Mexico, where she had a cache of weapons to use against Villa.[25] In March 1914, Capitana Parra and Capitana García also bucked their superior officers and guided their men to Saltillo.[26] Castillo and Gallegos were part of a hit-and-run band of irregulars who were eventually captured by U.S. authorities and sent to the internment camp.[27]

Federal regulars and irregulars were not the only women involved in frontline combat. The *Mexican Herald* reported on June 20, 1913, that a rebel band of four hundred included "about twenty women . . . mounted like men and [carrying] guns and cartridge belts."[28] John Womack describes a female rebel unit in Puente de Ixtla, Morelos, who fought under the command of "La China," a former tortilla maker who led them on ransacking raids throughout the Telecala district of Morelos. Relatives of slain Zapatistas, they had dedicated themselves to avenging the murders.[29]

Another important Zapatista fighter was María de la Luz Espinosa Barrera, born in Yautepec, Morelos, in 1887 of humble rural origins. Her mother died in childbirth and her father served as her lone parent and most important role model. Her childhood was lonesome and difficult. Her young companions laughed at her when she told them that her mother was a "favorite goat."[30] As a young woman she spent five years in jail for killing her husband's mistress; then she returned to Morelos and joined her father fighting for the Zapatistas. An immensely gifted horsewoman, she fought in many battles disguised as a man. She cursed like a man, and, according to historian Anna Macias, she "thought like a man." Emiliano Zapata was so impressed with her soldiering that he gave her a battlefield commission as lieutenant colonel. She had two encounters with male suitors during her army years. She was able to stop the unwanted affections of one but had to kill the other, who refused to leave her alone. After the Revolution she continued to wear men's clothing and became a successful traveling merchant in Morelos.

Colonel María Quinteras de Meras was one of the very few female officers respected by Pancho Villa. She enlisted in his army in 1910, and by 1913 she had fought in ten battles. In 1914 the *El Paso Morning Times* reported that she "shoots and throws a rope as well as any of the men in Villa's army. She wears a khaki suit and a broad-brimmed Stetson. Three belts of cartridges and a Mauser rifle are thrown over her shoulders. The colonel has led many desperate charges and her followers have come to believe she is endowed with some supernatural power."[31]

Twelve-year-old Elisa Grienssen became a legend in her hometown of Parral, Chihuahua. When she found out that the town's men were unable or unwilling to defend the community from General Pershing's expedition against Pancho Villa in 1916, she asked the municipal president, "Are there no men in Parral? If you can't get them out, we, the women, will do it."[32] She gathered the women and children, searched for weapons, and asked a man to teach her to fire a rifle. The Parral women and children surrounded U.S. Major Frank Tompkins and ordered him to shout "Viva Mexico! Viva Villa!" The U.S. troops beat a hasty retreat, chased out of town by the women and children of Parral.

Another outstanding female fighter was Angela Jiménez. Born around 1896 in Jalapa del Márquez, Oaxaca, she was the daughter of a Zapotec mother and a Spanish father, a political cacique in Tehuantepec. Jiménez was a soldier—not a soldadera—who disguised herself as a man and insisted on being called "Angel." She went to war against the federal army after her sister died during a rape attempt by federal troops. Rather than allow herself to be raped, the sister had shot her attacker, then killed herself. Incensed by this tragedy, Jiménez joined various rebel groups, soldiering first with her father against the Federales in Oaxaca, then fighting in the north with the armies of Venustiano Carranza. She earned the rank of lieutenant and the respect of her commanding officers and fellow troopers, who knew she was a woman. Her acceptance as a frontline soldier shows that women could and did successfully integrate themselves into the ranks, especially in the first years of the fighting. She was fearless and brave, a banner carrier, explosives expert, and firm believer that the Revolution was a struggle for justice. She prevented amorous assaults by assuring her fellow soldiers that if they tried to seduce her, she would kill them without remorse.[33]

Whether they fought among the federal regulars or irregulars or the rebel armies, however, women were denied the rank of general. Maderista fighter Petra Herrera was among several women soldiers who referred to themselves as "Generala." Herrera, who began her military career disguised as a man called "Pedro," proved her worth dynamiting bridges and guiding male troops on dangerous missions. After she led Maderista soldiers in the storming of Torreon and the routing of the federal forces in May 1911, her heroism was glorified in the "Corrido del combate del 15 de Mayo en Torreon":

> La valiente Petra Herrera
> al combate se lanzo
> siendo siempre la primera
> ella el fuego commenso.
>
> The brave Petra Herrera
> entered the battle
> always being the first,
> It was she who opened fire.[34]

When she was captured, Herrera defiantly shouted her loyalty to Madero. Heartened by her courage, the Maderistas successfully expelled the troops of Porfirio Díaz from Torreon, making this major victory for the revolutionaries a woman's achievement.

Unfortunately, Herrera received no general's rank for her effort. Like other women, she could not break through to the higher ranks. Angered, Herrera formed her own women's army (whose ranks numbered between twenty-five and a thousand members at various times) and made herself the generala. She allowed men from other rebel groups to visit her soldiers during the day but not at night. And she stayed awake at night to enforce her orders, threatening to shoot any man who defied her. Her actions might, perhaps, be seen as a woman soldier's retaliation to Villa's famed all-male Dorados. Villa allowed women to visit the camps only at night.[35]

The Masculinization of the Revolutionary Armies

As the officer corps began to gain control of the rebel armies after 1914, more emphasis was placed on cavalry units and the masculinization of the forces. During the Maderista revolution, women who owned horses (or stole them from haciendas or foreigners) rode with the cavalry as quality soldiers. But after the restructuring, especially in Pancho Villa's army, horses—purchased legally or obtained illegally—became Villa's to dispense. Villa created the

Dorados as an all-male cavalry. The new reliance on cavalry hurt women in many ways. Soldaderas had to vacate the interior of the railroad cars because these were now reserved for the horses, and army personnel now occupied the boxcar tops and the break beams under the cars.

Generals Villa, Obregón, Carranza, and even Zapata relegated soldaderas to riding mules or following the armies on foot. Only occasionally was a capitana or coronela seen riding a horse into combat. Cavalry units abandoned their soldaderas and children at will in order to evade capture. The abandoned soldaderas usually avoided massacre because every troop, federal and rebel, needed foragers and cooks; but the forced separation of families and loved ones caused distress for soldaderas and soldados alike. The incidence of rape increased when troops no longer soldiering with women plundered their way through villages and towns.

Villa was plagued by the soldaderas, whom he saw as a burden and an obstacle to swift cavalry movements. He wanted to modernize his army, improve the troops' mobility, and institute a more efficient supply system, and he believed a proper army should be composed entirely of men. A U.S. newspaper reported that Villa often forced women to leave the trenches and escorted them from the firing lines to places of safety only to find them racing back to the front when he was not looking.[36] He attributed his successful capture of Ciudad Juarez in 1911 to his refusal to allow soldaderas to accompany his soldiers.[37]

Villa once shot an officer for defying his orders and taking a soldadera with him into battle, and by this example he managed to stem the number of soldaderas in his ranks. When he formed the Dorados, he tried to relieve soldaderas of their function as cooks, foragers, and nurses by establishing official commissary and medical corps.[38]

Soldaderas sometimes fought among themselves—with deadly consequences. A soldadera who threw a bomb at a woman rival killed both her and a soldier much admired by Villa, who ordered the soldadera executed with "military honors."[39] His animosity toward women came to a climax in 1916 when he captured a railroad station and eighty or ninety soldaderas and children at Santa Rosalia Camargo, Chihuahua, from the Constitutionalist forces loyal to Venustiano Carranza. A shot rang out from among the soldaderas and hit Villa's sombrero. When Villa asked the women to point out his assailant, they were mum. He then ordered his men to kill all the women and children. "I was reminded of Dante's Inferno by that scene," recalled a witness, Colonel José J. Jurrieta. "I doubt if anyone could describe the panic and distress of those unfortunates, the tears, blood, and pain of 90 women slaughtered with Villista bullets."[40]

It is important to add that this brutal act occurred after Villa's major defeat at Celaya in 1915 at the hands of the Constitutionalist forces commanded by General Álvaro Obregón. Villa's army was on the defensive, and his power was in decline.[41] And he was not the only revolutionary general to abuse and disparage women. General Obregón was accused of putting soldaderas and children in front of his troops to shield them and the artillery from enemy fire.[42] In his memoirs, written in the 1960s, General Juan F. Azcarate denies that soldaderas ever fought with the insurgents. The cinema, he says, was responsible for creating the fantasy of their presence in the rebel armies.[43]

In 1917, the victorious Constitutionalists under Venustiano Carranza asked all the rebel factions to lay down their arms, have their ranks adjusted to regular army standards, and either retire or allow themselves to be incorporated into the government forces. When Petra Herrera requested that she be recognized as a general and allowed to remain in active service, General Jesús Agustín Castro made her a colonel and dismissed the other members of her women's army.[44] Policymakers for President Carranza and his successor, Alvaro Obregón, saw no future for soldaderas in the Mexican army. Second Assistant to the Secretary of War General Miguel Ruelas called for a military administration that would eliminate "from our armies the women camp followers who, in addition to their disadvantages and . . . lamentable backwardness. . . make us the butt of all writers."[45] Calling women the "chief cause of vice, illness, crime, and disorder," Minister of War Joaquín Amaro banned them from all military barracks in 1925.[46] The fact that thousands of women had died fighting in the Revolution had no bearing on policy. Nor did soldaderas mobilize politically for incorporation into the new army, recognition, or reward. Most were from poor families, and they were inexperienced in such organization. Middle- and upper-class women who might have provided leadership showed, on the contrary, a strong bias against the "*peladas*" of the lower classes and held the firm conviction that soldiering was a "male" activity. Although women who were able to get their commanding officers' verification did sometimes receive pensions for their military service, camp followers could not apply because their services were not considered combat related.[47] In general, the government favored giving pensions to women not for their own services but as relatives of male soldiers. In 1935, Ana María Zapata, the daughter of Emiliano Zapata, enlisted the aid of President Lázaro Cárdenas to form the Unión de Mujeres Revolucionarias. La Unión successfully pressed for pensions for widows, daughters, and sisters of dead revolutionaries. At one point, more than eight hundred women from Morelos, Oaxaca, Puebla, Guerrero, and Hidalgo belonged to the group.[48]

A more common fate of soldaderas, however, was that of Chepa Moreno and Dominga Ramírez, two Yaqui women who had been forcibly taken from Sonora and enslaved on Yucatán plantations before the Revolution. When the Revolution came, they joined Yaqui and Mayo soldiers who fought under Carranza. Both noted that as soldaderas their lives were hard, but they enjoyed a measure of freedom not previously available to them. Returning to Sonora, Ramírez especially faced downward mobility. During the Revolution she had been the pampered adopted daughter of an army officer and, later, a soldier's wife. After the Revolution she suffered impoverishment and discrimination.[49]

The Soldadera in Postrevolutionary Mexico: Imagined or Real?

After the violent phase of the Revolution, the Mexican mass media transformed soldaderas into either self-sacrificing, heroic camp followers or prostitutes. The Adelita corrido depicts the soldadera with a "heart of gold," the "sweetheart of the tropa." The soldaderas in fact became known as Las Adelitas. Often, when an artistic work is based on a corrido about a fearless, self-willed, and outspoken woman soldier such as Juana Gallo, the story line is compromised by adding a complicated love plot. The typical dominating soldadera has several romances and must overcome rivalries with other women. By the end of the story, the woman character has rechanneled her energies and become like Adelita: a valiant, pretty, sought-after lover and wife.[50]

In *Los de Abajo*, the best-known and most popular novel of the Revolution, Mariano Azuela creates two memorable female characters: an Amazon soldier/whore and a self-abnegating camp follower. Azuela calls La Pintada a "vulgar wench with rouged cheeks [and] dark brown arms and neck," while Camila, the camp follower, is maternal, submissive, and good.[51] The depiction of the soldaderas as "good" like Camila or "bad" like La Pintada demonstrates how realistic portrayals gave way to illusion and stereotype in male reconstructions of army women.

In the most important distortion of the soldadera in popular culture, camp followers were portrayed as prostitutes rather than cooks for the army. Most Mexican militarists have a difficult time accepting the fact that the soldaderas were crucial to the functioning of the armies. The soldadera as prostitute conforms with the patriarchal ideology of the Mexican revolutionary state, which suggests a moral and sexual understanding of women within a "good woman–bad woman" dichotomy. To acknowledge that soldaderas were essential to the armies as foragers and cooks would call into question the ideological constructions that make manhood synonymous with soldiering and military history a male sphere.

The ultimate reality, however, is that women as well as men have been actively involved in Mexican military history. The Revolution itself caused massive dislocation, to which women as well as men had to respond. Many women followed parents, brothers, husbands, and other relatives into the armies. Others were abducted, raped, and sexually abused and became soldaderas through no choice of their own. Some joined to make a living; working for soldiers paid more than begging on the streets or washing dishes for street vendors. Some soldaderas sought to serve officers, who could pay them more and foster upward mobility. But the perils besetting the soldadera were many. She could be abandoned by her soldier/consort by will or death. She faced pregnancy and the difficulties of caring for children in the midst of war. An unattached soldadera was often obliged to work long hours at hard labor such as laundering for meager compensation. After the Revolution, many soldaderas lived and died in poverty, without the pensions and hospital care awarded to male veterans.

The women soldiers also do not fit the stereotypes of prostitute, sweetheart, or subdued Amazon. Petra "Pedro" Herrera, who liberated Torreon from the federal forces, turned to espionage work in Chihuahua, where she died in a bar fight. María de la Luz Espinosa Barrera became a successful traveling merchant in Morelos. Angela "Angel" Jiménez, longtime combatant and explosives expert, migrated to San José, California, where she became a vigorous activist in the Chicano civil rights struggle. Dominga Ramírez may have faced poverty and racism when she returned to her native Sonora, but in her mature years she emerged as the strong and assertive head of her own household. Soldadera Manuela Oaxaca Quinn eventually moved to Los Angeles, California, where she raised her son, the actor Anthony Quinn. She had a simple explanation for joining the Revolution: "Maybe it wasn't God's law," she said, "that some people should starve while others had plenty. Maybe those who plant the lettuce can also eat the salad."[52]

Conclusions

Soldaderas came from diverse backgrounds and had different personalities and objectives. Although most were mestiza or indigenous women from rural areas and small towns, some also came from the cities. They lived through chaotic times and represent a migratory campesina culture in transition—stamping its own impression on Mexican revolutionary warfare. Militarists and bureaucrats were determined to eliminate them from the army to fulfill a patriarchal rationality. Mexican popular culture debased and distorted their role in a gender discourse that cast them as nonessential sweethearts, prostitutes, or domesticated Amazons. In the end, though, their contributions to Mexican history must be recognized.

NOTES

1. Vicente Blasco Ibañez, *Mexico in Revolution*, trans. Arthur Livingston and José Padin (New York: Dutton, 1920), 173.

2. Anita Brenner, *The Wind That Swept Mexico: The History of the Mexican Revolution, 1910–1942* (Austin: University of Texas Press, 1971), 49.

3. The Spanish word *soldadera* combines *soldada*, the pay of the soldier, with the -*era* ending reflecting a term used to refer to a servant. The pictorial works of the Agustin Casasola Collection and the seminal study of women soldiers by Angeles Mendieta Alatorre, *La Mujer en la Revolución Mexicana* (Mexico City: Talleres Gráficos de la Nación, 1961), have been crucial to this study.

4. Julio Guerrero, *La genesis del crimen en México* (Paris: Libreria de la Vd. de Ch. Bouret, 1901), 764.

5. Elizabeth Salas, *Soldaderas in the Mexican Military: Myth and History* (Austin: University of Texas Press, 1990), 28–35.

6. Katz, quoted in Eric R. Wolf, *Peasant Wars of the Twentieth Century* (New York: Harper and Row, 1969), 31–35.

7. Rosa E. King, *Tempest over Mexico: A Personal Chronicle* (Boston: Little, Brown, 1938), 93–94.

8. John Reed, *Insurgent Mexico* (New Mexico: International Publishers, 1914), 64, 189.

9. Herman Whitaker, "Villa and His People," *Sunset* 33.2 (1914):257.

10. Esther R. Pérez, James Kallas, and Nina Kallas, *Those Years of the Revolution, 1910–1920: Authentic Bilingual Life Experiences as Told by Veterans of the War* (San José, Calif.: Aztlan Today, 1974), 208.

11. Oscar J. Martínez, *Fragments of the Mexican Revolution: Personal Accounts from the Border* (Albuquerque: University of New Mexico Press, 1983), 232.

12. Enriqueta Longeaux y Vásquez, "The Mexican-American Woman," in *Sisterhood Is Powerful*, ed. Robin Morgan (New York: Vintage Books, 1970), 380.

13. Archivo de la Palabra del Instituto Nacional de Antropología e Historia, Departamento de Estudios Contemporáneos, Programa de Historia Oral [INAH, PHO], PHO/1/49, Major Justino López Estrada, 5.

14. INAH, PHO/1/66, Francisco Ruiz Moreno, 22; PHO/1/41, Major Adan Uro García, 20.

15. INAH, PHO/1/110, Major Constantino Caldero Vázquez, 28.

16. *New York Times*, Jan. 2, 5, 13, 14, 1914.

17. Ibid., Jan. 13, 1914.

18. *El Paso Morning Times*, Feb. 3, 1914.

19. *New York Times*, Jan. 13, 1914.

20. Captain George H. Estes, "The Internment of Mexican Troops in 1914," *Infantry Journal* (May–June 1915):747–69; (July–August 1915):38–57; (September–October 1915):243–64.

21. *Outlook*, Jan. 31, 1914; *El Paso Morning Times*, Jan. 21, 1914; *Los Angeles Times*, Jan. 19, 1914.

22. Ernest Bicknell, *Pioneering with the Red Cross* (New York: Macmillan, 1935), 158.

23. Peter B. Kyne, "With the Border Patrol," *Collier'sMagazine*, May 9, 1914, 21.

24. *El Paso Morning Times*, Jan. 24, 1914.

25. *Mexican Herald*, Feb. 6, 1914.

26. *El Paso Morning Times*, March 5, 1914.

27. Ibid., Feb. 1, 1913; Feb. 19, 1914; National Archives, Adjutant General's Office, Record Group 94, file cards on prisoners at detention camp, 1914.

28. *Mexican Herald,* June 20, 1913.

29. John Womack, *Zapata and the Mexican Revolution* (New York: Knopf, 1969), 16.

30. Anna Macias, *Against All Odds: The Feminist Movement in Mexico to 1940* (Westport Conn.: Greenwood Press, 1982), 43.

31. *El Paso Morning Times,* May 7, 1914.

32. Maria Barron del Avellano, "Habla Elisa, heroina parralense," *Sociedad Chihuahuense de Estudios Históricos,* Sept. 29, 1971, 16.

33. Pérez et al., *Those Years,* 159, 161, 170.

34. María Herrera-Sobek, *The Mexican Corrido: A Feminist Analysis* (Bloomington: Indiana University Press, 1990), 93.

35. *Mexican Herald,* Jan. 7, 1914; INAH, PHO/1/130, Eulalio Mendoza, 53; PHO/1/69, Major Medico Cirujano José Raya Rivera, 14.

36. *El Paso Morning Times,* Nov. 27, 1913.

37. Luis M. Garfias, *Truth and Legend of Pancho Villa,* trans. David Castledine (Mexico City: Panorama Editorial, 1981), 60.

38. Timothy G. Turner, *Bullets, Bottles, and Gardenias* (Dallas: South-West Press, 1935), 166.

39. Whitaker, "Villa," 252.

40. Quotation from INAH, PHO/1/98, Major Silvestre Cadena Jaramillo, 10; see also Garfias, *Truth and Legend,* 143; "Cleofas Calleros," in *Pancho Villa,* ed. Jessie Peterson and Thelma Cox Knoles (New York: Hastings House, 1977), 33–34.

41. Personal communication from Friedrich Katz, April 1993.

42. Pérez et al., *Those Years,* 169.

43. Juan F. Azcarate, *Esencia de la Revolución* (Mexico City: B. Costa-Amic, 1966), 80.

44. *Mexican Herald,* Jan. 7, 1914; INAH, PHO/1/130, Eulalio Mendoza, 53; PHO/1/69, Major Medico Cirujano José Raya Rivera, 14. INAH, PHO/1/69, Raya Rivera.

45. Manuel Calero, *Essay on the Reconstruction of Mexico* (New York: De Laisne and Carranza, 1920), 53.

46. Edwin Lieuwen, *Mexican Militarism: The Rise and Fall of the Revolutionary Army, 1910–1940* (Albuquerque: University of New Mexico Press, 1968), 94.

47. See Marta Romo, "Y las Soldaderas? Tomasa García toma la palabra," *Fem* 2.4 (1979):12–14.

48. Mario Gill, "Zapata: Su pueblo y sus hijos," *Historia Mexicana* 2.2 (1952):309–10.

49. Jane Holden Kelley, *Yaqui Women: Contemporary Life Histories* (Lincoln: University of Nebraska Press, 1978), 144, 172.

50. Among representative films are *La Enamorada* (1946), *Juana Gallo* (1960), and *La Valentina* (1965).

51. Mariano Azuela, *The Underdogs,* trans. Edward Munguia, Jr. (New York: New American Library of World Literature, 1915), 110.

52. Anthony Quinn, *The Original Sin* (Boston: Little, Brown, 1972), 24–28.

6

Rural Women's Literacy and Education During the Mexican Revolution: *Subverting a Patriarchal Event?*

Mary Kay Vaughan

*T*he Mexican Revolution of 1910 was a quintessentially patriarchal event for rural women, many of whom suffered physical violation during the prolonged struggle. Afterward, politics remained the dominion of men. Women were excluded from the postrevolutionary redistribution of land and water, except in their capacity as wives and daughters. Land reform helped to shore up the patriarchal peasant household unit of production, which had been threatened by prerevolutionary capitalist growth.

Still, the Revolution did give rise to processes that altered gender relations and behavior in the countryside, and this essay focuses on the education of peasant women as a window for viewing and understanding these processes. The crusade for literacy and schools undertaken by the revolutionary state's Secretaría de Educación Pública (SEP) after 1921 was not meant to alter women's subordinate role in the family, economy, and polity. The official curriculum promoted female domesticity to foster the creation of a competent labor force for capitalist growth and consumption through the modern marketplace. Educators sought to make campesino households healthier and more efficient by teaching nutrition, hygiene, and modern medicine and introducing corn mills and the waist-level hearth. However, in their efforts to win the loyalties and energies of youth for national development, federal educators threatened traditional patriarchal control over women, to whom schooling opened new areas of activity, interaction, and knowledge.

Sending thousands of women teachers into the countryside assisted this opening.[1]

Statistics suggest that in the short run, the state's campaign to school peasant women had disappointing results. In the densely populated central state of Puebla, women's literacy outside the capital city rose only six points, from 16 to 22 percent, between 1910 and 1940, compared with a significant rise in male literacy, from 23 to 38 percent.[2] After 1940, rural women's literacy acquisition accelerated and schooling became commonplace for peasant women.

In this essay I look at Tecamachalco, an agrarian reform district in central Puebla, and examine the factors that impeded women's schooling between 1900 and 1940 and accounted for their accelerated acquisition of literacy skills after 1940. In the final section I describe how revolutionary schooling opened new spaces and activities to women, and how families, community leaders, and teachers themselves negotiated these threats to traditional gender relations. I conclude that when changes seemed controllable, useful, and necessary to campesino household strategies for survival and improvement, women were able to secure new spaces for action and personhood.

I have depended upon a variety of sources. The census data suggest a series of socioeconomic variables correlating with women's literacy over time. Municipal and national presidential archives make it possible to reconstruct the political and economic contexts within which women acquired literacy during the years of revolutionary turmoil and state consolidation. School inspectors' reports contained in the SEP archives describe interactions between communities and teachers during the same years. I have also drawn upon oral interviews with teachers who worked in Tecamachalco in the 1930s and 1940s and upon the findings of anthropologists who studied communities similar to Tecamachalco during the same years.

Tecamachalco: The Setting

Located sixty kilometers east of the city of Puebla and the same distance west of Mount Orizaba, Tecamachalco is an area of low mountain ranges and cultivated valleys characteristic of Mexico's central highland plateau. In 1900, as an administrative district, it united eight municipalities and had a population of 48,000.[3] The majority lived in agrarian villages (*pueblos, rancherías,* and *barrios*) in varying degrees of subordination to the surrounding ranchos and haciendas, where villagers worked as wage earners and sharecroppers. All were engaged in dry cereal farming and the cultivation of maguey (for *pulque*), *ixtle* fiber, chiles, onions, and beans. One community was dedicated to weaving. In 1900, 23 percent of men over the age of twelve and 10 percent of the women could read and write.

Although in many ways typical of rural central Mexico, Tecamachalco had three important characteristics that affected the course of literacy and schooling in the region. First, although it was originally an area of indigenous settlement, it had undergone a long process of *mestizaje*, or acculturation. In 1910 and in 1940, 90 percent of the population spoke Spanish, and language was thus not an impediment to schooling in Spanish. Nevertheless, Tecamachalqueños guarded customs that urban educators classified as "Indian" and in need of transformation. In 1940, 90 percent of the population relied on a corn-based diet; two-thirds slept on the ground rather than on beds; and fully 70 percent of the women went barefoot while 75 percent of the men wore *huaraches* or shoes. These things, combined with other customs deemed backward by SEP modernizers, suggest that the cultural encounter between Tecamachalqueños and educators was likely to be contentious.

Second, Tecamachalco did not experience rapid growth during the Porfiriato. Although the Puebla-Oaxaca railroad ran through the region, providing new market outlets, Tecamachalco registered little increase in production between 1895 and 1910, perhaps handicapped by the lack of water, and exported people rather than attracting them. There was little occupational diversification in the area. These factors weakened both the demand for literacy and the area's capacity to sustain schools. They also encouraged an exodus of literate men, so that despite expanded schooling, men's literacy in Tecamachalco stayed at 23 percent between 1900 and 1910.

Third, Tecamachalco's insertion in the Revolution of 1910 can be regarded as positive, in contrast with regions where the Revolution was imposed from the outside, engendered strong opposition, and brought little reward to the disadvantaged. Although Tecamachalco peasants seem to have escaped dramatic victimization at the hands of voracious hacendados, they mobilized in 1910 to recover land, water, and political power. By 1930, one-third of the men were *ejidatarios* (recipients of land under the reform laws), although they had received only small parcels of land without water. In the 1940s and 1950s, various communities benefited from government-sponsored water projects and from increased possibilities for trade via the new highway from Puebla City to Tehuacán.

Historians argue persuasively that the Mexican Revolution as a social movement challenged the hierarchical structure with a defiant demand for access to the privileges and resources previously limited to a few. The people's demand for education has been interpreted as a part of this.[4] As a militant *agrarista* district, Tecamachalco should have responded enthusiastically to schooling and quickly increased its literacy rate, but other factors interfered. The variables muddying the neat equation between the demand for land and the demand for literacy are explained below with specific reference to women.

Factors Deterring Women's Education in Tecamachalco

In their study of literacy in France, François Furet and Jacques Ozouf explain the gender gap in rural literacy by suggesting that women's schooling poses a threat to the patriarchal order: it may lead women to deviate from their maternal, domestic vocation.[5] In late nineteenth-century rural Mexico, a socially constructed division of activity by gender justified a literacy gap. Men dominated politics, religion, property, and market relations, where literacy skills were useful. Girls were valued for their domestic work and their marriageability. Their mothers taught them the skills they needed in the sphere of the hearth, and these did not include reading and writing.

Yet, women's literacy rose from 10 to 18 percent in Tecamachalco between 1900 and 1910 in response to new educational opportunities. The literacy rate rose in conjunction with nonagricultural occupations (see Tables 6.1 and 6.2) and was also correlated with relative wealth at the individual and communal levels. The larger population centers (*villas* and pueblos) were more likely to be able to sustain separate schools for boys and girls than were the smaller, poorer rancherías. If rancherías had schools at all, they were usually coeducational, or *mixtas*. Few girls attended them for fear of mingling with boys.[6]

During the revolutionary years and just afterward, women's literacy in Tecamachalco appeared to reverse its course, falling from 18 to 15 percent between 1910 and 1930. The decline occurred because literate women, overrepresented in the propertied, urban sectors, fled the violence and commercial decline besetting revolutionary Tecamachalco. In 1930, only 11 percent of women over twenty-nine years of age were literate, compared with 34 percent of the men.

During the 1920s, literacy advanced rapidly among young girls in some municipalities but not in others, as the figures for 1930 in Table 6.3 show. Literacy tended to advance where it had been nurtured in the final years of the prerevolutionary period—in the weaving municipality of Tlanepantla, for instance, and the municipality of Tochtepec, where a substantial population of better-off peasants supported schooling. Although Tochtepec was an agrarian reform municipality, property redistribution did not automatically create a demand for schooling. In the land reform municipalities where women's literacy had been lowest in 1900 (Quecholac, El Palmar, and Yehualtepec), girls' literacy remained very low. These municipalities were characterized by scattered, impoverished rancherías culturally isolated from

Table 6.1

Tecamachalco Literacy and Socioeconomic Indicators, 1900–1950

	% Literate		% Active in agriculture	% Owners in agricultural labor force	% Males ejidatarios	% Population centers, rancherías[a]	% Religious marriages only[b]
	Males	Females					
1900							
Tecamachalco	29	16	71	8	—	—	—
Quecholac	16	8	91	8	—	—	—
Tlacotepec	19	7	92	4	—	—	—
El Palmar	19	9	84	10	—	—	—
Yehualtepec	24	5	95	5	—	—	—
Tochtepec	35	14	91	15	—	—	—
Xochitlan	22	7	85	5	—	—	—
Tlanepantla	26	11	10	1	—	—	—
Total Pop.	23	10	81	7	—	—	—
1930							
Tecamachalco	35	16	83	—	42	43	44
Quecholac	18	5	92	—	38	37	75
Tlacotepec	32	14	88	—	34	44	24
El Palmar	27	14	88	—	26	71	60
Yehualtepec	33	9	90	—	25	22	50
Tochtepec	56	25	86	—	42	45	37
Xochitlan	33	18	90	—	14	0	44
Tlanepantla	57	30	20	—	0	0	42
Felipe Angeles	22	7	86	—	71	0	79
Total Pop.	32	14	86	—	33	42	50
1940							
Tecamachalco	44	26	79	41	45	43	27
Quecholac	23	11	93	58	34	37	57
Tlacotepec	36	14	88	35	40	44	8
El Palmar	25	15	94	53	26	71	29
Yehualtepec	52	18	90	55	44	22	15
Tochtepec	57	35	87	30	40	45	22
Xochitlan	56	39	93	31	42	0	23
Tlanepantla	57	32	27	17	13	0	31
Felipe Angeles	22	6	97	74	65	0	64
Total Pop.	36	19	87	44	34	42	31
1950							
Tecamachalco	56	37	—	—	—	—	—
Quecholac	23	14	—	—	—	—	—
Tlacotepec	44	22	—	—	—	—	—
El Palmar	39	26	—	—	—	—	—
Yehualtepec	53	25	—	—	—	—	—
Tochtepec	68	48	—	—	—	—	—
Xochitlan	54	35	—	—	—	—	—
Tlanepantla	65	42	—	—	—	—	—
Felipe Angeles	34	14	—	—	—	—	—
Total Pop.	45	27	—	—	—	—	—

Sources: Censo general de la República mexicana, 1900; Quinto Censo de la población, 1930; Sexto Censo de la población, 1940; Séptimo Censo de la población, 1950 (Mexico City: Dirección General de Estadística).

[a] "Ranchería" refers to the proportion of this type of population center compared with other types (villas, pueblos) in a municipality.

[b] "Religious marriages" were marriages sanctioned only by the church, as opposed to those also confirmed by the state and to free unions. The incidence of "church-only" marriages indicates cultural isolation from modernizing processes.

modernizing processes owing in part to their geographical location and in part to their prerevolutionary domination by haciendas (see Tables 6.1, 6.2).

Between 1930 and 1940, women's literacy in Tecamachalco rose from 14 to 19 percent. The rise reflects the death of older illiterates and the coming of age of women who learned to read and write in the 1920s. It does not reflect gains among young girls in the 1930s, when literacy in children between the ages of 10 and 14 declined from 25 percent to 22 percent for girls and from 30 to 26 percent for boys. The collapse was gender-neutral, and it was not the result of school closings. On the contrary, the federal Secretaría de Educación Pública entered the region in force in the 1930s and increased the number of schools. The decline was due to worsening economic conditions throughout the region and, more importantly, the tumultuous political atmosphere as the region was incorporated into the emerging Mexican state.

Economically, the 1930s were years of duress, and parents had little to invest in their children's schooling. Ejidatarios had received a pittance of land from the government (an average of 1.5 hectares per family) and little or no water. Farmers faced rising prices for manufactured goods and productive inputs as the balance of trade turned against corn. Droughts and freezes alternately parched and ravaged the fields. Whole families boarded up their homes and left to look for work in Veracruz. Men lined up for weeks waiting to work on the new highway under construction from Puebla to Tehuacán. When the men left, women and children took up their work in the fields.[7]

If economic hardship made it difficult for children to attend school, the violent politics of state consolidation interrupted the development of schooling. Until 1934, agrarianism thrived in central Puebla because no urban political group was able to establish dominion over the rebellious countryside. In the 1930s, factional strife within Tecamachalco communities

Table 6.2

Tecamachalco Literacy Correlations, 1930–1940

	% Active in agriculture	% Males ejidatarios	% Population centers ranchos/rancherías	% Religious marriages only
1900				
Male Literacy	−.2234			
Female Literacy	−.3310			
1930				
Male Literacy	−.6628	−.3307	−.3849	−.5448
Female Literacy	−.7449	−.3595	−.3806	−.5073
1940				
Male Literacy	−.4863	−.2212	−.6615	−.3564
Female Literacy	−.4076	−.2838	−.5687	−.3143

Note: These are simple statistical correlations between the figures for literacy and other variables contained in Table 6.1. The closer the figure is to 1, the stronger the correlation. A minus sign indicates a negative correlation; the further away from 1, the more negative the correlation.

Table 6.3
Tecamachalco Youth Literacy, 1900–1940

	1930		1940		% Change	
	% Boys ages 10–14	% Girls ages 10–14	% Boys ages 10–14	% Girls ages 10–14	Boys	Girls
Tecamachalco	29	25	37	31	27	22
Quecholac	9	3	11	7	34	132
Tlacotepec	45	40	29	19	−36	−51
El Palmar	16	17	10	11	−35	−36
Yehualtepec	28	14	38	26	33	89
Tochtepec	59	58	43	50	−26	−14
Xochitlan	54	53	77	70	44	31
Tlanepantla	65	52	60	55	−8	6
Felipe Angeles	19	13	7	4	−61	−68
Total	30	25	26	22	−15	−13

Sources: *Quinto Censode la población*, 1930; *Sexto Censo de la población*, 1940 (Mexico City: Dirección General de Estadística).

intensified as representatives of the state-dominated political party, the Partido Nacional Revolucionario, and federal government agencies subjugated local politics to external control. Disputes over political power, land, and water disrupted the culture of schooling.[8]

The Secretaría de Educación Pública was particularly intrusive. In the 1920s, most children learned to read and write in locally controlled schools supported by villagers' donations, and the SEP's presence was weak. In the 1930s, the SEP quadrupled the schools it controlled and opened new ones in smaller population centers. The SEP's entry into local education sparked power struggles with local authorities. In addition, the SEP's modern learning-by-doing curriculum aimed at socioeconomic transformation clashed with local customs and provoked resistance. Teachers were instructed to change the way people farmed, marketed, consumed, organized households and family, ate, thought, cared for their bodies, and affirmed their communal identity. They were to do this by organizing schoolchildren to cultivate gardens and form cooperatives and hygiene brigades, by advising ejidatarios on scientific agriculture, by visiting mothers in their homes, and by organizing patriotic festivals.

Low-level resistance to the SEP's transformational project exploded into anger in December 1934 when the SEP's new policy of socialist education exhorted teachers to step up their struggle against religion: to replace religious beliefs and "superstitions" with scientific understanding of the natural world and to lambast Catholic ritual as a waste of time and money. In Tecamachalco, where religious faith ran deep and Catholic festival was a vital part of communal life, resistance to socialist education involved most sectors of the population, including many ejidatarios. Sporadic violence was interspersed with massive civil disobedience as parents removed their children from school.

If poverty, political dispute, violence, and opposition to official educational policy hurt schooling in general in the 1930s, certain factors impinged particularly on women's education. These factors emerge from a reading of the SEP school inspector's bimonthly reports. In 1935, the SEP controlled forty schools in Tecamachalco; two-thirds of these were in small towns averaging 335 residents—communities likely to be impoverished and unfamiliar with schooling. The other third were in larger towns with stronger schooling cultures. Between 1931 and 1935, around 30 percent of eligible children attended, ranging from 10 to 13 percent in small towns unfamiliar with schooling or where schooling cultures had been disrupted, to 68 percent in larger centers where schooling cultures were older and more intact. The ratio of female to male enrollments was one to three. Girls' attendance was higher in communities with older schooling traditions and female schoolteachers.[9]

Perhaps the most important factor hurting women's education in particular was the ubiquitous violence. Simply put, it was dangerous to travel the roads. Many mothers would not let their girls out of their sight. In Palmarito, Palmar del Bravo, robbery and kidnapping were so common that adolescent girls were whisked away in broad daylight. Rape was frequent. Throughout the region, women stayed away from adult night schools because of the dangers of darkness and their parents' fear of allowing them to mix with young men. Since the authorities hardly bothered to investigate crimes against women, parents were all the more reluctant to send girls to school once they had reached a certain age.[10]

The violence reinforced customs of female seclusion and provided an excuse for keeping girls out of the coeducational federal schools. Villagers told the school inspector that adults of the opposite sex should have no spiritual contact and that women did not need schooling anyway. Fears about coeducation were strong even in towns where schooling had a long tradition but boys and girls had been taught separately.

Not all parents objected to education for their daughters. They were less reluctant to send girls if the teacher was a woman, and a typical school roster showing a handful of girls enrolled in the first two years of school suggests a willingness to send girls briefly, at an early age. Girls over ten years old seldom attended school, in part because they were more useful at home, but also because girls at this age were considered to be entering puberty. Coeducation threatened parental control over sexuality, gender relations, and marriage.[11]

A third factor working against rural women's education was the SEP's campaign to transform campesina mothers into modern, market-oriented homemakers. If the school inspector had his way, women teachers would plunge through the doors of peasant homes to demand that children be inoculated against contagious disease, cured with modern medicines, fed more nutritious food, and bathed regularly. Teachers were to persuade women to clean their patios, burn their garbage, get the animals out of the house, and raise the hearth from the ground to waist level, and to introduce urban-style furniture, beds, and room partitions. Teachers counseled against early marriage and promoted the use of the civil register so that statistics on births, deaths, and marriages, essential to the state's reorganization of life and appropriation of the people, could be collected.[12]

In Tecamachalco, the teachers at first met with resistance. Campesina women often avoided their home visits, pleading work and scurrying off to the fields. More was at stake than lack of time, however. The teachers' aggressiveness offended the women's respect for household privacy. Further, there was no adequate resource base from which the teacher could demonstrate the effectiveness of her prescriptions. There was little water for washing hands and faces, let alone to install a modern sewage system or introduce a new vegetable to the garden.

A clash of cultures and belief systems aggravated these negotiations. Within its paradigm of "modern science," the SEP perceived a whole bevy of local customs as stupid, pernicious, and backward. Teachers wanted mothers to wash their children's clothes more often; mothers believed that frequent launderings would make the children sick. The SEP waged a relentless campaign against pulque, the popular alcoholic beverage of central Mexico which children drank in small amounts; and yet pulque, low in alcohol, was a nutritious substitute for water, which was scarce and contaminated.

Reproductive customs associated with health, nutrition, birth, and death rested on a shared conception of the body and natural phenomena. Infused with spiritual meaning, their practice gave women secular prestige and a sense of self-worth, power, and community membership.[13] Because SEP policy homogenized campesina women in their backwardness and ignorance, it ignored women with skills and prestige in such areas as curing. When teachers failed to discern hierarchies among women and to co-opt opinion makers and experts in local arts and sciences, their approach provoked resistance.

The school's campaign to inoculate children against smallpox illustrates the encounter between a "foreign" minority and a skeptical public. People feared the needle. Sometimes mothers hid their children, provoking health officials to demand their arrest. Misunderstandings abounded. Many believed the vaccine caused the disease. Teachers joined federal health agents in sanitary brigades that descended on the towns on market days to vaccinate en masse, often accompanied by the local police and federal troops.[14]

Women's resistance remained low and dispersed until socialist education challenged religious values in the name of science and rationality. The school inspector identified women as major players in organizing the opposition to this policy.[15] As offended guardians of reproductive rites and customs, they became political actors. This new domain of public life—the school—demanded their participation because it insisted on sharing in their tasks of socializing children. At first, mothers became visible as resisters, withdrawing their children from what they regarded as an unhealthy space. The Catholic religion gave them a propelling self-image, and the symbolism of Mary and the Holy Family, today identified by feminists with female subjugation, were more nourishing images for campesinas than those initially provided by revolutionary schools.[16] The latter could do little more than attack the way campesinas lived and thought about themselves, their families, and their future. As elsewhere in Mexico, the women of Tecamachalco were instrumental in forcing the government to retreat from its antireligious policy in 1936.

Factors Encouraging Women's Education

After 1936, school enrollments began to increase in Tecamachalco. Women's literacy rose from 19 percent in 1940 to 27 percent in 1950. According to the 1970 census, 50 percent of women born in the 1940s and 67 percent of those born between 1950 and 1955 could read and write. Although hidden beneath the global figures were the same differences between municipalities visible in 1900 (see Table 6.1), the overall growth in women's literacy may be attributed to five factors: state consolidation, government subsidization of schools, negotiation between teachers and communities over curriculum and the parameters of schooling, changing mentalities, and changing economic conditions.

The consolidation of the Mexican state in the late 1930s and early 1940s promoted women's schooling by subduing violence and institutionalizing local power. Greater security in the towns and on the roads increased women's mobility and school attendance. The ruling party, the PNR-PRM-PRI,[17] impressed upon village leaders the need to educate both boys and girls. Jurisdictional disputes between the SEP and local leaders were resolved. Campesino leaders, now ejido officers, took their places as judges at graduation exercises, distributing prizes to the students and tokens of appreciation to the *mentores de la niñez,* a nineteenth-century term for teacher indicative of the persistence and diffusion of tradition.[18] The state eased the burden of schooling for poor communities and families by paying teachers' salaries and providing textbooks, instructional materials, and supplies. Women began to attend adult evening classes initiated by government-sponsored literacy campaigns.

Women teachers became important brokers between the state and communities. Their presence in the classroom allayed fears about schooling girls. During the tumultuous negotiations of the 1930s, women teachers learned to respect local culture and the privacy of the campesino home.[19] Most teachers came from modest provincial backgrounds just a notch above the campesinas and were themselves recent products of the culture of schooling. While the teachers had internalized an ideology of modernization, they also shared certain values and customs with campesinas. They often used herbal medicines and traditional cures, censored the curriculum on issues of sex education and religion, and understood why mothers gave children pulque in small amounts. Evidence suggests that in the 1940s, teachers working with government cultural and health missions identified local health experts and trained them as disseminators of government programs. Moreover, as teachers stayed in communities, they befriended the women of the leading families who acted as opinion makers in their towns.[20]

New mentalities emerged from the intersection of political upheaval, state creation, and changing material conditions, facilitating the negotiations over women's schooling. Teachers, parents, children, and community leaders negotiated as the world changed around them. Between 1910 and 1940 local power structures were overturned in Tecamachalco. Resources were snatched from the hands of old owners and redistributed. Children contemplated new options and practices. This change came at a tremendous price: assassination, assault, rape, abandonment, property loss, material deprivation, death, and disease were everyday occurrences.

While the social convulsions hurt women, they also fostered women's mobility and allowed them to carve out new spaces. The response of Agustina Barrojas, a campesina from Cuaucnopalan in Palmar, is illustrative. Her husband was a sharecropper and agrarista. After he was killed by the hacendado's henchmen, she took to trading beans, fruits, and seeds between Veracruz and Palmar. With seven children to raise but no land and no grown sons to help her secure an ejidal parcel, she had few options. She wagered that the only patrimony she could leave her children was an education, and so she paid a private teacher in Cuaucnopalan to teach her boys and girls to read and write. When the public school reopened in the 1930s, she befriended the teachers. Unable to read herself, she joined the culture of schooling nevertheless.[21]

In general, changing economic conditions after 1940 made women's schooling easier and more necessary. In the 1940s and 1950s state policies and market development brought some economic relief to Tecamachalco. Various communities benefited from new irrigation works or obtained funding for deep-water wells.[22] Household economies diversified into fruit cultivation. Trucks and buses traversing the highway between Puebla and Tehuacán meant new mobility and trade. Labor-saving devices such as the corn-grinding mill, the sewing machine, the waist-level hearth, store-bought utensils, and water sources closer to home released girls for schooling and women for remunerative activities such as garden production and marketing, sewing, and temporary migration for urban domestic work.

Women's schooling took hold because it served the family welfare. After 1940, the schools' ideology of consumerism, change, and mobility became more synchronized with daily life. Mobile women in contact with city and marketplace had greater use for literacy and were more open to urban ways and consumer goods. Aspects of the school program had begun to demonstrate their efficacy. Mothers who saw that vaccinated children survived epidemics began to ask for vaccinations.[23] By 1940, smallpox and whooping cough had ceased to be important causes of infant mortality. Marketplace and school programs coalesced in improving health and diet. The introduction of antibiotics and canned foods, respectively, reduced infant death from diarrhea and infections and improved nutrition.[24] More children living longer meant more labor power for family sustenance. Investment in education—including that of women—had the potential for diversifying and increasing family income. Moreover, the pressures capitalist growth exercised against peasant family farming made this diversification necessary.

Literacy, Schooling, and the Subversion of Patriarchy

Postrevolutionary agrarian reform helped to shore up the peasant household as an agricultural unit until 1960, when market conditions and population growth began to seriously undermine it. By protecting the peasant household, the reform buttressed rural patriarchy. Yet schooling, in tandem with other processes etching themselves into daily life, challenged customary gender and age relations, affirmed change and mobility, and opened new spaces for women and youth at the expense of the traditional arbiters of rural life, the oldest men. Families, community leaders, and teachers themselves sought to control or eliminate these subversions, but changes that enhanced household strategies for survival and upward mobility often endured anyway. Insight into the challenges to patriarchy and how they were met can be derived from Tecamachalco data combined with observations made by Oscar Lewis and Robert Redfield in their studies of Tepoztlán and Chan Kom in the late 1940s.

Like Tecamachalco towns, Chan Kom and Tepoztlán were agrarian reform villages. Self-sufficiency and limited urban contact slowed the rate of change in Chan Kom. Insufficient land and proximity to Cuernavaca and

Mexico City accelerated change in Tepoztlán. In terms of agricultural resources and rural-urban exchange, Tecamachalco towns lay somewhere between these two extremes.

Overall, the school crusade was a corrective to a revolutionary struggle tarnished by its physical violation of women. The SEP deliberately set out to correct what it regarded as the debasement of peasant women in daily life. In its curriculum and through its teachers, the school appointed women to an important, if subordinate, place in Mexican development. Schooling implicitly empowered campesinas by creating a direct linkage between them as household managers and socializers of children and the state. The school requested their participation in the public sphere as learners and as parents serving on school committees.

Federal schools favored the principles of youth, choice, change, and mobility—all things in conflict with the "natural" order of rural patriarchy. In schools, women learned new skills and roles. They engaged in the same tasks as boys: cultivating gardens, keeping bees, reading history, keeping accounts, forming producer cooperatives. Girls held offices in these cooperatives, whose chief was frequently a female teacher. Women teachers promoted gender equality. Reyna Manzano, who taught in Tochtepec in the 1940s, worked to see that young girls excelled along with boys in academic contests. For her, the Revolution signified equality of opportunity.[25]

Extracurricular activities opened other new possibilities. In school fiestas, girls developed skills in oratory, theater, dance, and singing. Much as parents had feared, schools were places for girls and boys to intermingle. In Tecamachalco, school-sponsored basketball and baseball allowed boys to show off their prowess and independence from their elders and to learn a new ethic of competition identified with extravillage mobility. Young girls attended the sports competitions and interacted with the young men. In Chan Kom and Tepoztlán, Redfield and Lewis noted the emergence of a relatively autonomous adolescent space where young men and women interacted and enjoyed greater mobility. Redfield and Lewis believed this space promoted greater youth choice in marriage and a quicker separation of the newly married couple from the patrivirilocal extended family.[26]

Within a context of subtly relaxing parental control, greater mobility, and economic opportunity, schooling represented possibilities of choice and change for women. In Chan Kom, women in 1931 were "shy, almost voiceless . . . completely unassertive . . . [and] secluded in their homes." In 1948 Redfield observed a "new type" of girl, "who joins with zest in baseball with other girls at school, who may play a little ball with friends and neighbors, including boys, and who talks about the city and her wish to go there."[27] Lewis noted that schooling in Tepoztlán meant more to girls than it did to boys. An opportunity to escape their mothers' vigilance and the burden of housework, school allowed girls to play and make friends. By contrast, boys saw school as confining; they played hookey and looked forward to the day they would follow their fathers to the fields. Girls were not as enthusiastic about their future around the hearth. Many cried and became depressed when taken out of school to care for younger children and assist their mothers.[28]

In Tecamachalco, women teachers serve often as role models of autonomous women who stood up to male aggression. In Caltenco, Hermila Bravo Bañuelos challenged the ejido leaders when they took over her classroom for business and refused to let her handle the proceeds from the school plot's harvest.[29] Josefa Alva Hernandez blazed new trails in gender behavior. Married, abandoned, and now involved in a relationship with a male teacher, she raised her children alone. Her compañero was her source of protection from other men, but she did not allow him to participate in her family's affairs. As a teacher, she engaged in activities once off-limits for women. She was farmer to the school's garden, merchant to the children's cooperative, *bailarina* at community dances, and an expert basketball player.[30]

In Tecamachalco, Chan Kom, and Tepoztlán, threats to gender customs provoked suspicion, ravings about revolution against (male) authority, and fear of cataclysmic moral collapse.[31] Families, political leaders, and the teachers themselves moved to control challenges to male authority. One way was to limit girls' stay in school. In the 1940s and 1950s, most girls in Tecamachalco, as in Tepoztlán, attended school for two to three years, generally a shorter period than boys. Another tactic was to keep boys and girls separated as much as possible. In Tecamachalco, as in Chan Kom and Tepoztlán, coeducation was cause for concern. In Tochtepec in 1946, the ejido president told the school director that the community did not look favorably on laws requiring coeducation. The school director judged that schooling children was more important than coeducation: he taught the boys, and his wife taught the girls.

Although the school called women of the community into political life as the guardians of reproduction, the women of Tecamachalco resisted direct assumption of this role in the 1940s. In deference to patriarchal norms, they left men in charge of the education committees. Women negotiated face-to-face with teachers or entered through the familiar back door. They made the children's costumes and prepared food for school festivals. In Chan Kom and Tepoztlán, women were similarly excluded from public affairs.

Women teachers in Tecamachalco found their possibilities for autonomy and empowerment limited by communities, politicians, other teachers, their husbands, and their own mentalities. While male teachers joined the local power structure, female teachers did not. Municipal and ejidal officials avoided direct communication with them.

Communities had myriad ways of imposing standards. When teachers were invited into homes for a fiesta or a meal, the men ate with the men and the women teachers followed the wives to the kitchen to serve the men. Gossip and social disapproval acted as strong brakes on new female behavior. Only with tremendous force and constant strategizing was Josefa Alva, an unmarried woman, able to break into new territory as teacher, farmer, merchant, athlete, and dancer. Had she capitulated to a male suitor hot on her trail for her beauty and independence she would have lost her status and had to leave town.

The case of Elsa Rocha is a painful example of teachers' disciplining themselves.[32] She and her husband taught in a Tecamachalco town in the early 1940s. Her husband, a jealous man, abused her and confined her to ensure her fidelity, keeping her virtually locked up in the school where they lived with their four children. Upon waking in the morning, she dressed her children, prepared breakfast, and greeted the pupils who appeared at the door with their "Buenos días, Maestra." She organized more than a hundred girls into groups ranging from grades 1 to 4 and taught each until, at midday, her husband concluded his classes and wanted his *comida*. In the afternoon, she taught again. Each evening, she led adult classes or, with her husband, filled out certificates for campesinos seeking access to new irrigation water. Weekends she cleaned, washed, and ironed. She never left the house. Her children fetched water and ran errands for her. Her husband interacted with the community. She met campesina mothers only on the first day of school.

The ways communities, teachers, and local leaders muted the schools' challenge to patriarchy in Tecamachalco are illustrated by Mother's Day celebrations in the 1940s. Mother's Day became an important patriotic festival in revolutionary schools. By honoring mothers, the state recognized the family's importance to national development and sought to counteract women's loyalties to the church and to correct what educators perceived as the exceptional debasement of women in the countryside.[33] In Tecamachalco, communities fashioned their own Mother's Day celebrations around an image bathed in the pathos of suffering close to that of traditional Mexican Catholicism. As one teacher said, mothers were honored not as women but as symbols of unbounded love and sacrifice. The play performed on Mother's Day was intended to make the audience cry—"To value la mamá and let her cry for all she suffered" (or, as one male teacher said, "to let them sob in grief from their husbands' beatings").

The state, through the schools, injected new notions of women's work and personhood into this image, which Tecamachalqueños either appropriated or rejected. New spaces and behavior were more easily tolerated in women who left than in women who stayed behind. The revolutionary process enhanced women's mobility, and literacy and schooling were sources of empowerment for mobile women. Families of modest income sent daughters temporarily into domestic work in the cities. Better-off families took advantage of the expanding system of higher education to secure careers and training for selected daughters.[34] Agustina Barrojas's daughter married the teacher in Cuaucnopalan. Her daughters in turn obtained professional degrees in the city of Puebla in psychology, teaching, mathematics, and secretarial-notarial work. Josefa Alva's daughter became a teacher and a member of the national girls' basketball team. Reyna Manzano's daughter became a power in the state school system and teachers' union.

Literacy and schooling could empower women who remained behind in the villages as well. In Tepoztlán, Lewis argues, everyone knew that the most prosperous campesinos had become so through their wives' industriousness. Women played a more diversified role in family survival than before: as holders of purse strings, vendors, teachers, seamstresses, and domestic workers.[35] Literacy and schooling were useful tools in the execution of these roles. In the final analysis, economic need condoned women's invasion of new spaces and notions of personhood promoted by state education.

Conclusions

Contemporary studies of gender in rural Mexico have neglected education as an important variable in women's lives in part because they focus on economic processes to the exclusion of ideological, political, and social ones, and in part because they tend to underestimate the importance of even a little schooling in certain contexts. In this essay I have introduced rural women's literacy, basic schooling, and interaction with schools as skills and experiences empowering women in limited but significant ways. The politically motivated land reform of the Mexican Revolution partially shored up the patriarchally structured peasant family unit of production. Post-1960 economic growth transformed this family unit into one relying on diverse income-producing activities. Interpenetrating the political and the economic and critical to the survival of the campesino family unit over the span of the twentieth century were ideological and social processes linked to schooling which mitigated patriarchal practices and opened new spaces for women.

NOTES

I am grateful to Linda Montes and Betsy McEneaney for their help in compiling and analyzing the statistics. I benefited from comments on earlier drafts of this essay by Heather Fowler-Salamini, Refugio Rochín, Francie Chassen-López, Silvia Arrom, Soledad González, JoAnn Martin, and Patricia Arias.

1. On revolutionary educational policy toward women and the family, see Mary Kay Vaughan, "Women, Class, and Education in Mexico, 1880–1928," *Latin American Perspectives* 4 (1977):135–52; Victoria Lerner, "Historia de la reforma educativa, 1933–1945," *Historia Mexicana* 29 (1979):91–132. On teachers, see Vaughan, "Women School Teachers in the Mexican Revolution: The Story of Reyna's Braids," *Journal of Women's History* 2.1 (1990):143–68.

2. Between 1910 and 1940, female literacy in Mexico rose from 24 to 42 percent, and male literacy rose from 32 to 50 percent. Statistics used in this essay are from the following, published by the Dirección General de Estadística: *Censo general de la República mexicana verificada el 18 de octubre de 1900* (1900); *Tercer Censo de la población. Mexico. 1910* (1918); *Quinto Censo de la población. 15 de mayo de 1930, no. 21* (1930); *Sexto Censo de la población. 1940, no. 16* (1940); *Séptimo Censo de la población, 1950* (1950); *IX Censo general de población. 1970. Estado de Puebla* (1970); and *Estadísticas históricas de México,* vol. 1 (Mexico City: Instituto de Estadística Geográfica e Informática, 1986). The 1900 and 1910 censuses measured the ability to read and write in Spanish for people over twelve years of age; 1920–1940 censuses, people over ten; 1950 and 1970 censuses, people over six years.

3. In accordance with the Constitution of 1917, these municipalities became autonomous and the administrative district ceased to exist.

4. See, e.g., Alan Knight, *The Mexican Revolution,* vol. 2 (Lincoln: University of Nebraska Press, 1990), 517–27; Elsie Rockwell, "Schools of the Revolution: Enacting and Contesting State Forms (Tlaxcala 1910–930)," in *Everyday Forms of State Formation: Revolution and the Negotiation of Rule in Modern Mexico,* ed. G. Joseph and D. Nugent (Durham, N.C.: Duke University Press, forthcoming).

5. François Furet and Jacques Ozouf, *Reading and Writing: Literacy in France from Calvin to Jules Ferry* (Cambridge: Cambridge University Press, 1982), 243–45.

6. Archivo Municipal de Tecamachalco [AMT], Datos sobre la instrucción pública, Tecamachalco, Palmar del Bravo, Quecholac, Tlacotepec, 1909; Mary Kay Vaughan, "Economic Growth and Literacy in Late Nineteenth Century Mexico: The Case of Puebla," in *Education and Economic Development Since the Industrial Revolution,* ed. Gabriel Tortellar (Valencia: Generalitat Valenciana, 1990), 106.

7. On conditions in Tecamachalco in the 1930s, see Archivo Histórico de la Secretaria de Educación Pública, Departamento de Escuelas Rurales [AHSEP, DER], Jesús H. González, Tecamachalco [JHG], Informes: Caja 905, Aug., Nov. 1932; Caja 969, June, Aug., Dec. 1933; and Expediente [Exp.] 316.1, Jan. 1936; also Fondo Lázaro Cárdenas Rio, Archivo General de la Nación [AGN], Exp. 564.1/2091, Odilon Luna, Comisariado Ejidal, San Mateo Tlaixpan, to Cárdenas, Jan. 18, 1940; AMT, Presidencia, Caja 65, Celso Campos, Pres. Municipal, to Secretaría de Agricultura, Jan. 30, 1935; to Servicio Sanitario, Feb. 1, 1935. On terms of trade, see Arturo Warman, *We Come to Object. The Peasants of Morelos and the National State* (Baltimore: Johns Hopkins University Press, 1980), 160.

8. See Mary Kay Vaughan, "The Construction of Patriotic Festival in Central Mexico: Tecamachalco, Puebla, 1900–1946," in *Rituals of Rule, Rituals of Resistance,* ed. W. H. Beezley, C. E. Martin, and W. E. French (Wilmington, Del.: Scholarly Resources, 1994), for a discussion of political dispute and state consolidation based

on source materials from the Fondo Lázaro Cárdenas Ríos in the AGN and the municipal archives of Tecamachalco.

9. AHSEP, DER, Caja 905, JHG, Informe, Aug. 1932; Caja 969, JHG, Informe, Dec. 1933.

10. On violence and its effect on the schooling of women, see AHSEP, DER, Caja 905, JHG, Informes, April, June 1932, Instituto de Mejoramiento Profesional, June 30, 1932; Caja 969, JHG, Informe, March, 1933, Informe Anual, Dec. 1933; on crimes against women, see AMT, Presidencia, Caja 65, Carlos Maldonado to Ministerio Público, Aug. 6, 1935; Arnulfo Maldonado and Vidal María, Santiago Alseseca, to Pres. Municipal, April 11, 1935; Caja 74, Carlos Fuentes Miramon, Comandante de la Seccion Palmarito-Tochapan, Tecamachalco, to Gral. Comandante del Sector Militar, Tehuacan, Sept. 13, 1938.

11. On opposition to coeducation, see AHSEP, DER, Caja 905, JHG, Informes, April, Aug. 1932; interviews with Horacio Caro, Puebla, July 6, 1991; and Reyna Manzano Carmona, Puebla, July 5, 1991.

12. AHSEP, DER, Caja 905, JHG, Informes, April, June 1932; Caja 969, Informe, March 1933, Exp. 207.1, JHG, Informe, Aug.–Sept. 1935; Exp. 316.1, Informe, Jan. 1936.

13. For an excellent portrait of the social meaning of gender hierarchies and the reproductive sphere in rural communities, see Florencia Mallon, "The Conflictual Construction of Community: Gender, Ethnicity, and Hegemony in the Sierra Norte de Puebla" (Paper presented to the Latin American History Seminar, University of Chicago, May 1990), 14–20; also María Cristina Galante, Paola Sesia Lewis, and Virginia Alejandre, "Mujeres y parteras: protagonistas activas en la relación entre medicina moderna y medicina tradicional," in *Las mujeres en el campo,* comp. J. Aranda Bezuary (Oaxaca: Universidad Autónoma Benito Juárez, 1988), 357–59; Graciela Feyermuth Enciso, "Atención del Parto. Modificaciones en las practicas tradicionales y su impacto en la salud," in ibid., 355–61; María Teresa Guadarrama and Ruth Piedrasanta Herrero, "El papel de las mujeres en la medicina popular y tradicional," in ibid., 363–65.

14. AHSEP, DER, Caja 905, JHG, Informes: Caja 905, Nov., Dec. 1932; Caja 969, Dec. 1933; and AMT, Caja 68, Clemente Guevara, Jefe de la Unidad, Departamento de Salubridad, to Presidente Municipal, Jan. 2, 14, 1936.

15. AHSEP, DER, Exp. 207.1, JHG, Informes, Aug., Sept., Dec. 1935.

16. See JoAnn Martin, "Motherhood and Power: The Production of a Women's Culture of Politics in a Mexican Community," *American Ethnologist* 17.3 (1990):470–90; Marjorie Becker, "Torching La Purísima, Dancing at the Altar: The Construction of Revolutionary Hegemony in Michoacán, 1934–1940," in *Everyday Forms of State Formation: Revolution and the Negotiation of Rule in Modern Mexico,* ed. G. Joseph and D. Nugent (Durham, N.C.: Duke University Press, 1994).

17. The Partido Nacional Revolucionario, created in 1929, became the Partido de la Revolución Mexicana in 1938 and the Partido Revolucionario Institucional in 1946. Requests for schools, furniture, supplies, textbooks, and teachers increased dramatically after 1940; see AGN, Fondo Manuel Avila Camacho: Exp. 534.3/45, President, Comisariado Ejidal, San José Bellavista, Palmar de Bravo, to Manuel Avila Camacho, Jan. 9, 1941; Exp. 151.3/125, Gonzálo Bautista, Governor, Puebla, to Manuel Avila Camacho, May 16, 1941.

18. Interview, Reyna Manzano, Puebla, July 5, 1991.

19. Interviews, Victor Alva and Ida García Manzano, July 1991, Puebla; Vaughan, "Women School Teachers," 158–60.

20. Vaughan, "Women School Teachers," 158–61; interview with Reyna Manzano, Puebla, July 5, 1991; Judith Friedlander, "Doña Zeferina Barreto" (this volume).

21. Interview with Agustina Barrojas de Caro, Puebla, July 6, 1991.

22. On irrigation canals, see AMT, Legajo 74, Año 1938, Presidencia, Asamblea de la 4 Convención pro-Irrigación del Valsequillo, Tehuacan, Dec. 3, 1938; interviews with teachers Manuel Bravo Bañuelos, Tecamachalco, July 1, 1991; Horacio Caro, July 6, 1991; and Reyna Manzano, July 5, 1991.

23. AHSEP, DER, Caja 905, JHG, Informes, Nov. 1932, Aug. 1932.

24. See statistics on infant mortality in Raul Ayala and Carlos Schaffer, *Salud y seguridad social. Crisis, ajuste y grupos vulnerables* (Mexico City: Instituto Nacional de Salud Pública, 1991), 126–27.

25. Vaughan, "Women School Teachers," 158. On new activities for girls opened through schooling, see Elsie Rockwell, "Schools of the Revolution," 49–53; and Oscar Lewis, *Life in a Mexican Village: Tepoztlán Restudied* (Urbana: University of Illinois Press, 1971), 386–87.

26. Lewis, *Life in a Mexican Village*, 74–79, 386–89; Robert Redfield, *Chan Kom: Village That Chose Progress* (Chicago: University of Chicago Press, 1950), 79–81, 134–36; on sports in Tecamachalco, see Vaughan, "Patriotic Festival."

27. Redfield, *Chan Kom*, 134–35.

28. Lewis, *Life in a Mexican Village*, 383–93.

29. AHSEP, Archivo Particular, Escuela Rural Federal, Caltenco, Hermila Bañuelos to Inspector, April 16, 1934, Aug. 15, 1935.

30. Interviews, Victor Alva and Ida García Manzano, Puebla, July 2, 1991. Unless otherwise indicated, the information on Tecamachalco in the following paragraphs comes from interviews with the latter and with Horacio Caro Castillo, Agustina Barrojas de Caro, Reyna Manzano, and Manuel Bravo Banuelos. A *bailarina* is a dancer.

31. Lewis, *Life in a Mexican Village*, 108, 323, 327, 342, 389–98; Redfield, *Chan Kom*, 39–42, 134–45, 159–60.

32. The name of the teacher, interviewed in Puebla in July 1991, has been changed to protect her privacy.

33. Lewis, *Life in a Mexican Village*, 387.

34. Ibid., 389.

35. Ibid., 73, 323–24, 101–5, 170, 323.

7

Doña Zeferina Barreto:
Biographical Sketch of an Indian Woman from the State of Morelos

JUDITH FRIEDLANDER

Zeferina Barreto was born in 1905 in Santo Domingo Hueyapan, a bilingual (Nahuatl-Spanish) Indian village located in the northeastern corner of the state of Morelos. On August 26, 1993, she celebrated her eighty-eighth birthday with a traditional *mole* feast in her home, the same house where she grew up, married, and raised her four children. Although she has slowed down in recent years, Doña Zeferina continues to lead an active life. Every Tuesday she goes to the plaza to sell plastic toys, five-and-dime-store-variety dishes, and dried chile peppers in the weekly market, just as she has done for decades. She also maintains her practice as a healer, providing patients with a mixture of modern and traditional cures. When people tell her how remarkable she is for working so hard at her advanced age, she dismisses the compliment and reminds her admirers that she enjoys the strength she has today because she lived through the Mexican Revolution and the difficult times that followed. Growing up during the struggle for *tierra y libertad* (land and freedom), she spent many years on the edge of starvation, in a state of constant fear. As a mature woman in the 1930s and 1940s, she supported her children essentially alone by selling meat, fruit, and *pulque* (a beer of *agave* plant) in neighboring *pueblos* (villages), maintaining a schedule she was lucky to have survived.

I lived with Doña Zeferina and her children and grandchildren in 1969–70 while conducting anthropological research on Indian identity in contemporary Mexico.[1] Since then, I have continued to visit the family and keep in regular contact by telephone and mail.[2] In 1990, Doña Zeferina came to visit me in New York, accompanied by two of her grandchildren.

Given my long association with Doña Zeferina and her family, the story I tell may be different from those recorded by oral historians who usually interview their subjects in two or three sittings. The tale told here is one I heard many times in the intimacy of Doña Zeferina's home, usually in the evening as we sat around the hearth in the adobe kitchen, eating tortillas and beans and drinking herbal tea. The children and I loved to listen to the old woman reminisce about her life or tell one of the many fairy tales she has committed to memory from a published collection of stories a school teacher had loaned her when she was still a young girl, during the Mexican Revolution. Sometimes I taped Doña Zeferina while she talked, but only rarely, for she was self-conscious before the recorder. What follows, then, I have pieced together from copious notes taken during the many months I spent with Doña Zeferina and her family. Our close relationship has given me the courage to risk writing the story of this Indian woman in my own words, mostly, relying only occasionally on hers for descriptions of the most dramatic events in her life.

I believe my version of Doña Zeferina's story comes very close to the way she would tell it herself. Before publishing the Spanish translation of *Being Indian in Hueyapan,* I returned to the village with the manuscript in hand and read to Doña Zeferina what I had written about her, giving her the opportunity to correct any errors and to endorse or reject my interpretation of her life. After I finished, she gave me her blessings, only to regret having done so the following year when I returned with copies of the book for the pueblo: now everybody would know the full story, she complained—as if they did not already. Much to my relief, Doña Zeferina soon recovered and began to take pleasure in the fact that she had become a bit of a "star" with foreigners and upper-class Mexicans who, after reading about her experiences, wanted to meet her. Outsiders visiting Hueyapan looked up the woman whose stories had given them a glimpse at what life was like in Morelos for one individual during the Mexican Revolution and the turbulent years that followed.

Feminist scholars, historians, anthropologists, and others have been debating the value of recording life histories for many years. In the late 1960s when I recorded Doña Zeferina's story, I already had grave reservations myself, but I decided to proceed for two main reasons.

First, I saw Doña Zeferina's story as a corrective in a book dealing with broader issues about Indian identity. At the time I solemnly believed, and continue to believe, that anthropologists have to find ways to make theoretical arguments with—dare I say such a thing?—real people at hand. While refusing to generalize from the experiences and opinions of one individual and her family, I wanted to introduce readers to a few Hueyapeños, as I had come to know them, before offering my interpretation of how rural people in Mexico had been manipulated by the politics of ethnicity.

In the original sketch, and again here, I refer to Doña Zeferina as an Indian woman, even though the story I tell has little to do with her indigenous origins. If this sounds contradictory, it should, for that is precisely the point. In *Being Indian in Hueyapan,* I argue that Doña Zeferina is first and foremost a poor peasant woman who happens to live in a community where cultural vestiges of a pre-Hispanic past linger on. The fact that she speaks Nahuatl marks her as a descendant of those whose culture was destroyed nearly five hundred years ago and who have since been condemned to occupy the bottom rung of Mexico's socioeconomic ladder. While Doña Zeferina never expresses shame about her indigenous origins, she sees her life and the lives of her ancestors as a steady struggle to improve their economic circumstances, a struggle often requiring that they reject those traditions identified as Indian and acquire, when possible, attributes associated with upward mobility.

I never intended Doña Zeferina's story to stand alone. I expected it to be read as part of a book that also included historical and anthropological descriptions of her village, a community first conquered in 1524, three years after the fall of Tenochtitlán. For me, Doña Zeferina's life history provided one of several readings, all of them connected, of what it means to endure cultural, economic, and social domination for nearly five hundred years, first by Spanish *encomenderos* and the Catholic church, later by a number of governmental and private institutions, some trying to beat the Indian out of you while others tried to beat it back in.

My second reason for recording Doña Zeferina's tale was simple and direct: she had a wonderful story to tell. She gave texture, not information, to the world I wanted to analyze. In thinking about the problem of writing life histories, Ruth Behar puts it beautifully, paraphrasing Walter Benjamin. With her words I rest my case and turn to the story of Doña Zeferina:

> Information, in Benjamin's analysis, is a mode of communication linked to the development of the printing press and of capitalism; it presents itself as verifiable, it is "shot through with explanation," and it is disposable because it is forgettable. Storytelling, on the other hand, is "always the art of repeating stories," without explanation, combining the extraordinary and the ordinary; most importantly, it is grounded in a community of listeners on whom the story makes a claim to be remembered by virtue of its "chaste compactness" which inspires the listener, in turn, to become the teller of the story.[3]

Doña Zeferina's Story

Doña Zeferina's father abandoned his family when she was only two years old. She continued to see him occasionally, but Doña Zeferina shows little interest in the history of his family. On her mother's side, however, she has stories to tell that go back to the mid-1800s, many of them clearly fanciful, memories, so-called, of a "dream time" when people were supposedly healthier, richer, and stronger than they are today.

Doña Zeferina's story reaches back to the days of her great-grandparents, one of whom was still alive when she was a young girl (her grandmother's mother). What she learned about the period, however, did not come from this elderly relative but from her grandmother and mother, who told her, among other things, that people back then were much bigger than they are today. In her own family, for example, her great-grandfather Rafael Crisantos was apparently so enormous that he would eat half a sheep and a dozen eggs at one meal. His daughters used to take turns making tortillas for their father, who could polish off an entire basketful in one sitting.

Nahuatl was spoken almost exclusively in Hueyapan in the mid-nineteenth century. The language's grammar and vocabulary, however, had become very mixed with Spanish. Since virtually everyone was baptized, people had Christian first names but no last names.

When her great-grandparents were young, Hueyapan had a resident priest, and Catholic ritual was more elaborate than it is today. Doña Zeferina's mother told her that on Good Friday, men used to march in processions, carrying prickly pear cactus on their bare backs, to share in the agony of Christ. They also wore chains around their feet to make walking painful and to induce bleeding.

Virtually every woman wore a *xincueite*, the traditional long, black wool skirt of the region, woven on the backstrap loom. Men dressed in *calzones*, the white "pajamas" typically worn by *campesinos* (peasants) throughout Mexico. Unlike those of today, calzones then were fashioned out of one piece of fabric. The unfitted cloth was held together by a belt wrapped around the waist. Instead of shirts, men wore wool *gabanes* (serapes), which were sewn up the sides. Neither men nor women wore shoes or sandals.

In the old days, people were very rich. If you wanted to borrow money, you did so by the basketful. Doña Zeferina's great-grandfather Manuel Sardinias had a bull's skin filled to the brim with silver.

Using his considerable wealth, Great-Grandfather Manuel Sardinias bought some land on what is now called Calle Morelos. Three generations later, Doña Zeferina inherited part of this original purchase. In Don Manuel's time, the family had enough land that he did not have to split up this particular lot among his heirs. Instead, he passed down the entire property to Doña Zeferina's grandfather, Dionisio Sardinias, his eldest son.

Doña Zeferina's grandparents, Don Dionisio and Doña María, had three children. Soon after their third child was born, circumstances dramatically altered their relatively comfortable life: Don Dioniso was convicted of murder and sentenced to serve twenty years in the Cuautla jail. Before his arrest, Don Dionisio had been a *comandante,* a member of the pueblo's local police force. One day he learned that a Hueyapeño had stolen livestock from a cousin of his. When he went to see her about it, she told him who she thought had stolen the animals. Don Dionisio hunted down the alleged thief and ambushed him in the heavily wooded Amatzinac gorge about a kilometer away from the plaza. Unfortunately there was a witness to the crime. A woman saw Don Dionisio murder the man and reported it to other village authorities, who in turn alerted the federal troops. Within a matter of days, soldiers came to Hueyapan and took Don Dionisio away.

So that they would not forget their father, Doña María took the children to Cuautla as often as she could to visit Don Dionisio. Then, when Pablo Escandón became governor of Morelos in 1909, three years before the end of Don Dionisio's term, he gave all the prisoners in the Cuautla jail their freedom. The victim of terrible physical abuse, Don Dionisio was a broken man when he returned to the village. He died five years later.

Doña Zeferina was four years old when he returned and only nine when he died, so she does not have many personal memories of Don Dionisio. What she knows about him, she learned from her grandmother, who lived until 1932, by which time Doña Zeferina was a woman of twenty-seven. Listening to Doña Zeferina talk about her childhood, one gets the impression that Doña María influenced her more than anybody else, even more than her own mother.

Doña Zeferina has nothing but the greatest admiration for her grandmother, whom she describes as having descended from another "race" of people with dark skin and beautiful light hair. Doña María did not wear a xincueite because her husband did not want her or his daughters to dress like "Indians." Still, she followed the humble custom of walking barefoot, even though others in the village had begun to wear sandals. Doña Zeferina remembers that once she gave her grandmother a pair of *ixcacles* (agave-fiber sandals) and the old woman put them away, solemnly proclaiming that she would save them to wear on the day of her funeral, when she went to meet her Maker. Until then she continued to walk barefoot, carrying as much as twenty-five liters of corn on her back for very long distances. Today, Doña Zeferina notes with scorn, people cannot manage ten, with or without shoes!

After Don Dionisio went to jail, Doña María supported the family by selling pulque on market days in nearby villages. Even when she had grown quite old, Doña María kept working, traveling long distances by herself. When Doña Zeferina turned ten, she was granted the privilege of accompanying her grandmother on some of these trips.

On the days they sold pulque, Doña Zeferina remembers, her grandmother rose at three o'clock in the morning and went out alone into the fields to collect the juice (*agua miel*) from the agave plant. When people heard that she took such risks, they asked how it was that she was not afraid. "Why should I be scared?" she replied. "I have my dogs and my machete. If somebody attacks me, my dogs will help me, and if an animal attacks them, I can defend the dogs with my machete."

In the early 1900s, Doña Zeferina's mother, Doña Jacoba, settled down with José Ocampo, a man from Hueyapan who owned a small store. She moved into his home, and in 1905 gave birth to little Zeferina. Two years later, Don José left Hueyapan, abandoning mother and child, and moved in with a woman who lived in the neighboring village of Tlacotepec, about eleven kilometers away. Don José had several more children with this other companion. When he left, Doña Jacoba took her daughter and returned to her parents' home.

A few months later, Doña Jacoba accepted the advances of a second suitor, a man by the name of Lucio Barreto who came from the lowland community of Jantetelco. Don Lucio asked her to settle down with him in his village, but Doña Jacoba wanted to stay with her mother. Although they maintained their relationship for many years, the couple never really lived in the same home. Don Lucio would visit whenever he could leave his crops for a few days and make the trip to Hueyapan. Over the years, the couple had five children, three of whom died in infancy, and Don Lucio adopted little Zeferina, giving the girl his patronym so that she would not be different from the other children in the home. Don Lucio died in 1922, just after Doña Zeferina was married.

Like Doña María, Doña Jacoba supported her children essentially alone, without the help of a man. She found that she could make ends meet by working as a seamstress, and she purchased the first pedal-operated Singer sewing machine owned by anybody for miles around. Her reputation spread rapidly, and people came from many villages to commission her considerable skills. Although Doña Jacoba tried to encourage her daughter to become a seamstress too, Doña Zeferina preferred the life of a merchant, like her grandmother. When the time came to make a decision, Doña Zeferina chose to travel from village to village, selling meat, eggs, fruit, and pulque.

Since she grew up during the Mexican Revolution, Doña Zeferina hardly went to school. Nevertheless, she did have one excellent teacher, Maestro

Eligio, the son of the man who had founded the Hueyapan school in the 1870s. From him she learned history, most of which she still remembers. Doña Zeferina claims that what children learn in secondary school today, she received in the three years of primary school she was able to complete. Proud of her success as a student of history, Doña Zeferina admits she was less brilliant in math. Not until she became a merchant and had a practical use for numbers did she learn how to add, subtract, and multiply with ease. As for division, she never did master that skill very well.

As a child, Doña Zeferina was not permitted to go out of the house very often, an understandable restriction in the land of Zapata during the years of the Revolution. To keep her entertained, Doña Jacoba bought her daughter a book of prayers, and the young girl spent much of her free time reading and memorizing them. Doña Jacoba also borrowed a book of fairy tales from Maestro Eligio for little Zeferina, who devoured the stories and learned them by heart. To this day Doña Zeferina delights her grandchildren and great-grandchildren with the adventures of kings and princesses from foreign lands.[4]

In 1914, when Zeferina was nine, Doña Jacoba sent her to live with an aunt in Tlacotepec. The young girl stayed there nearly a year and now often wonders what life would have been like had she been a little older, met a man, and settled down permanently in this mestizo village.

In 1917, when she was twelve years old, Zeferina left home again, this time to live in Mexico City in the home of her godmother. Following the tradition of selecting a godparent with the social and economic means to help, Doña Jacoba had asked a school teacher temporarily working in Hueyapan to honor the family by becoming the godmother of little Zeferina. Soon after agreeing to assume the responsibility, the school teacher left the village, married, and settled down in her native Mexico City. During the Revolution, when it was hard to find food, Doña Jacoba called upon Zeferina's godmother to take the child in for a few months.

Doña Zeferina enjoyed her stay in Mexico City very much. Although she claims her godmother treated her like a member of the family, the way she describes her life there makes it sound as if she were one of the servants. Many years later, Doña Zeferina worked as a domestic—no nuances here—in the home of her godmother's sister, something she probably would not have done had she truly been considered a member of the family.

Doña Zeferina also spent a few of the war years in Hueyapan, where she, like everybody else in the village, had terrifying experiences. Here, in her own words, is one of her most traumatic memories:

Maestra,[5] I am going to tell you about what happened to me during the time of Zapata's war. Well, we were children then. I was about thirteen years old. In those days, everybody used to run away. The bells would ring to announce that soldiers were coming and everybody would run away. People used to run, because if government troops came, they killed villagers, and if the Zapatistas—you know, the rebels—came, they killed the villagers too. So, we would not wait for either of them. It was better to run. Finally, to bring an end to the war, a lot of government troops came to Hueyapan. One general came via Tetela. Another came from the hills we call El Monte. Another came from Tochimilco, Puebla. And still another came from this other place in Puebla called San Marcos. In this way, the five exits of the pueblo were closed off by government troops, so that the villagers couldn't escape.

Well, here in the house lived an uncle of mine, and he killed a pig. And this pig was fat and everything. I had my brothers. We were four, no more, and then my mamá . . . the poor thing, since she was pregnant, she couldn't run. Also she had to dismantle the sewing machine, the one that I still have. Well, I carried my youngest brother. And since it upset me to leave the meat, I grabbed a few pieces of meat, *xales, chicharrones,*[6] and a bag of tortillas. And in this way I took off, carrying the child on my back. I was carrying my little brother, who was about two or three. The government's soldiers were right behind me. And the rebels were in front. Then the rebels took a path to the left and disappeared. I took one to the right, toward the gorge, and the government troops followed me. They thought that I was the rebels' woman, or who knows what they thought. They used foul language with me, Maestra: "Stop, you daughter of a so-and-so!" And bullets whizzed by and more bullets. And then a bullet passed by my little brother's head and made a hole in his hat. But we weren't hurt. And when I got to the bottom of the gorge, I took this path in order to hide myself, my brother, and the food. In this path I leave everything: meat, tortillas, xales, chicharrones—I leave everything there. And I wait until that *pelón*[7] who was following me went by. And then I could hear that all the soldiers had left the gorge and gone over to the other side. Since it's so quiet, you can hear everything. Over there they were breaking windows, and well . . . it was ugly. I stayed hidden, but I heard that now they were gone. So I say to my brother, "You'd better not cry, because if you cry, they'll kill us. Don't cry."

I pick him up again and I travel around the entire gorge. Who knows where we ended up, Maestra. Afterward, I didn't recognize the area. And I didn't want to go down into the gorge again. I say, "Now, where can I go? There are nothing but gorges and more gorges. I just won't go." So I wait there. I was there awhile, and I was crying because I was scared. But then two men I know appear. One was Don Francisco Bautista and the other, who is still living, was Don Estebán Maya. I see them, and since I know them I speak to them: "Where are you going?"

"We're going over there now, back to the pueblo. Why are you crying?"

"Because I don't know how to return home."

"Let's go. Don't cry, child. Let's go." So they take me back, and as we are walking, they say, "The government troops have gone now. The bastards have gone."

We come to the spot where we had been hiding before, and I say, "I'll go see if the meat is still there." So I go down the gorge again and take the same little path. And there it is! The meat, the xales . . . everything. So, I pick up the food once again and I return to the pueblo. I go find my mamá, who, I am told, is now in Don Miguel's house. There I find her, and she is crying because they told her that they had killed us, that who knows what. I say to her, "But who could have seen that they killed us when nobody was there? No, here we are. And you, how did you defend yourself?"

"Well . . . I never even left," she says. "The government troops caught me." They put my mamá in the house of a certain man whose name was Don Pedro Escobar. It is said that all the people caught were simply put there. But nothing, absolutely nothing, happened to my mamá. Well, then we went home. And that is what happened to me during that period . . . when I was a girl. It was like that, all of it true; I saw it. We suffered many things during that time.

When her children became adults, Doña Jacoba divided the Calle Morelos plot among her three surviving heirs. Until their mother died in 1947, Doña Zeferina and her maternal half-brothers, Don Benjamín and Don Falconériz, remained together on the land. Once their mother was gone, the two men married and sold their shares to the Maya Cortés brothers; Don Benjamín moved to Cuautla and Don Falconériz to Tetela. Several years later the two half-brothers returned to Hueyapan to try to force Doña Zeferina at gunpoint to give up her part of the inheritance. By this time Doña Zeferina's son Rafael was a grown man, and he defended his mother against her brothers. After that time, Doña Zeferina had nothing to do with the two men.

In 1922, when she was seventeen years old, Doña Zeferina married Don Felipe Vargas. She was the first in her family to have an official wedding with both church and civil ceremonies. Most people in Hueyapan simply lived together in free union without going to the expense of having a formal ceremony. Then, as now, a religious wedding was costly, but it brought a great deal of honor and prestige.

Doña Zeferina told me that her mother tried to discourage the marriage, warning her daughter that as a wife she would have to work very hard. She refused to listen to Doña Jacoba, but once she was married Doña Zeferina was sorry. Every few days she had to rise at 4:00 A.M. to grind corn for her husband's tortillas. Don Felipe would then go to work in the fields, staying away two or three days at a time. When he returned, Doña Zeferina would have to serve him again and work long hours.

After five years of marriage, Doña Zeferina went on strike. She saw no reason to subject herself to this arduous routine any longer. She had infants by then, she complained, and she refused to add to her many burdens by getting up so early to make tortillas. Defiantly she told Don Felipe to find somebody else to cook for him, and this he did, turning to his sister, promising her many gifts in exchange for her help. For years Don Felipe's sister kept her side of the bargain, but according to Doña Zeferina she never received any recompense for doing so.

Doña Zeferina and Don Felipe had four children: Zeferino, Rosalía, Rafael, and Raúl. Zeferino, who died when he was seven years old, was born with three testicles. Everybody believed that had he lived, he would have grown into one and a half men. Rosalía died when she was five. Then, in 1931, a few years after their fourth child was born, Don Felipe died as well. He and Doña Zeferina had been married about nine years.

Soon after her husband passed away, Doña Zeferina, who was twenty-six at the time, left her children in the care of her mother and went to Cuernavaca to work as a maid for a year. She spent another two years in Mexico City in three different households, but finally she returned home, fed up with people ordering her about. "After all," Doña Zeferina told me, "I was not an orphan and did not have to put up with such treatment."

Although she complains about that time, Doña Zeferina clearly made the most of her life as a maid, delighting in her ability to cheat the mistresses she worked for. She enjoyed recalling the experiences she had in the home of one family in particular. Each time she started the story, Doña Zeferina would chuckle in her characteristic way, shake her head, and say to me, "*Soy bien canija, Maestra*" (I can be a sneaky so-and-so). The mistress of this house was notoriously stingy. No maid before her had lasted longer than a month, but Doña Zeferina stayed six. Apparently, Doña Zeferina added, the family was very rich, something she confirmed for herself one day when she saw the man of the house open a huge box filled to the brim with money.

In 1935, about a year after returning from Mexico City, Doña Zeferina left her children again, this time to join her maternal half-brothers Falconériz and Benjamín in San Juan Ahuehueyo, a rancho in the lowlands south of Hueyapan, near Tepalcingo, where the two men were working as peons. Doña Zeferina went there to keep house for her brothers, who were bachelors at the time, and to make a little money by doing laundry for the other peons.

From the beginning Doña Zeferina knew that she would not remain in the lowlands so far from Hueyapan. While she was there, however, she wanted to make as much money as possible, so she and several other women agreed to wash the dirty clothing of peons in a little stream located a good distance away from where they all lived.

One day, Doña Zeferina went to the stream by herself, a foolish thing to do. A man stopped her on the road and told her that he wanted Doña Zeferina to be his woman. If she would not agree to his proposal peaceably, he would take her by force. Although everyone knew she was no "señorita" and had children back home, several men still wanted to court her. Faced with the present threat, Doña Zeferina told the man that she would be happy to marry him, but she insisted on a proper ceremony. First he would have to go to Hueyapan and ask Doña Jacoba for Zeferina's hand. The man agreed, although he said he had heard that Doña Zeferina could not be trusted. He warned her that she had better keep her promise. Doña Zeferina reassured him, and he left without compromising her.

When Don Falconériz and Don Benjamín heard what had happened, they became very upset. They told their sister that she would have to stay in San Juan Ahuehueyo and settle down with the man. Doña Zeferina refused and told her brothers that they would just have to find a way to get her out of there. They wanted to send her home by train—the Salitre station wasn't far from the ranch—but they didn't have the money, so they decided to walk her back to Hueyapan themselves.

Doña Zeferina had caught malaria during her stay in San Juan Ahuehueyo and was suffering from severe bouts of fever. Nervousness about her imminent escape caused these attacks to worsen. Although she was uncomfortable and weak, at least the disease served as an excuse for not attending a dance that was held a few nights before her escape. Had she gone to the party, Doña Zeferina believes, she would have been abducted by her amorous suitor.

Finally the big day arrived. Doña Zeferina remembers that it was a Thursday, August 14. Leaving after dark, they walked all night long and arrived in Tlacotepec at seven in the morning. Too exhausted to continue, Doña Zeferina decided to stay put for the day and enjoy the fiesta celebrating the Ascension of Mary. Her brothers, however, kept going to let their mother in Hueyapan know what was happening. They returned the following day with a donkey to carry their sister the remaining eleven kilometers home.

In San Juan Ahuehueyo some men did come looking for Doña Zeferina on the morning of August 15, but by then it was too late. As for the enamored peon, he and Doña Zeferina corresponded for a while after she escaped, but nothing ever came of the romance. According to Doña Zeferina, if the man had been worth the trouble, something she had doubted from the beginning, he would have pursued her all the way to Hueyapan.

In 1936 Doña Zeferina began living in free union with Don Rosalío Noceda, a Hueyapeño. They settled down in Doña Zeferina's home and had one child, a boy named Ernestino. A year later Don Rosalío died, leaving Doña Zeferina a widow for the second time.

Since her two surviving children by her first marriage were old enough by now to accompany her on long trips, the recently widowed Doña Zeferina began working as a merchant, the trade her grandmother had trained her for. She depended on her eldest son, Rafael, in particular to help her sell pulque, eggs, fruit, and meat. By the time Rafael was nine, Doña Zeferina was taking the boy out of school several times a week so that he could keep her company over the lonely, rugged terrain that separated one community from the next. When he was about fourteen, Rafael started carrying some of the merchandise as well.

On Sundays, in the very early hours, Doña Zeferina usually asked a neighbor to help them pack the burros with sixty to eighty liters of pulque that she would sell in Zaculapan, twenty kilometers away, for twenty centavos a cup. On Mondays she and her son went to Atlixco (a small city in Puebla) to sell eggs. Doña Zeferina carried three hundred eggs on her back, and Rafael carried two hundred. They left Hueyapan at 5:00 A.M. and arrived in Atlixco around 2:00 or 3:00 P.M. The eggs, purchased at five centavos each, Doña Zeferina sold for ten. Mother and son spent the night in Atlixco and returned home the following day. On Thursdays, Yecapistla had its market day. Doña Zeferina and Rafael sold pears, peaches, and avocados there, purchased at ten pesos for a lot of one hundred and sold for twenty. They left Hueyapan on Wednesdays at noon and arrived in Yecapistla by 6:00, then spent the night and were ready to sell in the market early the next day. On Saturdays, Doña Zeferina and Rafael, or sometimes just Rafael and his younger brother Raúl, went to Ocuituco, a four-hour walk each way, to buy meat which Doña Zeferina's mother sold in the five barrios of Hueyapan during the week.

Although Doña Zeferina frequently kept Rafael out of school, she always saw to it that he did his homework. When mother and son returned to Hueyapan after their long and exhausting trips, Rafael would sit down and study the lessons he had missed. Quick like his mother, he always did well on exams, despite his extremely poor attendance record.

Doña Zeferina continued to support herself and her family as a traveling merchant until a market opened in Hueyapan in the early 1960s. In her late fifties by then, she decided to treat herself to a more sedentary life and began selling plastic toys, kitchenware, dried chiles, and other condiments in the market on Tuesdays and from her house on other days of the week. Once every three months or so she and Rafael, who had become a school teacher in the intervening years and was active in village politics, would go to the big open markets of Mexico City and replenish her stock.

In addition to selling, Doña Zeferina continued to make money as one of the village's local healers. According to Hueyapan tradition, one acquires the gift of healing by dying and returning from the dead. Doña Zeferina has come back to life twice, she says. That is why she "knows how to heal."

The first time she returned from the dead Doña Zeferina was only a baby, too young to remember the incident, but her mother told her about it. Apparently, when she was about one year old Doña Zeferina caught a serious case of whooping cough. Accustomed to high rates of infant mortality, Doña Jacoba gave the infant up for dead and lit a candle for her daughter. As luck would have it, an aunt stopped by, picked up the baby, and began rubbing little Zeferina's body all over, "bringing her back to life."

The second time Doña Zeferina returned from the dead occurred soon after the birth of one of her children. At the appointed time, Doña Zeferina went to clean herself thoroughly in the *temascal,* the traditional adobe steam bath. But she was still too weak to take the intense heat, and she fainted dead away. Doña Zeferina thinks she was unconscious for about an hour, during which time she dreamed that she was entering a large church. The doors opened wide to receive her. Drawing on memories of her grandmother in the dream, all of a sudden she grew deeply embarrassed and wanted to turn back, for she had forgotten to put on her sandals. When she woke up, Doña Zeferina understood that she had reached the Gates of Heaven.

For years Doña Zeferina cured people with herbs and eggs, using what was known as the rustic technique. Then, when the government nurses came to Hueyapan in 1945 as part of the federal government's social welfare program, known as the Cultural Mission, Doña Zeferina went to classes to learn how to give injections. Since that time she has changed over almost entirely to "modern" methods of healing.

The government nurses were very impressed with Doña Zeferina because she was not afraid of blood or of other people's diseases. They invited their star student to go to Mexico City for training as a nurse, but she refused because she had to stay home with the children. By this time her mother was old and sick and could not care for her grandchildren alone. Thanks to the nurses of the Cultural Mission, Doña Zeferina did learn how to give intramuscular and intravenous injections as well as how to bandage wounds. She already knew how to deliver babies by the rustic technique.

In addition to the everyday difficulties of supporting a family without the help of a husband, Doña Zeferina had to defend herself against the soldiers who were still pillaging the countryside. Although the Mexican Revolution had officially ended in 1920, agrarian fighters were still organizing peasants in the area as late as the 1930s. One latter-day Zapatista still stirring up the highlands of Morelos was Enrique Rodriguez, nicknamed Tallarín (Noodle). During the years 1936–38, Tallarín and his followers descended on a number of small villages and killed local government officials, in particular, school teachers and tax collectors. Tallarín had many sympathizers in Hueyapan, and as a result, the pueblo became embroiled in a new wave of violence reminiscent of the days of the Mexican Revolution.[8]

In 1941 Doña Zeferina had a brief affair with a man from Hueyapan by the name of Pedro Hernandez. When she became pregnant, Don Pedro asked her to settle down with him in his home, but she refused. Her mother was not well, and Doña Zeferina did not want to leave the old woman alone. As she says herself, "I loved my mother more than this man." Don Pedro soon married another, but he and Doña Zeferina remained friends. Doña Zeferina gave birth to a girl, whom she named Angelina. This was her only surviving daughter, and Doña Zeferina adored the child.

Soon after Angelina was born, Doña Zeferina began working in the lowlands, accompanied by her two eldest sons, Rafael and Raúl. For five years they spent June, July, August, and December living as migrant laborers. Doña Zeferina worked as a corn grinder, and the boys were peons. At times she and her sons served different people and had to live apart in separate caves provided for peons by postrevolutionary landowners.

In 1952, when Angelina was ten years old, Doña Zeferina went to live with Don José Flores, a widower who had a house in one of the outlying barrios of Hueyapan. Angelina stayed behind in the care of Rafael and his first wife in the Calle Morelos home. By this time, Raúl had been shot and killed in a drunken brawl, and Ernestino was in a boarding school, on scholarship, in the state of Puebla. Every day, Doña Zeferina returned home to make sure everything was going well. The following year she and Don José had a church wedding and moved to Doña Zeferina's home. They changed residences, Doña Zeferina explains, because she could not stand living so far away from the plaza, way up in the hills. Her regular patients stopped coming to see her, and, more to the point, she felt out of things. Although he agreed to do it, and even sold land and livestock to have capital to invest in Doña Zeferina's home, Don José never felt entirely comfortable there. It still remained his woman's place, he complained, not his own.

In November 1970, Don José fell off the roof of a bus in the plaza as he was trying to lower a basket of fruit from the rack. The poor man was drunk at the time, and he hit his head on the ground. A few hours later, he died. Widowed again, Doña Zeferina has never remarried. She continues to live in the same house off the plaza that has been her family's home for generations. Living there with her is the recently widowed Juana, Rafael's common-law wife and the mother of eleven children, and a few grandchildren. Rafael died in the fall of 1991 at the age of sixty-three. He worked most of his adult life as a school teacher and played a major role in the political life of Hueyapan. As for Doña Zeferina's two surviving children, they and their families live in Cuernavaca. Ernestino continues to work as an unskilled laborer at the Burlington Textile Mills, a job he has held for more than thirty years, and Angelina is a school teacher.

NOTES

1. *Being Indian in Hueyapan: A Study of Forced Identity in Contemporary Mexico* (New York: St. Martin's Press, 1975).

2. In the mid-1980s a telephone was installed in a store in the main plaza of Hueyapan, about a two-minute walk from Doña Zeferina's house.

3. Ruth Behar, "Rage and Redemption: Reading the Life Story of a Mexican Marketing Woman," *Feminist Studies* 16.2 (1990):227–28.

4. See "Pacts with the Devil: Stories Told by an Indian Woman from Mexico," *New York Folklore* 16.1–2 (1990):25–42, for translations and analyses of some of Doña Zeferina's favorite fairy tales.

5. Doña Zeferina and almost everybody else in Hueyapan called me "Maestra." Although she came to consider me her American daughter, she would still, out of habit, address me as "Maestra," adding frequently, "*mi hija*" (my daughter).

6. *Xales* and *chicharrones* are fried pork skin.

7. *Pelón* (baldy) is one of the peasants' derogatory names for government soldiers.

8. In Morelos, a number of local rebels took the name Tallarín. Some have tried to attribute these rural rebels with a latter-day Cristero movement. See Jean Meyer, *The Cristero Rebellion: The Mexican People Between Church and State, 1926–1929*, trans. R. Southern (Cambridge: Cambridge University Press, 1976). For Doña Zeferina's dramatic encounter with soldiers hunting down Tallarín, see the longer version of this life history in *Being Indian in Hueyapan.*

8

Seasons, Seeds, and Souls: Mexican Women Gardening in the American Mesilla, 1900–1940

RAQUEL RUBIO GOLDSMITH

*W*e all know the world is one, that the past in all its complexity is one. As we learn to study the past, however, we learn to divide and analyze; and, of course, there are good scientific reasons to do so. But life is also art, imbued with the spirit. I learned this obvious fact several years ago when I was invited to participate in a series of talks sponsored by the Arid Lands Department at the University of Arizona. The series organizers sought funding from the Arizona Humanities Council, which at that time mandated the inclusion of ethnic minority scholars or topics. My research on the history of Mexicanas living in Arizona appealed to them, and I was asked to speak on Mexicanas' use of land.[1] My immediate response was to explain that the number of Mexicanas who owned any land was minuscule, and that Mexicanas worked lands belonging to others. One could scarcely describe that as land use. It was more like exploitation!

For several years I had conducted ten in-depth oral history interviews, but nothing close to land use had ever come up . . . or had it? I suddenly remembered one woman's remarks: "I don't know if I'll prune it or not. I've been thinking about it for two weeks now; it hurts me to do it, but it's too bushy now. I don't mind cutting off the dry leaves or branches . . . but when they are green, alive, well . . . poor plant. I'm sure it will hurt it. Plants are a marvel; if one part dies, then a new one comes forth. Not like me. I get older and I don't see any new life growing in me."[2] These words of an old Mexicana, inhabitant of La Mesilla[3] since 1918, were uttered as we walked amidst the organized chaos of dozens of plants, large and small, all potted in metal cans. The plants overran the boundaries of the small yard and spilled over into a vacant lot. In one corner, an enveloping profusion of roses emerged . . . red, white, yellow, pink, deep burgundy . . . every color except blue. Suddenly, a whiff of something unseen—the aroma of orange blossoms from around the corner. The birds were chattering. They all seemed to respond to Doña Maria, pushing her to prune the unsuspecting plant. Then she answered, "Tomorrow I'll prune it. It's the Day of Holy Cross and she will not feel it."

The "garden" where I sat for hours listening to Doña Maria over a period of four years took shape from my memory and my notes. And not only her garden, but also the outdoor spaces of seven of the ten Mexicanas I had interviewed during the same oral history project. Reexamination of the dozens of hours of tapes of all the interviews reaffirmed my memory. Listening with a new ear, checking my copious notes of the interviews with a new eye, I slowly began to understand the meaning of the words I had heard. References to planting, plants, gardening, uses of the garden, and visions of its place and beauty emerged. My search for the Mexicanas' experiences in southeastern Arizona, after they had taken refuge from the violence and chaos of the Mexican Revolution of 1910, had been so filled with my own visions that I had been blind to the actual lives of the interviewees. To most of these women, gardening became, if not a central activity, an important way to carve out a tiny piece of cultural space in an alien town.

Why was gardening so important to so many of the interviewees? Where did they learn to garden? Why those plants and not others? How were their gardens different from those of Anglo women? or Indian women? Were these Arizona gardens like their gardens back in Mexico? What could these gardens, created by refugees on foreign soil, tell me about the world of Mexicanas? Would it be possible to learn from these green, colorful patches snatched away from the dusty desert surroundings?

The search for answers to these questions carried me over ancient roads, from ranchos to pueblos, in deserts and sierras of Sonora and Chihuahua, as well as the routes over the Atlantic that tied Spain to the northern reaches of nineteenth-century Mexico. Since the sixteenth century women had parted from Spanish towns and cities, following husbands or fathers into the northern frontier of New Spain. The oral histories indicate that women coming from Spain and central Mexico included seeds and cuttings as well as other treasures of civilization in their trunks. Seeds from Mediterranean lands arrived to feed hunger, soothe the palate, cure the body, and nourish the imagination. Along with techniques for nursing seeds passed from mother to daughter from time immemorial came visions of paradise on earth with the plants given by the Christian God.

Historical studies of gardens usually focus on large public or private plots cared for by professional gardeners and sometimes designed by landscape architects. The small individual *jardincitos* planted by working-class women rarely command attention. In this essay I do not try to answer all questions I asked above; rather I concentrate on three themes: (1) the historical development of gardens from seeds and plants from Spanish arid lands that crossed the Atlantic to the high and low deserts of northern Mexico; (2) Norteña gardening as part of women's efforts to nourish and heal the bodies of their families; and (3) Norteña gardening as an expression of the aesthetic and spiritual relationships between these migrant gardeners and their earthly paradises.

Methodology

This essay is based on seven of the ten in-depth, open-ended oral histories that I conducted between 1978 and 1982 in southeastern Arizona and southeastern New Mexico.[4] The ten Mexicanas were all refugees of the Mexican Revolution of 1910. Three came from the sierra of Chihuahua, one was from the city of Chihuahua, and the other six came from various pueblos in northeastern Sonora. All but one were from what is classified as rural Mexico. As fate would have it, the one woman who was born and raised in the city of Chihuahua ended up living most of her life in rural New Mexico. The other nine, having escaped the violence in Mexico, spent the rest of their lives in mining communities in southeastern Arizona.

All the interviews were conducted in Spanish, the native tongue of the interviewees. Their words were taped, and I wrote extensive notes after each session to record dress, space, and ambience. Both tapes and notes were used to re-create the spaces and activities described in this essay.

In addition to the interviews I used archival documents, ethnobotanical studies, and private letters to reveal the long road that seeds and visions of the good and the beautiful had traveled to bring familiar sights and smells to new homes. The oral and written sources find validation in the material expression as seen in the *corrales* created by Mexicanas in Arizona.

DEFINITIONS

The terms *corral* ("yard" or "corral" in English use) and *patio* are used interchangeably in the oral histories to describe spaces covered with flowers, corn, trees, and vegetables. In central Mexico, a patio is an enclosed space surrounded by walls on at least three sides, usually four; a corral is a space enclosed by a fence, or sometimes the space behind a rural house. Why use the word *corral* in urban settings? The mining towns of southeastern Arizona follow Midwestern American urban plans, in which house lots are set back from the street, leaving a front yard between the house and the street and a backyard in back of the house. Calling the latter "corral" denotes an experience of space akin to the rural Mexican corral, not the patio. When the interviewees used the word *patio*, correction followed, as if a mistake had been made.

The interviewees did not use the word *jardín* (garden) to refer to their gardens. In Mexico, into the mid-twentieth century, the word *jardín* was reserved for formal, usually public gardens. Home gardens were grown in the patio or corral. Planting around the house tended to be in pots called *macetas*. The clay macetas used in central Mexico were not common in the ranchos and pueblos of northern Mexico, however, and when one was found, it was used for cooking beans rather than growing plants. More often than not, the macetas were tin cans. The Spanish word *huerta* was used for fruit tree groves, and a corral became a huerta even if it had only four or five trees.

Patio, *corral*, and *huerta* are words that describe the experience of gardening in central Mexico. Away from the benign climate and urban public services, however, on rural rancherías and pueblitos, words took on their own meanings, and *patio* and *corral* became somewhat interchangeable.[5]

Seeds Crossing the Ocean: Spanish Expansion in the Sixteenth, Seventeenth, and Eighteenth Centuries

The Spaniards found that the cultural and geographic area composed of Sonora, Chihuahua, southeastern Arizona, and southern New Mexico experienced similar life patterns. These faraway desert lands, inhabited by descendants of ancient cultural traditions long adapted to life in arid lands, were invaded by Spanish soldiers, missionaries, and settlers, who imposed Spanish and Mexican ways of life. The Spaniards' search for mineral wealth, souls, and, later, fertile lands established patterns of violence and hostility as the indigenous people defended their domains.

With the newcomers came seeds. Whether in official baggage or simply in the bowels of horses, cows, or sheep, European seeds had been falling upon the soil of the Western Hemisphere since Cortés and his army set foot there. In the lands named "of the Chichimecas" by the Aztecs, and Nuevo Mexico or Tejas by the conquistadors, European seeds made their appearance in a systematic fashion in the sixteenth century. Jesuit and Franciscan missions dotted the landscape of Sonora, Chihuahua, and Arizona (and Texas, California, New Mexico, Coahuila, and Nuevo León). Missionaries came not only to bring the Word of God but also to "civilize" the indigenous people. The first seeds and cuttings of European plants came in the supply bags of missionaries. Wheat, grapevines, olives, oranges, and lemon trees shared the sun with apricots, basil, mint, and rosemary. Mission fields, patios, and corrales shared their seeds with incoming settlers, who also brought along their "civilized" plants.

The migration routes from Spain to central Mexico to the north are amply documented. Families following *presidio* (fort) military personnel and people in search of gold or new ranching enterprises found their way to the north. Seeds and cuttings were often their most valuable belongings.[6] Along with material possessions came visions of beauty and nature. As we shall see, the women in these migrations—criollas, mestizas, and *mulatas*—held on to their views of the proper foods, flowers, and herbs necessary to have on hand. No matter where—presidio, rancho, or pueblo—Mexicanas carved out a corner, a plot, or even a field to plant their seeds. Food, fruit, flowers, and herbs burst forth.

In ancient Spain, part of the river of Mediterranean cultures, women were at the center of horticulture, the first providers of grains for the family. But the land tenure policies that emerged from the patriarchal Roman Empire, reaffirmed by the Visigoths and later by the Moors, deprived Spanish women of their ancient role as principal cultivators and producers of family food. This patriarchal system of land use and tenure was imposed by the Spanish in their American colonies.[7]

Inheritors of the Spanish colonial system, Norteñas at the end of the nineteenth century did not own land, as a rule, nor did they control food production, even on the hostile, isolated northern frontier. This does not mean that women were not active participants in the actual work, merely that their participation was seen as "helping" their men or families. Wives did not control production. In their corrales, however, Mexicanas decided what to plant, how to plant it, and what to do with the produce, although this was never considered a major element of the family's domestic economy. Such was the European tradition as it was brought to Mexico.

This was not the only way women in northern Mexico and, later, the U.S. Southwest gardened, however; indigenous women of these lands were legitimate participants in their communities' food production. In Arizona, for example, Hopi women planted the first corn of the year in small gardens by springs at the base of the mesa. These plots provided food during the lean months of early summer, before the corn planted in the fields by men was ready for harvest. Corn from these gardens also was important in religion. Some indigenous women remote from Spanish domination were able to maintain their roles as equal participants in the production of food and in the religious, social, and political lives of the villages. It was not until after the Second World War that Hopi women planted flowers on their lands.[8]

Mexicanas began trekking northward long before the northern lands hung out Anglo road signs, and they continued to settle in these areas, which were, geographically at least, a mere continuation of their own northern Mexican states. In the dry lands of Sonora and Chihuahua, mineros, rancheros, and pueblerinos learned survival techniques from Mayos, Yaquis, Papago, Pimas, Opatas, and others. They ate *bellotas* (acorns), *pinole* from mesquite bean pods, and *tunas* (prickly pears). But never were they allowed to forget the unrelenting dangers of the desert, and these were not just lack of water. Although the U.S. government had promised to protect the international borders designated by the Treaty of Guadalupe Hidalgo in 1848 and the Treaty of the Mesilla of 1853, settlers in Sonora, Chihuahua, Arizona, and New Mexico continued to be threatened by Comanche, Apache, and Yaqui raiders. This life of insecurity and isolation reinforced Spanish ways, including the corral.

The Corral as a Hymn to Work: Nineteenth-Century Mexico

The bond between the nineteenth-century Mexicana housewife and her corral has been amply documented. Whether it was the urban corral behind the living quarters, the patio of a doctor's, lawyer's, or merchant's home or the plot surrounding the one- or two-room dwelling of a common laborer, the woman of the house demonstrated her talents as housekeeper and mother by harvesting grains, fruits, and herbs, as well as eggs and meat from domestic animals. Writing in a magazine published by Mexicans in exile in Kansas in 1917, a Mexicano nostalgically recalls the corral of his home in Mexico.

> From the *zaguan* one can see the patio, broad and filled with light with a "bugambilia" covering a good part of the wall . . . the orange trees in bloom . . . the traditional well and . . . birds singing. Beyond the kitchen there was that something, that something that made one smile knowing of its comforting feeling . . . that something was the corral. . . . The corral has so much of that feeling of "home" . . . it is that maternal tenderness, instinctual in the woman that awakens in her love for the corral. Here she spends a good part of her time taking care of the animals . . . caring for the chickens, cleaning the dovecote, feeding the mule, rabbits . . . here in the corral one eats from one's work . . . surely the corral is a hymn to work. At that moment of great sadness, when one is so homesick, the memory of the birds, the flowers comes to mind.[9]

For the nineteenth-century Norteña, however, the challenge to reproduce a civilized way of life, including the corral, was often overwhelming. She may have succeeded in creating a green earthly paradise, but along the way she had to incorporate some "uncivilized" indigenous foods. For Norteñas, as for other Mexicanas, the types of plants grown and the techniques used to grow them were determined by the socioeconomic status of the gardener. Distance from the Mexican metropolis, harsh conditions, and hostile indigenous populations did not erase differences in social standing. For women married to *hacendados* (large landowners), it was possible to create the traditional Mexican setting: a home with a real patio, a space surrounded by walls and filled with potted plants and caged birds. The domestic labor was in the hands of servants and peons, and the lady of the house could spend as much time as she liked pampering her potted plants. For the wives of men who owned small ranchos or small houses, the patio was often a series of potted plants arranged against the wall, and the corral may have been crammed into a tiny corridor between dwellings or a back corner of the minuscule lot. Other Norteñas, those married to laborers with little or no property, had to make do with a few pots crowded around the front or back door of a one-room pueblo dwelling.

Frances Douglas de Kalb, the wife of an American mining engineer, described the household activities of a working-class housewife she met in a Sonoran mining camp.

> The housewife spent most of her day in the clearing in front of a tiny house. A fire for cooking and several rude stools under a huge oak tree provided kitchen and dining rooms. Dogs and chickens coexisted with several children. The children's mother made paper-thin wheat tortillas (cakes). A comal (grill) and an olla (clay pot) of simmering beans shared the small grilled fire. Sometimes, when there is time, she gathered some of the wild amaranth growing on the edges of the nearby spring.[10]

This Mexican housewife knew which desert plants could be added to the table. *Verdolagas, quelites* (wild greens), *pechitas* (mesquite pods), and bellotas were all edible. Not far away was a family with several cows, and cheese and milk were added to the diet on special occasions. Money to buy anything other than wheat flour for tortillas, beans, coffee, and sometimes sugar was scarce.[11] Centuries of hostility had made Norteñas—inhabitants of pueblos, mining camps, and ranchos as well as urban centers—uneasy with indigenous women, and exchanges were limited. Although Mexicanas did learn to use some of the foods indigenous women gathered from the desert, in their own corrales they planted seeds of foods and flowers known to their grandmothers and mothers from central Mexico or Spain. Indian women planted corn, beans, and squash, varieties known to them for generations, but until the middle of the twentieth century, no flowers. Norteña gardens have always had flowers.

Nourishing and Healing the Body: Corrales in Arizona, 1900–1940

In 1900 the economic policies of Mexican president Porfirio Díaz were affecting the lives of many Norteñas. The buying power of the peso had plummeted. Government attempts to remove Yaquis from their rich lands in Sonora and Sinaloa resulted in continued resistance and violence. The Díaz government's stringent control made political participation difficult, if not impossible. All these things acted together to push the Mexican population into armed revolt.

As the hardships imposed on the lower classes during the Porfiriato became more acute, Mexican families followed the lure of economic well-being into the U.S. Southwest. When the Revolution began in 1910, the constant trickle turned into a river.[12] Then it was not only families or single men migrating but also lone women, fleeing the violence and chaos of the Revolution. Some sought refuge with their husbands, but many came alone or with small children. The growing mining towns of southeastern Arizona welcomed women because there were many single men who needed domestic help. Relatives and friends from the *patria chica* helped the newly arrived refugees. Most came from Sonora or Chihuahua, but some were from as far away as Durango and Zacatecas.

The new homes were in arid lands where hardship and isolation were a way of life. The Mexican refugees were connoisseurs of desert living, accustomed to the physical struggle for survival in adverse conditions and well schooled in the practice of a domestic economy that utilized every possible resource for the family's survival. Livelihood meshed with desert, either on its flat expanses raising cattle or wheat, or in the mines of its rocky mountains. The separations between cattle ranches, farming, mining, and commercial enterprises were blurred in most peoples' lives. Whether Norteñas came from ranchos or pueblos, however, corrales were an important part of their lives.

The Arizona mining towns in which the refugees arrived were very different from the pueblos of Mexico. Some towns had emerged overnight with no planning. Often Mexicanos had to live in shanties or even tents. Other towns, such as Douglas, had better housing, but segregation existed everywhere. Mexicanos in Douglas lived in the southern and western parts of town, clearly outside the city limits. The buildings in Pueblo Nuevo came right up to the street and had corrales in back, not unlike Mexican pueblos. In some towns houses were built on lots in Midwestern urban–style tracts, with front and back yards. Mexicanos who could afford a house usually left the front yard plain, perhaps with a shade tree or two. The backyard was the corral.

Between 1900 and 1940 this use of front and back yards by Mexicanas changed very little. Whatever the size, whoever the landlord, Norteñas kept house and planted vegetables, fruit trees, and herbs to nourish and heal the body while creating a space of beauty to nourish the soul and spirit.

If the desert landscape presented endless horizons to Mexicanas in Arizona, the political, economic, and social realities of their lives drew rigid boundaries. The struggle for survival in patriarchal Anglo America was usually conducted in small barrios. Weekly excursions to the local church and rare visits to the Anglo bastions in the outside community were the only escape. While men left the barrios daily to work in the mines, on railroads, or in construction, women mostly tended to the household and its corral, re-creating tried-and-true forms to save money or to earn a bit extra for the household. Traditional foods unavailable in the company store could be grown at home. Norteñas confined to small urban lots tried to re-create their Mexican corrales by combining the subtle effects of birds singing, crackling fires, chickens scratching, and water running, all under the fragrance of blooming honeysuckle, wet desert earth, and overpowering whiffs from the patch of *yerba buena* (mint) growing under the outdoor faucet. In the early fall, bursting corn, ripe pomegranates, squash, and chiles shared the space with marigolds, late-blooming zinnias, and roses. All was ready for All Souls' Day (Dia de los Muertos). Even if the local priest warned against pagan practices (in Tucson, one bishop prohibited food and music at the cemetery), the flowers had to be ready.

Mexican Sonoran and Arizona households grew up with the seasonal rhythm of *tamales de elote* in late summer, *tamales de carne* at Christmas, *buñelos* for New Year's, and *capirotada* for Lent.[13] Most foods used at least some produce from the corral. Market fruits were usually beyond the Mexicana's budget, so the bounty of the *higuera* (fig tree), *albaricoque* (apricot), *parra* (grape vines), and *granada* (pomegranate) were all appreciated and used in a variety of ways. Those lucky enough to have an orange tree could brew *azar* (orange blossom tea) to calm the nerves and bring on sleep. The diversity of the foods grown in the corrales is astonishing: beans, squash, chiles, corn, cucumbers, melons, figs, oranges, lemons, pomegranates, grapes, *nopalitos* (tender new leaves of cactus), as well as *verdolagas* (purslane) and quelites.

To this was added a variety of herbs, most originally from Europe, such as yerba buena, *romero* (rosemary), *ruda* (rue), and *albaca* (basil). From indigenous people Mexicanas learned to use *toloache* (jimsonweed) and *canutillo* (Mormon tea). Yerba buena tea was good for stomach discomfort or simply to warm the body and soul. Mint does not grow well in dry climates, but spreading clumps hung on at the base of the *asequias* (watering ditches) or the outdoor faucet. Romero was good for *rheumas* (rheumatism), and, of course, for seasoning food. Ruda, albaca, and even toloache were all associated with specific and general curative powers.

Unable to follow the traditional Spanish custom of planting cypress trees, Norteñas planted *nopaleras* (cactus) to delineate the borders of the corral. Nopaleras were used for the favorite spring and early summer suppers of nopalitos. The epicenter of the corral was located under the deepest shade of the largest tree. *Moras* (mulberry) were often preferred because they grow fast, spread easily, and are deciduous, letting the warming winter sun shine through their bare branches. It was under the shady mora, or sometimes a ramada, that all the summer cooking was done over an open fire. Prized ollas held frijoles simmering over the constantly burning fire. To one side, on the comal, huge, paper-thin wheat tortillas cooked over aromatic charcoal. Even today, in some Mexican homes, ramada cooking is not confined to the weekend barbecue.

In those years, when hard domestic labor was the rule, a second fire burned beneath a large tin tub to boil the laundry. The tin washboard and tub had replaced the rock at the river, but it was not until the 1950s that washing machines with manual rollers became more or less standard. And even then, often these were outside under the mora on Mondays.

A number of unique uses were found for Arizona corrales in the first decades of the century. One Mexicana leased an empty lot, fenced it, and planted it with fast-growing trees, then built paths, had a cement slab poured for a dance floor, installed electricity for Chinese lanterns, built trellised booths, and rented the space for weddings and parties. It was a very successful enterprise for some twenty years and made her widowhood less lean. During Prohibition, at least two Mexicanas in Tucson made even more profitable use of their dense, overgrown garden. Their helter-skelter backyard growth camouflaged two homemade stills. A granddaughter remembers:

> Although my grandmother was Catholic, she was not very religious. She would not let her children go to church and as a result they never made their First Holy Communion until they made it on their own at an older age. The reason she never let them go to church was that she always had them working in her bootleg business. My mother and aunts had to wash and scrub the bottles for the beer. They would use long bottle brushes to scrub the insides . . . washing them in a large galvanized tub. My aunt said they had the best and cleanest beer in town. They would put them under the trap door to ferment . . . hidden from the law. Sometimes at night when they were asleep they would hear the corks pop off the bottle tops. When the beer was ready, they would fill large

tubs with ice, cool it, and sell it. At this time, they lived near the immigration station on Ninth Street. Immigrations officers were their best customers.[14]

Corrales as Social Spaces

Unless the space was painfully cramped, the corral provided the family with a hospitable and pleasant site for cooking, laundering, and visiting. At times the corral was opened to everyone—men, women, neighbors, and friends—for celebrations: feast days, name days, birthdays, and weddings. The hard-packed earth was watered and swept clean so that not a speck of dust would disturb the dancing. The guitar or accordion player, usually a friend or relative, would arrive and select the coolest spot under the mora or *nogal* (walnut). Dancing, conversation, jokes, gossip, and declamation accompanied *tesguin* (fermented drink), pollo, tortillas, chile, frijoles, and a *quequi* (cake). Anything that could be sat on—chair, bench, packing crate, or stool—was pressed into service for the comfort of the elderly and the pregnant. Younger unmarried women flew around serving, talking, flirting, and dancing. The young men hovered together in corners drinking tesguin or beer, and even mescal or tequila, while out of the corners of their eyes they scouted the scene for a dancing partner. Usually someone was invited to sing, and a good part of the evening passed listening to music.

Grief also came to the corral. During wakes, women stayed inside in candlelit rooms, lightheaded with grief and lack of oxygen, praying and lamenting over the deceased loved one. Outside, the men talked, drank, and often laughed loudly. Then, suddenly remembering the place and circumstances, they shifted into profound silence. Such were the uses Mexicanas found for their corrales while they cared for the bodies of their families.

Nurturing and Healing the Soul: The Corral as an Expression of Beauty and Spirituality

As Mexicanas remembered and described their corrales to me, a complex set of visions emerged. They spoke of comfort, solace, privacy, and even, in somewhat oblique terms, of spirituality. Born out of their words and silence, memories of visions, ideas, beliefs, and perceptions came forth. David Lowenthal says that "the geography of the world is unified only by human logic and optics, by the light and color of artifice, by decorative arrangement and by ideas of the good, the true, and the beautiful."[15] Mexicanas who came to or were born in the Arizona Mesilla at the turn of the century expressed a systematic view of the desert landscape they inhabited. Even in isolated frontier pueblos and ranchos, Norteñas—*ricas* and *pobres*—were born into the cradle of Spanish language and Christianity. Mexican girls grew up listening to Mexican echoes of Iberian and Moorish views of the land. Mediterranean visions of the landscape passed down by their mothers and grandmothers colored their eyes. Just as Christianity sought to impose itself on "savage" or "primitive" indigenous religions, the collective memory of the beautiful as that which is green and lush renewed the desire to re-create paradise on earth.

In the missions and churches on the northern frontier, on ranchos, and in well-to-do pueblo homes, Spanish patios with a central fountain or well, fruit trees, flowers, and herbs were re-created. For many Norteñas, these patios were echoes of landscapes they remembered in central Mexico. Others had encountered the image of green beauty in desert mountains during their travels from pueblos to mines to ranchos.

These women lived and died submerged in Iberian visions of the landscape defined many centuries earlier in terms of the division between *natura* and *cultura*. The ancient classical cultures, reinforced by Christianity, gave to Spain an image of human beings as the center of creation, above nature. Later came the Saracens, who viewed the desert as untamed wilderness, knowable but best left in the hands of Allah. It was only in the walled garden, the patio, that humans could re-create paradise.

Moorish gardens were walled squares or rectangles that closed out the untamed desert wilderness. This civilized space was divided into four equal areas by a cross pointing to each of the cardinal points and centered with the element that brings life to the desert: water. In the middle of the garden stood a round pool, often with a fountain adding the sound of trickling water. Each quarter boasted at least one tree—olive, apricot, orange, lemon, date, or fig; a proper garden held one of each.[16] In traditional Spanish gardens, lines of cypress pines hugged the high walls and provided the necessary green frame to shut out the blinding desert sun. Under the protecting branches, in half shade, arose a profusion of flowers and herbs filling the air with perfume. Truly it was a space to reach all the senses. And a place where tranquility, silence, and beauty reigned.

Mexicanas, heirs to these cultural scripts, also knew that the "good" is that which is civilized, European, Christian. "Bad" is wilderness, indigenous, pagan. Beauty emerges from carefully cultivated growth, from trimmed and tamed greenery. Ugly is the extension of infinite wilderness, plants with thorns and without leaves, that which is barren, dry, and colorless.[17] Despite the need to adopt new foods and new farming techniques, and in direct contradiction to views of the world and landscape held by indigenous peoples, the Mexicans maintained their European cultural visions. They sought to reproduce a tiny piece of civilized paradise in the immense desert. They wanted color, a landscape of green with roses, sweet peas, daisies, carnations, geraniums, poppies, lilies, honeysuckle, and irises—plants new to the desert, plants that required water and more water. Desert plants, they thought, were no more than weeds that produced tiny flowers—sometimes only once every five or six years, when the rains became deluges on the command of pagan gods.

All the while, the Mexicanas knew the desert as it existed in the Christian conviction. They learned that this life is not for happiness. Life here is but preparation for the next one. And it is in the desert that Christianity puts penitence, fasts, and prayer. When the soul enters the desert, it leaves only with the waters of grace from God. Geographer Yi-Fu Tuan explains that premodern visions of the landscape are vertical.[18] Such were the Mexicanas' visions of the landscape—the heavens, the earth, and, below, hell.[19] The premodern vision of the world as a vertical universe with a hierarchy of good and evil begins with gods in the heavens, traverses through earth, and ends with demons in the darkness below.[20] Norteñas in Arizona expressed this view.

Those born to landowning families may not have experienced the hardships known by Norteñas born into landless poverty. To plant what is one's own can never be the same as harvesting for another. But the spiritual beliefs that put God and the Virgin in all lands brought joy and solace to all, rich and poor, the horizon, skies, land, and the worlds below.

Patricia Martin Preciado has written of the visions seen by Maria Carrillo de Soto. Maria, who was born in Tucson in 1868, saw the Virgin descend onto the Soto lands and appear on a rocky hillside. Her daughter describes what Maria saw.

My mother claimed that the Blessed Virgin appeared to her at the ranch many years ago. It was in the summertime. She was young and newly married and somewhat lonesome. She had just given lunch to the cowboys and she was resting—reading a novela, a love story. Then, all of a sudden, she turned to one side and she saw the Virgin appear at the window. My father was in another room reading the newspapers. "Ramon, Ramon!" she called. "Come here! I have just seen the Virgin. Her mantle moved!" My father tried to calm my mother. He tried to comfort her. But my mother believed the Virgin was trying to tell her something—that she was about to die. She used to go out to the arroyo and pray to the Virgin and ask the Virgin if she had a message. So she came to town and confessed and the priest told her that even if it was a dream, nevertheless, it was a beautiful one.

We always knew the story of my mother and the Virgin, and so, after many, many years had passed, we bought her a statue of La Virgen Milagrosa and built the grotto. And the grotto is still there, and the statue of the Virgin is still there. Many people have come and gone, but the Virgin remains. She is looking after the ranch; she is protecting it. It is as if the Virgin were saying, "I belong here. And you must let me stay."[21]

God, the Virgin, and the saints from heaven are in all places—even the desert—and they can be counted on for protection. Mexicanas living on the land sensed God's hand in terrestrial fruits and bounty. Submerged under God's endless sky, the Norteña planted. She planted flowers for God and she planted flowers for civilization. Every time a rosebush blossomed, it spoke to a woman's care and "good hand." Gardens vibrant with petunias, azaleas, daisies, sweet peas, *espuelitas,* and laurel testified to all that the woman of the house was surely a good woman. She made sure that desert plants were never admitted, except for those one could eat.

As in all material cultural manifestations, the ideal vision is one thing and the actual possibility is another. Classic Spanish gardens with spacious plots, fountains, and paths dividing the quadrants were mostly in churches or public parks. Only a few rich families continued the practice for themselves. In southeastern Arizona, however, between 1900 and 1940, Norteñas used the spaces surrounding their rented urban dwellings to re-create whatever it was possible to grow of an earthly paradise.

Civilized and domesticated beauty, embroidered desert patches filled the eyes with wonder before the advent of Technicolor films and color television. The eye feasted on the landscape, far away or at one's fingertips. But beauty must be returned to God, whence it came. Flowers followed the religious calendar as well as the seasons. Early spring blooms were for the Virgin Mary in her month of May. Every evening for a month, the rosary was offered, accompanied by music and with processions of young Mexicanas carrying bouquets of freshly cut flowers. Girls wearing white dresses and garlands of daisies in their dark hair followed angels, messengers of the Virgin, and gave up all the barrio's flowers. Then came the Feast of Corpus Christi—another long procession and more flowers. In November, marigolds and autumn zinnias were ready to go to the cemetery for All Souls' Day. The best gardeners tried to keep something available at all times for funerals. Florists and nursery keepers were rare in mining communities, but Mexicanas could always be counted on for a flower arrangement for the dead.

Because plants were difficult to come by, corrales were living quilts of social relations. Practically every plant had a social history. "The rosebush is from my sister. She brought it from California." "This one, the hibiscus, is not from her. Doña Maria gave me a cutting from hers. She got her hibiscus from a friend in Albuquerque." And so on, and so on. Then, of course, there was always that favorite plant that had been "stolen"; the temptation had been too great.

Flowers for beauty and for ritual connote public uses. To these we can add private uses of gardens. After all, big families in little houses meant that mothers could not easily justify (or meet) their need for privacy. Amazingly, children did not often offer to help dig, water, weed, or prune. In their gardens, Mexicanas could close their hearts and minds to the outside and look into themselves. From chore to routine, gardening for many became a necessity. Call it meditation, prayer, or simply moments to think and plan. Whatever it may have been—the joy of solitude or "talking to God," as one said—the gardens afforded privacy. One Mexicana's garden started as a burial ground. Her first child, stillborn, was buried there. She never moved from that house. Another's garden was a monument. In it was a huge pine tree her eldest son had planted as a young boy. He was shot down over the Mediterranean during the Second World War. For another, her garden was the joyous wedding party for her daughter, when everyone danced under the mora. She left as a bride and died before she could return. Every year, the mother planted her daughter's favorite poppies.

For some Mexicanas, private expressions of devotion to a particular saint materialized in garden shrines. Often, a man in the family would build the shrine and the woman would care for it: shrines to Saint Joseph, patron of families and workers; Saint Rita, patron of impossible causes; the Virgin of Guadalupe, mother and protector of all. When news of miraculous devotions spread, the shrine became public, and on the saint's feast day the Mexicana celebrated by sponsoring a Mass at the shrine and serving *menudo* (tripe stew) or some other Mexican dish. The garden celebrates, and flowers and food abound.[22]

Conclusions

Mexicanas brought seeds and visions of beauty with them when they entered North American lands. Their homes in the pueblos, ranchos, and mining camps of northern Sonora and Chihuahua provided a rich cultural life centered in Spanish beliefs and ways. Denying the arid reality of the desert environment, their corrales reflected their unwillingness to incorporate indigenous cultures, and the gardens planted by Norteñas who immigrated to Arizona and New Mexico in the wake of the Mexican Revolution of 1910 followed these Spanish traditions until the 1940s. The Norteña showed her domestic prowess by creating a bountiful corral, which supplied fruits, herbs, and flowers to meet the family's physical and spiritual needs.

1. A Mexicana is a Mexican woman. The women I interviewed were all Mexican women who left Mexico as a result of the Mexican Revolution of 1910 and remained in the United States. A Norteña is a Mexicana from northern Mexico (Sonora, Chihuahua, etc.).

2. Interview with Maria Concepción Montaño in La Mesilla, New Mexico, 1980.

3. La Mesilla is a strip of land on the international border dividing Mexico and the United States in southern Arizona and New Mexico. The treaty defining the Mexico–United States border in 1853, called the Gadsden Purchase in the United States, is El Tratado de la Mesilla in Mexico.

4. From interviews with Rebeca Gaitan, Refugio Vasquez, Maria Concepción Montaño, Maria Luisa Elizondo, Reyes Bustamante, Mariana Camacho, and Lavinia Quijada, 1980–82.

5. Joan Corominas, *Diccionario Crítico Etimológico Castellano e Hispanico,* vol. 1 (Madrid: Editorial Gredos, 1980), 202–6; vol. 4 (1981), 432–34.

6. Interviews with Rebeca Gaitan and Refugio Vasquez, Douglas, Arizona, 1980–82; C. Radding, "Ciclos demográficos, trabajo y comunidad en los pueblos serranos de la provincia de Sonora: Siglo XVIII," in *Historia e População: Estudos sobre a América Latina,* ed. S. O. Nadalin, M. L. Marcilio, and P. P. Balhana (São Paulo, 1990), 265–75; Cynthia Radding "Pueblos errantes: Formación y reproducción de la familia en la sierra de Sonora durante el siglo XVIII," in *Familias novohispanas; Siglos XVI al XIX,* comp. Pilar Gonzalbo Airpuru (Mexico City: El Colegio de México, 1991).

7. J. Vicens Vives, *Aproximación de la Historia de España,* 2d ed. (Barcelona: Editorial Teide, 1960), 115–27; Ann M. Pescatello, *Power and Pawn: The Female in Iberian Families, Societies, and Cultures* (Westport, Conn., Greenwood Press, 1976), 15–30, 132–45.

8. Interview with Emory Sekaqaptewa, professor of Hopi language and culture, Department of Anthropology, University of Arizona, 1986; see Ramon A. Gutierrez, *When Jesus Came, the Corn Mothers Went Away: Marriage, Sexuality and Power in New Mexico, 1500–1846* (Stanford: Stanford University Press, 1991).

9. Cited in Fernando Tapia Grijalva, "Ideología y Poesía en el Exili: Cuatro Poetas Mexicanos en el Suroeste Norteamericano (1900–1920)" (Ph.D. diss., University of Arizona, 1991), 178–80. The author of the quotation, a Mexican exile from Oaxaca, supported Venustiano Carranza with his newspaper work.

10. Frances Douglas De Kalb, Diary of a Trip to Nacozari. Unpaginated manuscript in the Special Collections, University of Arizona Library.

11. Ibid.

12. Lawrence A. Cardoso, *Mexican Emigration to the United States, 1897–1931* (Tucson: University of Arizona Press, 1980), 35, 53.

13. Tamales are a steamed cake made from either green corn (*elote*) or cornmeal with meat. Buñelos are fried cakes. Capirotada is a catchall casserole with varying ingredients. Staples tend to be dried fruits and cheese and other meatless goodies.

14. Isabel Doe, pers. comm., Tucson, Arizona, 1986.

15. Cited in Tuan Yi-Fu, *Topophilia: A Study of Environmental Perception, Attitudes and Values* (Englewood Cliffs, N.J.: Prentice-Hall, 1974).

16. Christopher Thacker, *The History of Gardens* (Berkeley: University of California Press, 1979), 36–41.

17. Ibid. See Paul Shepard's discussion in *Man in the Landscape: A Historic Review of the Aesthetics of Nature* (New York: Knopf, 1967); also Ronald King, *The Quest for Paradise: A History of the World's Gardens* (New York: Mayflower Books, 1979); Clarance Glacken, *Traces on the Rhodian Shore: Nature and Culture in Western Thought from Ancient Times to the End of the 18th Century* (Berkeley: University of California Press, 1967).

18. Tuan Yi-Fu, *Topophilia,* 129.

19. Interviews with Rebeca Gaitan, Maria Luisa Elizondo, and Refugio Vasquez, in Douglas, Arizona, 1978–80.

20. Ibid. Tuan's excellent study of the relationships between people and their physical surroundings, placing culture at the center, is the basis for the theoretical concepts presented in this section.

21. Patricia Preciado Martin, *Images and Conversations: Mexicans Recall a Southwestern Past* (Tucson: University of Arizona Press, 1982), 41–42.

22. See James S. Griffiths, *Beliefs and Holy Places: A Spiritual Geography of the Pimería Alta* (Tucson: University of Arizona Press, 1992), for an extensive discussion of shrines and Mexicans.

PART THREE

Rural Women, Urbanization, and Gender Relations

9

Three Microhistories of Women's Work in Rural Mexico

Patricia Arias

*T*he always fascinating encounter with the color, harmony, and abundance of native markets dotting the roads from Mexico City to Chiapas and Yucatán ends abruptly in the western part of the country, where open-air markets are scarce, especially in places where rancheros farm meager lands. There are few market stands with fewer products. The day goes by monotonously and ends early. Unlike the indigenous world, where the presence of women in the markets is overwhelming, in western ranchero societies marketing is the job of men. The difference suggests the predominance of different commercial institutions. It also suggests a deeper and more persistent diversity in the rural world—a heterogeneous Mexican countryside where it is possible to trace the different ways people relate to their environment, establish relationships, and construct institutions that limit the spatial, social, and gender spheres of their public and private behavior.

The notion of diversity helps to clarify a concern and provides a context for rethinking an image dominant in studies of rural women. In the early 1980s, Fiona Wilson pointed out a persistent tension in research: on the one hand, a conceptualization that emphasized the "impact" of capitalist development in agriculture on women's condition; and, on the other, a desire, certainly political, to uncover women's active role.[1] The prevailing hypothesis in the past was that women's daily lives and destinies were controlled from outside, by powers operating at a great distance from the rural world. Although the notion of gender has permitted a more subtle, complex approximation of the relation between capitalism and attitudes about women, the tension persists. The ghost of "impact" still haunts research. Still dominant is the idea that life and work in the countryside have been and are defined by macroeconomic factors and extraregional instances that bring homogeneity to the past, present, and future of the countryside.

The notion of impact is linked to an image of the rural world almost exclusively identified with agriculture. Rural ethnography is defined by the rhythms of agriculture, and peasants leave, stay, fight, and win or lose as dictated by agricultural work and agrarian destiny. This view, common in studies of peasant economy and society, adversely influenced past investigations of rural women and their roles. Although research uncovered the incidence of women in rural history and looked at women within the dynamics of peasant economy and the organization and gender division of labor markets, it could not free itself from the position that agricultural work defined rural society. A whole universe of other tasks carried out by women in the diverse societies of the Mexican countryside was cast into a vast gray area known as "complementarity" and "assistance." And yet, deciphering this gray area is necessary to understanding rural traditions and transitions in their greatest diversity.

The notion of female work as "assistance" has tended to hide two irreversible and conflictive processes: in peasant society, the loss of agriculture as the organizing axis of economy and family life and the subsequent monetization of both; and, in peasant and ranchero societies, the tendency toward feminization of labor markets. The notion of assistance as a marital obligation and a feminine attribute is a fiction—although, in authoritarian societies undergoing an intense process of economic change, the concept seems to have eased women's entry into new areas of work by reducing social and marital costs.

The notion of complementarity has obscured an older, more general phenomenon: the heterogeneity of economic processes and dynamics in rural societies; that is, the diversity of rural trajectories and destinies. Within the great, hazy area of complementarity one can discover and reconstruct a richer and more complex history of rural activities in Mexico. In the area of complementarity, more than in agriculture, one encounters the multiple microhistories of women's work. One could even hypothesize that rural women's history and culture can be understood only by poking around in the big closet where the many examples of rural complementarity have been stored. Not only is the notion of a microhistory of women's work a way to approach and capture rural diversity, it can shed light on local social mechanisms and the ever-changing demands imposed by extralocal economic and political contexts.[2]

The notion of microhistory in Mexico owes much to the historian Luis González, the author of *Pueblo en vilo,* who also suggested a novel way of examining rural diversity. He detected the imprint of at least three rural societies and cultures: the peasant, the indigenous, and the ranchero, each representing distinct ways of working and producing, appropriating space, organizing family and social life, and transmitting and modifying customs and values.[3] In using his typology in my three microhistories, I am not suggesting absolute differences or immutable borders between these three cultures, but rather nuances that punctuate diversity and suggest differences visible in rural women's work today.

Rural Space During the Porfiriato (1880–1910)

The building of railroads during the regime of Porfirio Díaz initiated a profound restructuring of rural space and its internal and external articulations. This new means of communication and the ensuing economic boom broke down the barriers of rural isolation.[4]

It could be argued that the railroads and the government's export-promoting policies favored the lowlands in almost all regions of the country. Here, plantation crops such as coffee in Chiapas, sugarcane in Morelos, and henequen in Yucatán were grown and easily transported to new markets.[5] This reorganization of productive space affected interregional relations by emphasizing labor recruitment as never before. By legal and illegal means, coercion or choice, increasing numbers of indigenous people and peasants left the highlands year after year for lowland plantations and haciendas to compensate for losses in their own agricultural production, which was carried out under increasingly unfavorable conditions.

In the case of indigenous societies, migration to the lowlands may have acted as well to stimulate artisan production among women. Alice Littlefield notes that the greater poverty and dependency of workers on the sisal haciendas in Yucatán dynamized artisan production and specialization, an area in which women participated actively.[6] From the mid-nineteenth century through the end of the Porfiriato, household production and artisan communities prospered in the Purépecha region of Michoacán.[7] Porfirian industrialization may have contributed to dynamizing the production of traditional handicrafts, if not to improving the living standards of craftspersons. Such was the case with palm weaving among the Mixtecs, when, at the turn of the century, the hat factories of Tehuacán, Puebla, contracted out palm weaving to Oaxacan Mixtec households in order to meet export demands.[8]

Until now, the presence of indigenous women in marketing has been better documented in pictorial testimony than in written ethnohistory. Beautiful antique photographs show the overwhelming presence of women in the marketplace, in contrast with written descriptions, which insist that men handle indigenous production. There are exceptions. Judith Friedlander has shown that marketing can give rise to specialized commercial careers for women, as in the case of Doña Zeferina's grandmother in Hueyapan, Morelos.[9] Beverly Newbold de Chiñas documents successful commercial histories among the Zapotec women of the Tehuantepec Isthmus.[10] John Durston has noted the more modest treks of the Purépechas and the colorful stalls they set up all over the state of Michoacán, especially at the great Friday market at Pátzcuaro.[11] Soledad González's studies in the district of Tenango, México, show that women (mostly indigenous women) prefer ambulatory trade to any other economic activity after agricultural wage labor.[12]

The available ethnohistory does not provide a specific definition of women's "complementary" work; nor does it document women's contribution to the indigenous family economy. However, examples like that of Heliodora, the woman from Tlayacapan, Morelos, who through petty trade in coffee managed to buy a parcel of land in her pueblo, lead to speculation about the important role female income may have played in improving the rural family's condition, even in the difficult final years of the Díaz regime.[13]

Indigenous women's commercial activities appear to have been recognized and supported by their spouses and families. In Hueyapan and the Isthmus, for example, men facilitated women's marketing activities, and family collaboration permitted them to leave and stay away even for extended periods.[14] Increased female participation in regional markets of production and labor does not appear to have caused great ruptures in social and cultural frameworks. On the contrary, this participation fit within socially accepted norms: an acknowledged economic role and accepted geographical mobility expressed in household production of goods, field labor on small plots, and the possibility of marketing this production.

The wide repertoire of possibilities open to indigenous women in the face of change appears to contrast with the situation of their peasant counterparts, women from primarily agricultural communities that had begun to shed their ethnic identity at the end of the nineteenth century. Our lack of knowledge about this period permits no more than conjecture.

In the Morelos lowlands, the loss of land intensified the need for men to perform wage work on haciendas.[15] In this context of precariousness and dispossession, women seem to have increased their collaboration, mostly by helping their husbands with the farm work on their own land, but also by helping their men meet work obligations as peons and tenant farmers on larger estates. Only one record exists of direct female wage work in agriculture: on the hacienda of Tepextenango, near Tepalcingo, women were *gaña-nas* (field hands) and even *capitanas* (overseers) in charge of corn planting. They received less pay than the men but a little more than the children.[16]

Something similar happened in the other lowland areas favored by the railroads. The expanding cereal haciendas of Irapuato, Guanajuato, operated on the basis of tenancy and sharecropping, precarious occupations for peasants. During the Porfiriato, wives and daughters participated more often and more regularly in family agricultural labor. Women's participation became indispensable when the men began working as migrant laborers in the United States. Intense population growth, agricultural insecurity, and the direct availability of transport lines to the northern border led boys barely sixteen years old to take the trains north from the enormous Irapuato rail station. But in contrast to what happened in indigenous societies, the men's absence did not stimulate women's commercial activities, even though Irapuato became the major trade depot of the Bajío. Only 12 percent of the registered *comerciantes* in 1900 were women. Ethnographic information suggests that the presence of women in commerce was a factor of chance and need (i.e., they were widows or spinsters). Women of that time and place preferred domestic service: in 1900, there were 1,486 domestics and 83 laundresses in Irapuato, versus 177 women in commerce.[17]

In certain regions of Morelos and Guanajuato, precarious conditions brought on by articulations with the larger society and economy were met with intensified agricultural labor within the domestic unit—above all, an increase in female field labor. Thus, women's work in peasant societies may be the clearest example of "assistance"—contributions made through agricultural work that are incorporated into and reflected in the family's income and production.

Recalling his fieldwork in Morelos, Jorge Alonso touches on a sensitive point germane to this distinction between peasant and indigenous women's work. The peasant women he met in Tenango insisted that what made them different from the next town's indigenous women was their absence from the market.[18] This insistence on a difference suggests a necessity to establish distinguishing criteria as part of the process of ethnic differentiation. The market as an attribute of indigenous women could have been one of those criteria. For peasant women, it was a Pyrrhic victory. By shunning the market and restricting their labor to agriculture, women lost the right to carry out a number of tasks that might have resulted in independent production and geographic mobility.

In the ranchero regions, where livestock defined the pace of rural work, the situation differed. In highland Guanajuato, Jalisco, and Michoacán, the hacendados' tendency to sell off less productive land stimulated greater male participation in the market and male migration to the United States. These became useful mechanisms for purchasing poor, highland properties, or, with luck, becoming a tenant farmer in the enclosures since the haciendas concentrated in the fertile lowlands continued contracting tenant farmers.[19]

Here too, however, even in the face of economic duress and male emigration, the patriarchal authoritarian society permitted few openings for women, who helped very little in agricultural work and much less in trade. While their men were working across the border, women remained in the homes of their in-laws, where conflict was unavoidable. Their spaces were confined to home and church. The women's expert skills at embroidering cut down on expenditures and contributed to meeting social commitments, but their sewing resulted more in savings than in income.[20]

Despite their restrictions, women found a way to obtain monetary resources. The railroad made it possible to transport food from the highlands of Jalisco and Michoacán to Mexico City and generalized and feminized the old traditions of raising and fattening pigs and chickens and selling eggs. After 1890, a network of intermediaries went daily to every highland house, purchasing animals or eggs to be shipped through Ocotlán, in the case of towns in western Michoacán, or through the lowland stations of Pénjamo and San Francisco del Rincón, in highland Michoacán and Jalisco. Behind this network were a multitude of women at home tending their animals. The money they earned was used to cover the endless round of daily expenses, but it also allowed the purchase of novelties, which reached even the smallest and most distant places during the Porfiriato. The most coveted novelty of all was the Singer sewing machine.[21]

In these proud and segmented societies, women's money was not transferred openly to male activities and investments; instead it was used to help meet the needs of the next generation. Many children left for the United States thanks to women's industry in raising and selling animals. Thus, without leaving their restricted space or altering their domestic condition or marital obligations, western rancheras observed the opportunities in their environment and constructed ways to turn them to profit.

From Agrarian Revolution to Green Revolution (1920–1960)

During the Porfiriato, the restructuring of rural space was economically determined and carried out in a relatively short time. The Revolution years (1910–17) interrupted this process and eventually transformed the arenas in which country women lived and worked. The period afterward, from 1920 to 1960, was a time of confusion and drawn-out change. More often than not, land reform had more to do with politics than with economics.

Land distribution started earlier and ended sooner in regions like Morelos where inhabitants had participated decisively in the Revolution. And land reform was relatively simple in the north, where a sparse population inhabited extensive lands. Owing to the power of northern politicians within the emerging state, portions of the north were earmarked for government investment to lead in the Green Revolution and the national agricultural modernization.[22] The situation was different in western, southern, and central Mexico. In these areas of dense population and age-old conflicts, the land distribution satisfied few people.

The emphasis on land and agriculture ignored other problems that had deepened during the Porfiriato. Communities had lost water, woodlands, and farmlands to greedy hacienda owners. At the same time, the rural economy had begun its inevitable march toward monetarization in relation to wage labor and the exchange of goods. The limitations of agrarian reform between 1940 and 1960, combined with industrial urban growth, unleashed rural-to-urban migration on an unprecedented scale.

In indigenous areas of Hidalgo, Michoacán, Puebla, and Tlaxcala, the departure of men and even women became frequent, although their destinations and goals differed. Male migration tended to be seasonal, and men returned to the community weekly. When possible, as it was in Puebla and Tlaxcala, men preferred a daily commute.[23] This mode of migration allowed men to continue their relations to agriculture, a crucial factor because the right to land was the basis of the access to other rights within the community. By working outside the community men also obtained resources that could be used to improve their farms. The situation was different for women. Indigenous women seem to have been the great losers in this stage of rural history. Industrial products and new distribution networks undermined the market for crafts and the interregional systems of exchange in which these women had honed their skills.

Worse still, almost any urban improvement resulted in deterioration for some small-scale producer. Every river diverted to a city and every conversion of rural land to urban destroyed raw materials. In San Pedro Tlaltizapán, México, for example, a pond originating in the Río Lerma supported a wide variety of aquatic flora and fauna. Fishing and the manufacture and sale of products from the pond's reeds (mats, hats, winnowers) brought income to the local inhabitants, who took their products to the market at Santiago Tianguistenco every Tuesday. When the pond was drained to distribute ejido lands and to facilitate the distribution of water to Mexico City, a habitat that had allowed peasants to survive through a mixture of farming, gathering, fishing, crafts, and trading activities was destroyed forever.[24]

The protection of natural resources, so much a part of consciousness and politics today, would have saved many microregional cultures of labor from extinction. But at that time conservation was not fashionable, and the indigenous people had no political strength to defend their right to carry on rural work other than farming.

Stripped of production and trading possibilities, indigenous women drew on the last option permitted by their society: geographical mobility. They became migrants, a part of the domestic landscape of practically every urban middle-class household. Their migration and wages, unlike those of men, did not help to improve their conditions in their home villages. Rather, their income helped to alleviate the growing insecurity of family farming: it went to educate a younger brother or to solve a pressing problem.[25] I know of no example of female migration that resulted in the purchase of lands or resources assuring a more favorable return for the women themselves. Instead, just the opposite is true: there were many cases of permanent migration and returns without improvement.[26]

Women were incorporated into wage labor in many rural regions. Lack of alternatives pushed peasant women more rapidly than others into the agricultural wage work they knew best. In depressed regions, the need for income meant geographical dislocation. Whole families moved, temporarily at first and permanently later, to regions of agricultural prosperity such as the lowlands of Zamora and the modernized agricultural and horticultural areas of the north.[27] In the crowded municipality of Irapuato, an abundant female labor force in the surrounding microregion of Guanajuato resulted in a steady expansion of work alternatives in agriculture and agroindustry.

Peasant society faced two processes simultaneously: women's incorporation into wage labor outside the home and the acceptance of women's money income. For the first time, female work and wages were disconnected from *family* work and income, traditionally managed by male members of the household. Fathers and husbands had difficulty adjusting. With women working outside the home, notions of assistance and corresponding authoritarianism began to lose their grip. Negotiations and adjustments were necessary to reduce the unpleasant implications for cultural, social, and family life.[28]

The situation in Irapuato was particularly severe. Women who went to work outside the home were called nasty nicknames by threatened males, who alluded to the proliferation of single mothers and abortions and accused women of infidelity, promiscuity, and bigamy. As far as men were concerned, something very serious was at stake: the need to keep women from transforming their now independent economic status into demands at other levels of social, family, and marital life.

At this stage of economic development, rancheras caused the least worry to families and neighbors. Their access to cash income continued, although it became more restricted and erratic. Technological improvements in aviculture made chicken farming big business and reduced women's domain to raising and fattening pigs. These women lacked the social alternative of working outside their households or communities. If a woman got along with her husband, who went annually to the United States to work, she could dream that he would stay there and take her with him. There, she knew, husbands "allowed" their women to work.

Despite all obstacles, women sometimes discovered that their skills at embroidering, weaving, and sewing could be turned to profit. Women in Capilla de Guadalupe in the Jalisco highlands began to send their work out by the same exit route used by the livestock. Once again, from their homes, women honed their managerial skills; the majority found a new way to obtain resources badly needed by their families.

Between 1920 and 1960, despite the government's emphasis on land reform and farming, rural families experienced a constantly increasing need for cash income. Frequently the need was met through women's incorporation into regular wage labor inside their home regions, as in the case of peasant women from prosperous areas, or outside them, as in the case of indigenous and peasant women forced to leave depressed areas. Although they were not incorporated into the regular wage-earning world, rancheras intensified the household activities that provided regular cash income.

Although precarious economic conditions were something two generations of rural Mexican women faced in common, their responses were different, and they reflect not only changing economic opportunities but the imprint and strength of local societies and microregional cultures of work.

Three Microhistories (1970–1990)

The decade of the 1970s was the period when rural society was most studied and, ironically, the time when it stopped being understood. Social scientists know little about what happened after we internalized the image of a deteriorated and destroyed rural world. Perhaps for the first time in many years, country people did not want to leave their land. But they knew that if they were to stay, they would have to find a means of support other than agriculture. Land concentration and the centralization of infrastructural services had led to a situation in which agriculture was the business of a few, who monopolized resources.

After 1970, a process of diversification and specialization in rural economies began. Without agriculture disappearing, and in some cases with it actually prospering, medium-sized and small cities and rural towns began to organize themselves around specialized activities related to manufacturing, livestock raising, or commerce.[29] The process was vigorous in western Mexico, but it also occurred in the central region (Puebla, México, and Tlaxcala) and in the indigenous south.

The search for alternatives that would allow people to remain in their communities coincided with a transformation in development policies, which in turn led to a profound redefinition of regional space and the relation between city and countryside. During the late 1970s and the 1980s, industrial dynamics came to be based on spatial dispersion and fragmentation in the production process. Multiple microregions have been appropriated as spaces for new industrial, livestock, and agricultural models. The old functional dichotomy between agricultural countryside and industrial city has broken down. The image of industry associated with large concentrations of people and technology has disappeared. In contrast with the situation thirty years ago, the clothing and shoemaking industries in Mexico are dispersed over several rural areas rather than being concentrated in big cities. At the same time, changes in the production of animal and vegetable foodstuffs have stimulated the appearance and proliferation of new work systems in rural areas.

Although linked to extraregional phenomena, this new production process responds to local dynamics. The way each local society orients its diversification and specialization relates to a combination of three factors: a generalized improvement of service and communication infrastructure, the ever-changing demands of the extralocal economy, and the possibilities defined by often deeply embedded microregional cultural histories of work. A common trait is the generalized widening of the market for female labor through two mechanisms: wage work outside the home and remunerative work within the household. Also involved is the generalized loss of agricultural income and the precariousness of male employment in several rural regions.

The migrations of previous decades encouraged some indigenous people to find new niches in the city for the products and skills of their homelands. The Purépechas of Nahuatzen, Michoacán, began to sell—and to transform—their traditional dress (the *huanengo*) as a fashionable item of women's clothing in the popular markets of Mexico City.[30] In the early 1980s, the production of huanengos extended to other Purépecha communities and the process of production fragmented, giving rise to a microregional system of piecework, or *maquila*.

Tourism in indigenous regions sparked the revitalization of handicrafts and their conversion into piecework systems of manufacture. In the early 1970s, two-thirds of the four thousand people of the Maya community of Cachalquén made hammocks in their homes, an activity and system of production they shared with eleven other towns in the sisal-growing region.[31]

Something similar happened in the central valleys of Oaxaca. The ancient textile traditions of Santo Tomás Jalieza became the predominant economic activity, providing full-time work for whole families. The average of three weavers in every household attests to the predominance of crafts and the breakdown of agriculture.[32]

Today, women's presence in indigenous production is notable not only in salaried craft production but in management and administration. In Motul, the most populated municipality in the henequen zone of Yucatán, five clothing factories (maquiladoras and independent) are run by women.[33]

Apparently, new industrial and market conditions encourage the versatility of indigenous women's skills and activities, and two traditional characteristics: their individualism and independence. In contrast with the collective rights and work connected with land, handicrafts and trading depend on the individual. Although women may travel and sit together in the marketplace and exchange small favors, the life of the artisan or trader is not subject to the rules and agreements that dominate other areas of social life.[34] Perceptions of indigenous women's work as collective have been misleading and may well account for the failure of projects that have tried to promote collective organization and separate women from the domain of independent trading.

Economic and family dynamics are acting to turn indigenous women into wage workers in their own homes, however. Although the women much prefer to sell their products themselves (thus ensuring that any income comes directly to them), their husbands are taking over that aspect of production. In fact, in Santo Tomás Jalieza, a trend is apparent. As soon as a feminine activity becomes economically viable, the male head of the household takes it over and separates the woman from what has been her vital domain—marketing her product—often using family responsibilities or the birth of a new child as a pretext.[35]

The process seems to be different in peasant regions. The 1980s saw a demand for female workers in the prosperous new agricultural field of horticulture. In Quiringüicharo, Michoacán, an area from which many men migrate to the United States to work, the current generation of women has moved into the strawberry-packing industry in the city of Zamora,[36] and women's work has become socially acceptable. Women have won the right to control their earnings. In rural areas, women employed in agroindustry stop working after they get married, but in the lower-class neighborhoods of urban Zamora there is a tendency for women to stay on the job even after marriage.[37] Important changes can occur within peasant society from one generation to the next. The Zamora example suggests that the division of labor by civil status may break down with time; that is, more and more married women will continue to work outside the home.

In neighboring Irapuato, the intensification of export horticulture has dramatically increased women's employment. Of the twenty packing industries operating year-round, some, like Jolly Green Giant, hire 1,200 workers in the processing plant in the peak season apart from field laborers, workers in the "cutting centers" during harvest, and greenhouse workers. The agricultural and agroindustrial labor force is mostly female. The demand is so great that young women are trucked in daily from all over the state to work in the packing plants.

The capitalistic logic of employing women as cheap labor is well known. But women themselves feminized the market. Faced with deteriorating conditions in agriculture, they had no choice but to enter the labor market, thus increasing the supply of cheap labor. They know the limitations of the local job market and the reasons they were hired. Their decision was in large part shaped by the men's situation. Unable to work as independent farmers or to rely on agricultural income for family sustenance, men nonetheless avoid local wage labor. Some continue to "do the rounds of the ejido" (i.e., tend their plots), but in reality they have very little to do. Younger men go to the United States to work and do little or nothing during periods at home (although some pick up inferior service jobs in the city). Many men live in a conflictive, cynical state—off the earnings of the women of their households. Usually three or more women from one household, spanning two generations, work in the fields, the harvest areas, and the packing plants.

With the extinction of agriculture as an economically viable and socially prestigious activity, peasants seem to have lost the central axis of their public and private lives. This process has been perverse not only for men but for their families and for women's work. Underemployment, violence, cynicism, and marriage breakups are the dark side of women's employment in Irapuato, and it is to this world that they return daily after work. Although men have always transformed their work situations into domestic demands, women working outside the home have not. The tensions in domestic life thus keep work from being a pleasant experience that women wish to continue and improve over the long run.

Still, very little is known about the long-term dynamics of this situation. Ethnography provides insight into the options of other peasant women. In poor rural regions close to large manufacturing centers, especially in the garment industry, women have responded to the extralocal job market by going to factories and workshops in nearby towns and by taking in piecework. Single women tend to predominate among the former, and married women among the latter. For example, in the early 1980s, maquiladora workers in Caderetya, Querétaro, came from twenty hamlets within a fifteen-kilometer area. The majority were single women from large families facing a lack of land and work options for the men outside of seasonal migration.[38] In northeastern Guanajuato, precarious agricultural conditions and the absence of the men stimulated women to turn to piecework knitting of baby clothes.[39]

South of the Toluca Valley in the state of México, at least four localities have combined to sew pants for the factories and workshops of Santiago Tianguistenco. In 1982, Claudia Cuéllar found that a third of the families lived exclusively on piecework income. She found that in San Pedro Tlaltiza-pán, the labor market split along lines of civil status, with underage and single women preferring the maquilas, or workshops, in the town and married women predominating in home piecework.[40]

The evidence at hand indicates that male migration, especially to the United States, has favored the expansion of the female labor market. The departure of men made the step toward employment less conflictive for women, whether they left the home or worked within it. Women who turn to wage labor are not only accused of neglecting their household chores, they are public proof of men's inability to support their families. Male migration to the United States is an act that seemingly restores the social and familial security once afforded by owning and farming land. Many a migrant proudly details his work on "the other side," even in farm labor or urban services he would never undertake in Mexico. Further, migration guarantees the maintenance of male rights as sons, husbands, and fathers. It allows men to remain idle during their stays at home. On the other hand, men's absence and the concomitant need to engage in wage-producing labor have increased women's decisiveness and ability to act, although these are subject to restriction by long-standing gender norms.

The interrelationship between male migration and female labor is especially clear in farming regions subjected to spatial decentralization and fragmented manufacturing. In the 1980s, several cities and microregions of western Mexico became part of a new industrial geography.[41] Santa María del Valle and San Julián, in highland Jalisco, are now production centers for blown-glass Christmas ornaments, an industry that became feminized as it left urban areas. Faced with the option of migrating to the United States, men rejected the wages and work offered by this industry. Women, burdened with the insecurities of livestock raising and agriculture but without the alternative of migration, accepted the work. Local social and family organization immediately imposed a division of labor based on marital status. Single women could work in the ornament factories. Married women had to work at home, packing the ornaments—the more irregular and worst paid of the tasks. The punishments meted out to the few transgressors of this norm serve to confirm it. Married women cannot go outside the home to work even in the worst of economic circumstances.[42]

Married women have been eternally in search of income-generating activities they can carry out at home: the combination of raising pigs and some task associated with clothing or shoe production is currently most common in the rancherías where the states of Guanajuato, Jalisco, and Michoacán come together. This situation does not seem to change with time. In San Francisco del Rincón, a ranchero area of western Guanajuato that is the center of an old hat-making industry and a flourishing shoe industry, women have always left the factories and workshops when they married. Once married, they take up piecework. Frequently, husbands carry the piecework home to their wives, although they consider this work unacceptable for themselves. It seems that new manufacturing processes depending on rural women's domestic work have helped to expand a feminine condition in one respect: a portion of the population which according to its marital status ought leave the job market stays within it.

Conclusions

In contrast to the notion linking rural women's "complementary" activities to agriculture, recent ethnography has unveiled the wide spectrum of non-agricultural work now available to women in the countryside. Reconstructing this complementarity has helped us to unearth the diverse microhistories of labor that rural women have constructed. In these microhistories women contend with two vital realities: the ever-deepening economic hardships of family life and the options permitted by their social and cultural environment.

In the diversity of their responses is a common thread: women's difficulty in transforming economic activities into social and cultural resources that can modify their position within their families and societies. According to the possibilities within their culture, women have traveled, traded, brought money and goods home, and earned a regular income, but this did not lead to a modification in their domestic roles or their traditional community roles, where obligations and rights are defined by land possession and agricultural work and status hierarchies are ordered according to age and sex. Although in recent years ethnographers have begun to detect significant changes in rural women's condition, there is still much to explore.

NOTES

This essay was translated by Neicy Zeller. The information presented here is part of a wider research project on family and women's conditions in the region of Irapuato, Guanajuato, carried out in 1991 and 1992 with the support of the John T. and Catherine D. MacArthur Foundation and the Asociación Mexicana de Población. References to Irapuato in this essay are based on my own fieldwork there.

1. Fiona Wilson, "La mujer y las transformaciones agrarias en América Latina: Revisión de algunos conceptos que fundamentan la investigación," in *La mujer y las políticas agrarias en América Latina,* ed. Carmen Diana Deere and Magdalena León de Leal (Bogotá, Colombia: Siglo XXI Editores, 1986), 265–90.

2. Patricia Arias, "Dos nociones en torno al campo," in *Ajuste estructural: Mercados laborales y TLC* (Mexico City: El Colegio de México, Fundación Friedrich Ebert, El Colegio de la Frontera Norte, 1992), 229–42.

3. Luis González, *Pueblo en vilo* (Mexico City: El Colegio de México, 1987), 6–11; and "Gente del campo," *Vuelta* 151 (1989):22–29.

4. See John Coatsworth, *El impacto económico de los ferrocarriles en el Porfiriato* (Mexico City: Ediciones Era, 1976), 11–19; González, *Pueblo en vilo,* 6–11.

5. For Chiapas, see Henry Favre, *Cambio y continuidad entre los mayas de México* (Mexico City: Siglo XXI Editores, 1973), 59–68; for Yucatán, Alice Littlefield, *La industria de las hamacas en Yucatán* (Mexico City: Instituto Nacional Indigenista, 1978), 52–54.

6. Littlefield, *La industria de las hamacas,* 53–54.

7. John Durston, *Organización social de los mercados campesinos en el centro de México* (Mexico City: Instituto Nacional Indigenista, 1976), 43–44. *Purépecha* refers to the original indigenous inhabitants of the state of Michoacán.

8. Patricia Arias, *Nueva rusticidad mexicana* (Mexico City: Conaculta, Colección Regiones, 1992), 191.

9. Judith Friedlander, *Ser indio en Hueyapan* (Mexico City: FCE, 1977), 55–56; also see her "Doña Zeferina Barreto" (in this volume).

10. Beverly Newbold de Chiñas, *Mujeres de San Juan* (Mexico City: SepSetentas, 1975), 84–102.

11. Durston, *Organización social,* 81–89.

12. Soledad González Montes, "Trabajo femenino y expansion de las relaciones capitalistas en el México rural a fines de porfiriato: El distrito de Tenango del Valle, Estado de México, 1900–1910," in *Haciendas, pueblos, y comunidades,* ed. Manuel Mino Grijalva (Mexico: Conaculta, 1991), 284.

13. Guillermo de la Peña, *Herederos de promesas* (Mexico City: Casa Chata, 1980), 96.

14. Friedlander, *Ser indio,* 34–42; Newbold de Chiñas, *Mujeres de San Juan,* 55.

15. See Arturo Warman, *Y venimos a contradecir* (Mexico City: Casa Chata, 1976).

16. Elena Azaola, *Los campesinos de la tierra de Zapata. III. Política y conflicto* (Mexico City: Sep Inah, 1976), 45.

17. See Antonio Penafield, *Censo General de la República Mexicana verificado el 28 de octubre de 1900. Estado de Guanajuato* (Mexico City: Oficina Tipográfica de la Secretaría de Fomento, 1903).

18. Jorge Alonso, pers. comm., 1992.

19. Arias, *Nueva rusticidad,* 111–52.

20. González, *Pueblo en vilo,* 58–68.

21. Ibid.; and Arias, *Nueva rusticidad,* 111–52.

22. Cynthia Hewitt de Alcántara, *La modernización de la agricultura mexicana, 1940–1970* (Mexico City: Siglo XXI Editores, 1978), 120–32.

23. Hugo G. Nutini and Barry L. Isaac, *Los pueblos de habla Nahuatl de la region de Tlaxcala y Puebla* (Mexico City: Instituto Nacional Indigenista, 1974), 425–26.

24. Claudia Cuellar, "El papel de la mujer en la producción maquilera y su importancia en la reproduccion de la fuerza de trabajo de la unidad familiar" (Licenciatura thesis, Universidad Autónoma Metropolitana-Iztapalapa, 1983), 32–33.

25. See, e.g., Lourdes Arizpe, *Migración, etnicismo y cambio económico* (Mexico City: El Colegio de México, 1978).

26. On women in domestic work, see Mary Goldsmith Connelly, "El servicio doméstico y la migración femenina," in *Trabajo femenino y crisis en México,* ed. Elia Ramírez Bautista and Hilda R. Dávila Ibañez (Mexico City: Universidad Autónoma Metropolitana-Xochimilco, 1990), 257–65, 267–71.

27. Gustavo Verduzco, "Crecimiento urbano y desarrollo regional: El caso de Zamora, Michoacán," *Relaciones* 5.17 (1984):9–40; Sara Lara, "Las relaciones de género en el proceso de producción de hortalizas de exportación en el estado de Sinaloa" (Discussion paper, Programa de la Mujer, El Colegio de México, 1991).

28. Lourdes Arizpe and Josefina Aranda, "Las obreras de la agroindustria de la fresa en Zamora, Michoacán," in *Las mujeres en el campo,* ed. Josefina Aranda (Oaxaca: Instituto de Investigaciones Sociológicas de la Universidad Autónoma Benito Juárez, 1988), 232; Gail Mummert, "Dios, el norte y la empacadora: La inserción de hombres y mujeres rurales en mercados de trabajo extralocales," in *Ajuste estructural,* 243–56; Georgina Rosado, "Las mujeres de San Pablo: trabajo y vida cotidiana," in Aranda, *Las mujeres en el campo,* 147–62.

29. See Arias, *Nueva rusticidad.*

30. Jorge Alonso, *Lucha urbana y acumulación de capital* (Mexico City: Casa Chata, 1980), chap. 3; Lucía García, *Nahuatzen* (Zamora: El Colegio de Michoacán, 1984), 75–76.

31. Littlefield, *La industria de las hamacas,* 67.

32. Josefina Aranda, "Género, familia y división del trabajo en Santo Tomás Jalieza," *Estudios Sociológicos* 8.22 (1990):5.

33. Florencia Peña and José M. Gamboa, "Mujer y trabajo industrial en Motul, Yucatán," *I'NAJ* (Mérida) 2 (1991):2.

34. Newbold de Chiñas, *Las mujeres de San Juan,* 133–45.

35. See Aranda, "Género, familia y división," 5.

36. Mummert, "Dios," 248–49.

37. Rosado, "Los mujeres de San Pablo," 155–61.

38. Martha Lucila Ceja Barrera, "Efectos de la incorporación de la mujer campesina al trabajo industrial," in Aranda, *Las mujeres del campo,* 177–88.

39. Sandra Treviño Siller, "Reflexiones sobre el trabajo a domicilio en la zona noreste de Guanajuato," *Estudios Sociológicos* 6.18 (1988):583–601.

40. Cuellar, *El papel de la mujer,* 32–33.

41. Arias, *Nueva rusticidad,* chap. 1.

42. Patricia Arias and Jorge Durand, "Santa María de las esferas," *Sociedad y Estado* 1 (1988):5–16.

10

Intergenerational and Gender Relations in the Transition from a Peasant Economy to a Diversified Economy

Soledad González Montes

*S*tudies during the 1980s in Mexico showed the expansion of rural women's participation in wage work within the context of the crisis suffered by peasant economies since the 1960s.[1] My own research examines how changes in women's work have contributed to the transformation of family dynamics, particularly with respect to intergenerational and gender relations. The context within which these changes take place is the transition from a peasant to a diversified economy, in which women's incomes have gained central importance.

In order to understand changes in family relations we must examine the cultural background against which they occur, taking into account values, family morals that speak about rights and obligations and, ultimately, people's notions about the social order and the places men and women should occupy in it at different times of their lives. In this essay I focus on the interplay between ideology and economic conditions.

Given a peasant economy in which capital and sources of income other than agriculture are scarce, land is undoubtedly the most valuable resource. Such was the case in Xalatlaco until the late 1960s. In this community in central Mexico, the domestic cycle and the hierarchy of authority inside the family were organized around the control and hereditary transmission of land. I will show that the correlation of power with genders and generations changed once agriculture ceased to be the basis of the family economy and as women took advantage of the new possibilities for earning money that opened for them.[2]

I used seven sources of information in my research: (1) open-ended interviews conducted with some thirty informants with the purpose of reconstructing their life histories and their ethos; (2) the genealogies and histories of fifteen family groups; (3) the national population censuses, including a detailed sample of five hundred homes from the 1990 census; (4) two local population censuses, conducted in 1933 and 1974, which were used to analyze the composition of 257 and 512 domestic groups, respectively; (5) marriage and birth records from the parish archive and the civil register for the 1920–90 period; (6) Records from the local justice of the peace, which I used to study marital conflicts and land inheritance cases for the same period; and (7) the lists of landowners in the public land registry.

The Transition from a Peasant Economy to a Diversified Economy

The municipality of Xalatlaco, where my research was conducted, lies on the southeastern rim of the Toluca Valley, about sixty kilometers (forty-eight miles) from Mexico City. It belongs to the district of Tenango del Valle, which until the 1950s had the largest concentration of Nahuatl speakers in the state of México. The 1940 census indicates that three-fourths of Xalatlaco's population spoke Nahuatl, a proportion that decreased rapidly in the following decades; by 1990, only 2.3 percent of the population spoke Nahuatl. Its use is now limited to religious rituals, which in Xalatlaco as in most Mexican villages continue to have great importance in local social life and absorb much of the village's collective expenditures.

Even though language is no longer an element of ethnic identification, the Indian past has undoubtedly left its imprint on social relations and on the local culture. Until a couple of decades ago, this meant, for instance, a collective effort to avoid the loss of municipal resources held in communal tenancy (*bienes comunales*), such as woods, water, and grazing grounds, to outsiders. These efforts were not always successful, but they were an important element in the group's concept of community.[3] Family history in these situations cannot be disentangled from community history, since both mutually constructed each other through perennial encounters between individual and family interests, on the one hand, and collective interests, on the other.[4]

According to the 1990 census, about 75 percent of Xalatlaco's total population (about fifteen thousand) resides in the municipal county seat (*cabecera*), and the rest is scattered over several rancherías. Approximately half of the municipality's territory is a wooded area 2,700 meters above sea level that is held communally. The other half consists of arable land divided into small private holdings. Agriculture and sheep raising for wool were the basis of Xalatlaco's economy until the end of the 1960s, with wage work contributing variably at different times.[5]

Wage work was of great importance at the end of the nineteenth century and in the first decade of the twentieth, when land became concentrated in the hands of a few families. This situation forced a segment of the population to sell its labor as farmhands and day laborers (*jornaleros*). At the end of this period one out of three day laborers in the district of Tenango was a woman.[6] "To hire oneself out" (*alquilarse*) was particularly important for women in the poorest segment of the population, who had to work for the wealthier families grinding corn, washing clothes, or planting and harvesting.

The economic polarization of the community during the Porfiriato created strong internal tensions which found an outlet in the Zapatista movement. The eight years of war during the revolution that ensued destroyed the fortunes of the few families who had become rich and served as a leveling mechanism. After the 1910 Revolution, land was never again concentrated. Families with little or no land were able to gain access to it, as half the population died during the war or afterward as a consequence of famine or the 1918 influenza epidemic.

From 1920 until the end of the 1960s, Xalatlaco's economy was a typical peasant one in which corn, beans, potatoes, and barley were grown for home consumption and for sale. During this period, lumber, charcoal, turpentine, and other forest-related products were more important sources of male income than wage labor. Relatively few men migrated to the city, whereas most of the women spent part of their youth in the capital working as domestic servants, returning to the village when it was time to get married.

The third period, from the 1960s to the present, has been marked by a series of swift transformations: the growing importance of nonagricultural incomes; the increase in the number of homes without land and without members dedicated to agriculture; the appearance of a truly free land market, open to anyone, even outsiders; and an increase in paid work for women. In 1960, almost 90 percent of the economically active population of Xalatlaco devoted itself to agricultural activities. Twenty years later, the 1980 census proved that less than half of the economically active population was composed of peasants.

Extremely rapid and profound transformations occurred in the occupational structure of the municipality between 1960 and 1990. The root of these changes was not so much that land had become scarce as the population multiplied, but rather that the cost of agricultural production rose while prices for peasants' products remained low. It soon became obvious to peasants that nonagricultural work was more remunerative than agriculture. As a result, at the end of the 1950s, as soon as public transportation connected Xalatlaco with the capital, men and women began to go to Mexico City to work and sell their products.

Proximity to the capital is a great advantage to the district. The city constitutes an enormous market with a great capacity to absorb products and workers. The trip takes less than two hours, making it possible for those who work there to commute daily. In many cases, workers with stable employment stay in the city for five days and return to Xalatlaco to spend weekends with their families. Since the mid-1970s, the industrial area of Santiago Tianguistenco (which lies six kilometers, or four miles, from Xalatlaco) has offered employment to a considerable number of young men and women. Salaries are very low and working conditions are bad, but at least unemployment and underemployment are not the problems here that they are in so many other regions of Mexico.

Analysis of a sample of five hundred domestic groups from the 1990 census shows that about half of the households do not have members devoted to agriculture. One-third of the households declared that all of their employed members worked exclusively in agriculture (of these, the majority live in the rancherías, in the outskirts of town); the remaining households combine agriculture with other income-generating activities. For most of the families that still cultivate, the share of produce destined for sale has diminished while that destined for home consumption has increased. In other words, for half of the population family agricultural production provides a large part of the family's food, but it is no longer the main source of income, as it was through the 1950s. Agriculture has become complementary to wage work and commerce.

Women in the Occupational Structure

In the traditional conception of the "natural" division of labor, men worked in the fields and women worked at home. But the truth is that only in the better-off homes were women able to abstain from working in agriculture or as domestic servants. Given that there were few alternative sources of money during the 1920–50 period, incomes from *sirvientas* were particularly important in reconstructing the productive infrastructure destroyed by the war of 1910–18. Up to the beginning of the 1970s, working in Mexico City as a domestic servant before marriage was a normal phase in the lives of most women. Mothers received their daughters' salaries directly from the employers, and the money was used to buy livestock, land, seed, fertilizers, trucks, and, more recently, to pay the university expenses of male siblings. On the other hand, Xalatlaco women have always worked side by side with men in all stages of cultivation: taking food to workers in the fields, planting, weeding, and harvesting (the task requiring the largest number of laborers, since it is done by hand and in the shortest time possible). In this municipality women did not substitute for men in agriculture, as happened in areas where males left to become migrant workers. Women from the poorest households not only worked without pay on family plots, they also hired themselves out for wages on other people's lands, especially during the harvest. The emergence of new, better-paid alternatives during the 1980s, however, greatly reduced the number of women working in agriculture.

One of the fundamental aspects in the transformation of the occupational structure of Xalatlaco since the 1960s is the incorporation of an increasing number of women into the nonagricultural labor force. According to national population censuses, which have always tended to underestimate women's work, women made up barely 6 percent of Xalatlaco's economically active population in 1960; but by 1980 one out of every four economically active persons was a woman.

In 1990 the proportion of women registered by the census had dropped slightly, to 17 percent of the total labor force. Their proportion also decreased in each sector of the economy compared with the number of men, but this is only in relative terms and is due to the fact that the number of male workers increased at a faster pace. In absolute terms, the number of women in nondomestic occupations grew notably between 1980 and 1990, especially in industry, services, and trade (see Table 10.1).

Men say that "the road came to open women's eyes," because it allows the women to go into Mexico City to sell food and beverages that they themselves prepare (*tamales, atole*, etc.) or that they buy at the local market (sausage, salted beef, cheeses, etc.). Almost half of all the traders in the municipality in 1970 were women, according to the census.[7] Eventually, the new income allowed many families to open stores in town, so that in many cases a fixed trade replaced peddling during the 1980s.

Women's participation in the service sector grew likewise, though to a lesser extent than in trade. The types of activities included in this sector have been changing. Originally, practically all women classified under "Services" worked as domestic servants, but since 1980 the number of women teachers, secretaries, and nurses has increased. With the opening of industries in Santiago Tianguistenco in the mid-1970s, young women stopped going to the city to work as domestic servants and turned to industrial work instead. There has also been an increase in the number of small workshops that assemble clothing for large commercial chains. Industrial, workshop, and secretarial jobs have replaced domestic service, with its lower wages and lack of status.

Table 10.1
Male and Female Participation by Sector in Xalatlaco's Economy, 1940–1990

	1940	1960	1970	1990
Agriculture				
Men	99.3%	96.5%	94.5%	98.5%
Women	0.7%	3.5%	5.5%	1.5%
N	1,202	1,410	1,627	1,442
Industry				
Men	100.0%	90.0%	80.0%	81.0%
Women	0.0%	10.0%	20.0%	19.0%
N	13	69	182	929
Trade				
Men	84.6%	70.0%	54.0%	65.0%
Women	15.4%	30.0%	46.0%	35.0%
N	26	66	170	482
Services				
Men	100.0%	62.0%	51.0%	62.0%
Women	0.0%	38.0%	49.0%	38.0%
N	4	37	121	596
Other				
Men	50.0%	87.5%	52.8%	96.0%
Women	50.0%	12.5%	47.2%	4.0%
N	14	8	178	97

Sources: National population censuses. The 1980 census does not separate the working population by gender and therefore is not included in this table.
Note: N = total number registered by the censuses.

Male Control over Land

Women's contributions to the domestic economy in Xalatlaco have not been rewarded with equivalent control of land and money. Throughout the period I studied, the main mechanism of access to land was through inheritance, and—as is common in peasant villages in Mexico and elsewhere—heredity patterns tend to favor sons.

The 1884 Mexican Civil Code established freedom in the designation of heirs and so ended the legal protection given to women under colonial law through the obligatory legitimate share and the system of equal division.[8] The few historical studies of inheritance show that from early times there were differences between indigenous and nonindigenous practices. Among the nonindigenous urban sectors, the tendency was equal inheritance by children of both sexes.[9] Among the indigenous population, however, the tendency—frequently mentioned in ethnographies—was to leave to the sons the bulk of the land, the work tools, and the livestock.[10]

Xalatlaco is no exception: women are secondary, residual heirs; they receive less than their brothers—either little, nothing, or the worst portion.

Women receive a substantial inheritance only under certain conditions, the most frequent being the absence of male siblings. Another possibility is that some female relative (almost always the mother) has property to pass on— bought by her, inherited by being an only child or not having any brothers, or inherited from another female. In Xalatlaco it is the custom for women to will their property to their daughters (or, if they have none, to other female relatives) in the same way that men favor their male offspring.[11] A third condition under which a woman may inherit occurs when she makes an exceptionally important monetary contribution to the parental household; for example, taking on large medical or funeral expenses. As long as women had no money of their own this was not possible, but things changed when women began to participate in paid work.[12]

As a consequence of the practices mentioned, land is not distributed equally between the sexes. Men are the main proprietors. The data from the Public Registry of Property confirm that this pattern continues to be important in Xalatlaco: until the mid-1980s, only about 20 percent of the registered land belonged to women.

Although land has been losing its economic value in relation to non-agricultural income since the 1960s, it is not completely valueless: it constitutes a form of savings and also holds social and symbolic value. For these reasons families that have little or no land try to buy it. Given today's economic conditions, inheritance has lost ground to purchase as the main mechanism of access to land. Women's wage work contributes to land purchases, which then, according to family morals, gives them the right to receive a share in proportion to the amount invested. This means that within the new economy, women's work is "visible" because it has a cash equivalent.

Occupational changes in Xalatlaco are too recent to show quantitative proof of the transition from a strongly patrilineal heredity pattern to a more bilateral, egalitarian one between children of both sexes. But data on heredity from communities where the process has a longer history suggest that although cash incomes do not necessarily guarantee land inheritances for women at the same level as for men, they do favor a change in that direction. A comparison of data from several communities within a region of Altos de Chiapas shows an absence of preference toward males in communities where land no longer contributes the bulk of most families' income.[13]

Headship of the Domestic Group and Authority Within the Peasant Context

An inheritance pattern that favors men is of great importance not only because it limits women's control over resources but also because it influences postmarital residence, the domestic cycle, and the headship of household. The custom by which the man takes his wife to live for some time in his parents' household is related to the fact that he has to continue contributing his labor to the parental household for a while in order to deserve his eventual reward of a piece of his father's land. It has to do, therefore, with intergenerational exchanges in which women's domestic work is not taken into account (as opposed to their cash income, which is).

Inheritance and residence are linked through labor: the men live (and invest their labor in agriculture) in the place where they expect to inherit, and finally they inherit where they have lived and worked—where they earned rights. Land ties people down. After they are married a couple will go to live in the household where the possibility for inheriting the most land exists. The spouse who will not inherit or who will inherit less is the one who moves away from her or his paternal home. Women inherit less or not at all because they leave their parents' household at marriage, and they leave because they are not going to inherit. . . . The patrivirilocal postmarital residence pattern and the predominantly patrilineal inheritance mutually reinforced each other and were widely practiced among the Mexican peasantry.[14]

On the other hand, the transfer of the bulk of the patrimony does not take place until the owner dies or is unable to continue agricultural labor due to old age, sickness, or accident. Parents can turn over some of the land to be used for residence or agriculture, but this is always a small portion. They reserve the greater part of the property for as long as possible, since land is the means by which they can back up their decisions; it allows them to exercise their will. While he is the head—the *jefe*, the father leads the productive process. Until the 1960s, he also managed the incomes of the household's members.

An important aspect of the father's rights as head was to decide whom his children would marry, and when. Arranged marriages still occurred in the 1950s. Marriage was a family matter, not a question of individual selection based on romantic attraction. The elders' will had to be taken very much into account because one lived in their household and worked on their land, without much alternative to this situation.

Concerning the socialization of children, the parents had the right and the obligation to instill in them early the principles of hierarchical authority on which society was organized. It was customary to impose severe and even brutal punishments to obtain a discipline of "respect," which meant obedience and submission. Until recently, physical repression was common and included beatings, forcing the child to inhale chile smoke, rubbing with *chichicastle* nettles, and, in extreme (though not rare) cases of offenses considered very grave (like stealing or losing something valuable), suspending the culprit from a beam.

The hierarchy arranged by generation (age) and by sex had to be respected. The young had to display constant signs of submission, such as not raising their eyes in the presence of elders. Even today, many still kiss an elder's hand. Those who did not obey their elders or accord them the requisite respect were punished or received supernatural sanctions in the form of curses, which were thought to bring accidents or sickness. Thus elders were even attributed with magical power.[15]

There were many ways to display hierarchy in the man-woman relationship: women went barefoot while men wore sandals; if the couple owned a riding animal, the man rode it while the woman trotted along behind. Violence against women was frequent and intense.[16] Males might be subordinate with regard to other segments of society, but in the home the man was the boss. He had people to serve him (the women of the domestic group) and he controlled the material and human resources (the children), which served him equally as labor and political support.

Beyond the domestic sphere, senior males' control extended to the public sphere. In effect, the reins of community government were held by elders or *principales*, the heads of extended families who lived within the same compound or in the same neighborhood. Their opinions were sought in all public or private matters of importance. They occupied the positions of judges, municipal presidents, and mayors, and they also held the important posts within the civic-religious hierarchy (the cargo system), so they combined economic, political, and religious powers.

Women's Position Within the Peasant Domestic Cycle

A woman's position within the authority hierarchy varies according to her place within the domestic cycle, her age, and her civil status, but women's life courses are not the same as men's. As long as a man lives within the parental household, he must accept his father's authority, work for him in the fields, and turn over practically his entire income for the father to manage. Once he breaks away and sets up his own domestic unit, the man becomes the head of the household. Very few women ever become heads of household, nor do they get to control a significant part of the more valuable resources. As long as there is a male head of household above them (father, father-in-law, husband), they cannot "govern" (make decisions by) themselves. They can, however, influence decisions, and they can obtain control over their children and daughters-in-law when they reach the stage of wife of the jefe.

In Xalatlaco's family system, children did not establish a separate household at the time of marriage. This implies that most women moved in with their in-laws when they married. Thus families formed extensive household groups comprising more than one couple and their children. The fact that it was the woman who had to move means that it was she who had to adapt to living in a strange household and had to submit to a new family head, just as she had done before with her parents. It was said that the woman went as a daughter-in-law to *serve* in the father-in-law's home. She had to go through a period during which her work capacity was tested, and she had to ask her father-in-law for permission to go out or do anything out of the ordinary, even to visit her own parents. Her mother-in-law directed her domestic activities. Even today, as long as they live with their elders, she and her husband must turn over their earnings to his parents.

The man who has to move in with his in-laws falls into a similar position, but one which is especially humiliating to a man. It is said that he left his home to become a male daughter-in-law, or more disparagingly, an *atolero*,[17] a position proper for women but not for men. The "male daughters-in-law" have to accept their in-laws' decisions just as female daughters-in-law do.[18] Only men who know they are not going to inherit or who will inherit very little because they belong to very poor families are willing to move in with their in-laws (patriuxorilocal residence). In these cases, usually the woman is an only child or her parents had only daughters. Sometimes it is convenient for the parents to attract the son-in-law to live with them because they still have small children to raise, and another adult male adds an important contribution to the family budget.

The Xalatlaco municipal census shows a clear pattern: the overwhelming majority of extended families were formed because wives came to live with their husbands' parents. In a sample of 512 households from the 1974 census, 120 married men lived in extended families, but only 8 were living with their in-laws; the rest lived in their original household with their own parents. Of those 8 men, 2 were workers, 2 were artisans, and 1 was an "employee"; that is, they owned no land. In the other three cases, I was told that the wives were sole heirs.

Only after a period of residence within the extended family—patrivirilocal or, exceptionally, patriuxorilocal—can the couple move away from the original household. On doing so they stop turning over their incomes to the common fund of the parental household. The establishment of a separate household marks the beginning of a new stage for the woman. For the first time she stops being under the authority of the previous generation. Her husband is the head, but she can usually find a way to influence his decisions. Her authority is augmented when her sons bring daughters-in-law into the home. This happens quite early in her life, since by the age of forty or forty-five a great number of people have marriageable children. Thus the cycle begins again.

Nonagricultural Incomes and the Transformation of
Relations Between Generations and Genders

The massive rush to work outside the municipality that began in the 1960s extended young people's social lives beyond the narrow confines of the neighborhood. The new workplaces were outside parents' control and presented new opportunities for young men and women to interact with non-relatives who could be potential marriage partners. A rapid decrease in the overly high percentage of endogamic marriages began at that time,[19] and between 1970 and 1980 the proportion of people marrying outside the area practically doubled.

This trend also contributed to weakening the control that senior males had over the younger generations, as evidenced in changes in the way marriage partners were selected and couples were formed. The transition was from a pattern of marriages arranged between families to one with freedom of individual selection, opening a space that did not exist before: courtship and betrothal as a socially acceptable stage. Even during the 1970s couples found in the act of courtship were physically punished, and some were forced to marry. Today young people can back up their wishes with the income they receive from jobs away from their parents' lands. They have earned more individual decision-making power over their own lives.

The 1990 census data indicate that the custom of a man taking his spouse to his parents' house at the time of marriage continues, but the duration of the cohabitation now depends mainly on the domestic group's economy. In landless households the tendency has been toward a reduction of the coresidence period, making it more symbolic than real. In households devoted exclusively to agricultural labor no substantial modifications have occurred. Among households with a diversified economy (i.e., that combine agriculture with other economic activities), however, the period of cohabitation has been prolonged (as compared with purely agricultural households), and more than half of these domestic groups have an extended family structure.[20]

Of the households analyzed from the 1990 census, 26 percent were extended families. Although the period of cohabitation is the most conflict-laden stage of the life cycle for women, it also has advantages. The presence of several adults allows for a more efficient division of labor among household members; for example, between those who work in the fields and in the home and those who work outside. A great number of women who work outside the home live in extended families. This domestic structure also allows a favorable balance between producers and consumers during the difficult period of child raising, when expenses frequently exceed a couple's income-generating capacity. This is the stage of greatest hardship and toil for a woman if the nuclear family is on its own and none of her daughters is old enough to help with the housework and child care.

On the other hand, my interviews suggest that nonagricultural incomes have affected intergenerational relations in the extended family. Before, land and agricultural production were the uniting elements between the members of the domestic group. Children, even after they were married, were dependent on their fathers, who gave them shelter and work on the land and eventually left them an inheritance. Now, young people's incomes are crucial for the productive process; without this money fertilizer cannot be bought, plows cannot be rented, and so on. Moreover, young people's jobs provide access to medical insurance and senior care. That is, the relation of dependency has been inverted.

The fact that the ability to generate an income has become so important is modifying parents' attitudes toward sons and daughters. Because outside incomes can be obtained by individuals of either sex, from the point of view of the older generation a child's gender is no longer important. This did not happen when land was the fundamental means of subsistence because agriculture was considered men's work par excellence. Men were seen as the producers of the means of exchange, while women were perceived as limited to the reproductive sphere. Parents preferred male children, who could work alongside them in the activity considered the most valuable.

Now, men *and* women can obtain incomes, and daughters and sons are valued more equally. Illiteracy by gender is a good indicator of this process. Fewer than one-third of the women sixty-five years or older in 1990 could read or write, as compared with 60 percent of the men within the same age group. The percentage of those who can read increases as age decreases, and the difference between the sexes diminishes. In 1990, according to the census, 95 percent of Xalatlaco's men and 91 percent of the women aged thirty to thirty-four could read and write. Between 1980 and 1990 almost the same number of girls as boys finished grade school. Around 45 percent of the population between twelve and thirty years of age completed some type of middle school or higher. Still, fewer than half of the graduates are women, except among teachers, but compared with their grandmothers, women have taken a great leap forward.

It is not only for outside work that women need more education. Within the new economic context, domestic groups have been losing importance as production units and have gained as consumption units, a process that has in turn modified the roles of the wife and the head of household. Previously, the male head organized production, sold the surplus, and managed the money derived from these sales; he went to the regional fairs and markets to buy tools, raw materials, and other items needed for family production, given that the greater part of everyday goods, such as clothing, were manufactured within the household. Now it is the wife who is in charge of managing the incomes, which go into the common fund. She buys or directs the purchase of consumer goods.[21]

Women even manage the surpluses derived from family production, when these exist. For example, the greater part of the corn a family grows is devoted to household consumption; the rest is no longer sold directly but rather is used by women to make traditional foods (*gorditas,* tamales, and tacos) and beverages (atole), which they sell in Mexico City.[22] The income from these sales is added to the common fund used for the maintenance of the domestic group; but now it is the wife who decides what will be done with it.

New Options for Female Residence

Other processes within the last decade have also had a direct bearing on women's situation and position. As long as agriculture was the economic base of the municipality, there were few options for women as far as residence and cohabitation; only a few exceptional women escaped the typical stages within the peasant domestic cycle. The local censuses for 1933 and 1974 show a great deal of homogeneity in this sense. In the 1990 census, however, we find four new possible life courses: (1) an increased number of men who live with their in-laws rather than bringing their wives to live with their own parents, (2) more single mothers who continue to live in their original household, (3) an increased proportion of female heads of households, and (4) an increased number of married women who separate from their husbands and return to their paternal homes.

Each option is the result of a complex process and would require more space than I have here to discuss properly. For this reason, I will discuss only the last two. An insignificant phenomenon in the 1933 census, female heads of household represented 7 percent of homes analyzed in 1974, and 10 percent in 1990. Of the fifty-one female heads of household in the 1990 sample, twenty-one claimed to be widows; eleven were single, almost all with children; twelve were married; and three were common-law wives. When a woman declared that she was married (legally or by common law) but also declared herself the head of the home, it was for one of two possible reasons: either the husband worked and lived in the city most of the time and returned to his family only on weekends; or the husband had two households, one with a legal wife and the other with a common-law wife. The second woman would then declare herself the household head, since the man did not live there.

There is no particular pattern in the ages of the heads of household. Contrary to what was happening in 1933 and 1974, when almost all female heads of household were aged widows, female-headed households in 1990 showed greater diversity in the head's civil status as well as in her economic condition.

In the sample of five hundred households from the 1990 census I was able to identify a total of thirteen homes with women who were separated from their husbands—something I could not detect in the samples from the 1933 and 1974 censuses. In four of these homes the woman was the head and lived alone with all or some of her children. The other nine women returned to the parental household to live with their parents and their married and unmarried siblings. The numbers seem small, but a review of the records of the local justice of the peace shows that it is an important overall trend. Sixty-eight cases of separations were brought before the judge in 1990,[23] a sharp increase with respect to 1984 (thirty-eight cases) and 1970 (nine cases).

The majority of women who were separated in 1990 were under thirty years of age, and the presence of children or pregnancy was no hindrance to abandoning the conjugal home. The most common reason separated women gave for not returning to their husbands was that the husbands continued to live in an extended family with their parents, a conflictive situation which they were no longer willing to accept. The second most frequent cause for separations was that the husband did not fulfill his obligations to support the household, was an alcoholic, and/or beat his wife. The appearance of such a modern cause as incompatibility of character is very significant.

Conclusions

The information analyzed above suggests that whereas many of the homes and individuals of Xalatlaco continue to follow the same phases of the "typical peasant" cycle as in the past, a growing proportion of the population has new possibilities for action, an especially important situation for women. Taken together, the transformations described here point in one direction: the transition from a strong patrivirilocality in residence, which characterizes the peasant family system, toward a more flexible system in which women have begun to experiment with the possibility of returning to live with their parents or, more rarely, on their own. A woman can even pressure her husband to bring her parents to live in their home, something that was very exceptional in the past, when elderly parents lived with one of their married sons.

This transition has brought about profound changes in thought and attitudes. In the past, a woman's return to her parents' home after marriage or elopement was practically impossible. Single and married male siblings continued to live there, but the general view was that a married woman had no right to leave her husband and return to her parents' home. In the past, women were socialized to think that living with their in-laws and "serving them" was a natural part of the life cycle. They also were taught that husbands were substitute fathers with the right to physically punish them if they did not fulfill their roles as wives and daughters-in-law adequately.

Such punishments were considered abuse only when they were too harsh. In the family moral code, the husband's right to be obeyed ceased only when he did not fulfill his obligations as provider. Under this system a woman could not expect support from her family of origin. Even if mothers wished to help and protect their married daughters from ill treatment at the hands of husbands and in-laws, they were hardly in a position to do so.

Conditions have changed. Single women have increased their monetary contributions to their parents' home, and they stay home longer.[24] Their contributions have made their work more visible and entitle them to reciprocal support. At the same time, there are more opportunities for women who leave their husbands to work and support their children (and practically all separated women have children), so that their return to the paternal home is not seen as a burden. The foundations have been laid for a change in the conception of womens' obligations and life courses: what in the past was considered "normal" destiny now is just one possible road, definitely not acceptable to—and not accepted by—many.

NOTES

This essay was translated by Neicy Zeller.

1. See Josefina Aranda, ed., *Las mujeres en el campo* (Oaxaca: Universidad Autónoma Benito Juárez, 1988); Lourdes Arizpe et al., "Efectos de la crisis económica de 1980–1985 sobre la condición de vida de las mujeres campesinas en México," in *El ajuste invisible, Los efectos de la crisis económica en las mujeres pobres* (Bogotá, Colombia: UNICEF, 1989); Sara Lara, "El papel de la mujer en el campo: Nuevas estrategias," in *Las sociedades rurales hoy*, ed. J. Zepeda (Zamora: El Colegio de Michoacán, 1988), 297–305.

2. S. González Montes, "Familias campesinas en el siglo XX" (Ph.D. diss., Universidad Complutense, Madrid, 1992). An earlier version of this essay appeared in *Textos y pre-textos. Once estudios sobre la mujer*, ed. V. Salles and E. McPhail (Mexico City: El Colegio de México, 1991).

3. Alejandro Patiño and S. González Montes, *Memoria campesina. La historia de Xalatlaco contada por su gente* (Toluca: Instituto Mexiquense de Cultura, 1994).

4. Arturo Warman, "Notas para una redefinición de la comunidad agraria," *Revista Mexicana de Sociología* 47.3 (1985):5–20. González Montes, "Trabajo femenino y avance de las relaciones capitalistas en el Mexico rural a fines del porfiriato," in *Pueblos, haciendas y comunidades en el centro de Mexico. Los valles de Toluca y México entre 1580 y 1910*, ed. M. Miño (Toluca: El Colegio Mexiquense, 1989).

5. Wage labor and other forms of nonagricultural work were always present in the peasant world and were crucial for family livelihood. What has varied are the types of work available and their contributions to family budgets.

6. González Montes, "Trabajo femenino."

7. A 1975 survey calculated that about seven hundred women went into the city one or more times a week to sell, a much higher number than that shown by the 1980 census; see José A. Paoli, "Dinámicas políticas en un municipio de México central" (Master's thesis in Sociology, Universidad Iberoamericana, 1980).

8. Silvia Arrom, "Cambios en la condición jurídica de la mujer mexicana durante el siglo XIX," *Memoria del segundo congreso de historia del derecho* (Mexico City: UNAM, 1981); Ingrid Brena, "La libertad testamentaria en el Código Civil de 1884," in *Un siglo de Derecho Civil mexicano* (Mexico City: UNAM, 1985).

9. Asunción Lavrín and Edith Couturier, "Dowries and Wills: A View of Women's Socioeconomic Role in Colonial Guadalajara and Puebla, 1640–1790," *Hispanic American Historical Review* 59.2 (1979):280–304.

10. This inheritance pattern, associated with a strong tendency toward patrilocal residence, has been documented in communities in the states of Puebla, Tlaxcala, Morelos, Guerrero, Chiapas, and Oaxaca; see L. Arizpe, *Parentesco y economía en una sociedad nahua* (Mexico City: Instituto Nacional de Antropología e Historia, 1967); J. Taggart, *Estructura de los grupos domésticos de una comunidad de habla náhuatl de Puebla* (Mexico City: Instituto Nacional Indigenista [INI], 1975); H. Nutini, *San Bernardino Contla: Marriage and Family Structures in a Tlaxcalan Municipio* (Pittsburgh: University of Pittsburgh Press, 1968); D. Dehouve, "Parenté et marriage dans une communauté nahuatl de l'état de Guerrero," *Journal de la Societé des Americanistes* 65 (1978):173–208; J. Collier, *Planos de interacción del mundo Tzotzil* (Mexico City: INI, 1976); J. Ravics, *Organización social de los mixtecos* (Mexico City: INI, 1965).

11. These practices in the Toluca Valley go back to at least the beginning of the eighteenth century; see Margarita Loera, *Calimaya y Tepemaxalco. Tenencia y transmisión hereditaria de la tierrra en dos comunidades indígenas* (Mexico City: Dirección de Estudios Históricos del INAH, Cuadernos de Trabajo no. 18, 1977). For a broader discussion of this "homogeneous" inheritance pattern, see Jack Goody, *Production and Reproduction. A Comparative Study of the Domestic Domain* (Cambridge: Cambridge University Press, 1977).

12. In Xalatlaco's family system the women receive no dowry, which represents an advance on the inheritance. The parents usually give them pots, mats, blankets, clothing, or, in the case of wealthier families, small animals and jewelry.

13. See Collier, *Mundo Tzotzil*.

14. The persistence of patrivirilocal residence in contexts where family agriculture is secondary in the domestic economy can be attributed to the economic advantages of living within the extended family, but above all to the role it plays (if only symbolically) in the preservation of an authority hierarchy that privileges men and subordinates women.

15. A. Villa Rojas, "Kinship and Nagualism in a Tzeltal Community," *American Anthropologist* 49 (1947):578–87, discusses elder men's use of supernatural power as a form of social control.

16. People's stories regarding the use of footwear by men and women coincide with information from the national population censuses. For a study of violence against women in the past, see González Montes and P. Iracheta, "La violencia en la vida de las mujeres campesinas. El distrito de Tenango, 1880–1910," in *Presencia y transparencia. La mujer en la historia de México* (Mexico City: El Colegio de México, 1987).

17. An *atolero* prepares atole, a sweet, warm drink made of ground corn.

18. Nutini, *San Bernardino Contla*; and Taggart, *Estructura de los grupos domésticos*, 168; among others, found the same phenomenon in the communities they studied.

19. Even in 1960, 50 percent or more of marriages took place between people from the same neighborhood; in 1970, 70 percent of people marrying in the municipal capital were from the same town (according to the marriage records from the Xalatlaco Civil Registry).

20. As a point of comparison, Lutz Berkner considers that 25 percent of extended households is a very high figure, indicating an important phase of the domestic cycle; see "The Stem Family and the Developmental Cycle of the Peasant Household, an Eighteenth Century Austrian Example," *American Historical Review* 77 (1972).

21. An equivalent strengthening of the mother's role as organizer of the family unit of consumption is described for Yugoslavia by R. First-Dilic, "The Life Cycle of the Yugoslav Peasant Family," in *The Family Cycle in European Societies,* ed. J. Cuisinier (The Hague: New Babylon; Paris: Mouton, 1977), 77–89.

22. Paoli ("Dinamicas políticas," 29) estimates that toward the end of the 1970s, less than 15 percent of the corn produced in the municipality was sold outside, mostly in the form of foods such as *gorditas* (cakes made of corn with a bean paste filling), tamales, tacos, and *atole* (a corn gruel beverage).

23. The sample of households analyzed represents approximately one-fifth of the total registered for the municipality in the 1990 census. Therefore, the number of separations found through the census and from the legal records is almost equivalent ($13 \times 5 = 65$). Sixty-eight separations is truly an impressive number if we take into account that there were 143 marriages in 1990.

24. The average age at marriage for women has gone up in Xalatlaco, according to the civil registry: it fluctuated between 17.5 and 18 in the 1910–50 period and has been around 20 since 1960.

11

From *Metate* to *Despate: Rural Mexican Women's Salaried Labor and the Redefinition of Gendered Spaces and Roles*

GAIL MUMMERT

Van a la congeladora al despate de la fresa pero se van porque le tienen miedo al metate.
—LINE FROM A CORRIDO

*I*n 1965, when the strawberry boom hit the Zamora region of Michoacán in central-western Mexico, Ruth was one of hundreds of women from small villages in the surrounding countryside who flocked to work in the first packing plants. Her entry into salaried labor in the urban center sparked severe criticism from her fellow villagers, much like the line above sarcastically suggests, that women went to work destemming strawberries in the packing plants to escape the *metate*, the stone used to grind corn for tortillas, and a symbol of female duty. Tongues wagged, insinuating that Ruth's father was no longer able to support his family and that she and the other women were prostitutes who would return to the village with twins.

Today, several of Ruth's granddaughters who commute daily by bus to the plants during the six-month strawberry season encounter no such resistance. The packing plants are now considered suitable workplaces for young women, and the job has become a rite of passage for teenagers (often barely out of elementary school) anxious to earn money.

How the perceived challenge to existing gendered spatial divisions and roles was resolved over the course of two generations by a rural population is the subject of this essay, which is based on an anthropological case study of the village of Quiringüicharo.[1] From the vantage point of the anthropologist, my purpose is to understand the mechanisms through which the gradual molding of new gender roles occurred in a particular setting.[2] On a broader scale, I will deal with the issue of what this reshaping of male and female domains has meant for the different generations of rural working women themselves, their families, and the community. By exploring the historical peculiarities of one village I hope to relate the changes now under way to a wider context. I will show, for example, how family structure and organization have been affected by women's involvement in the wage economy on a substantial scale.

From a life course perspective that privileges "transitions in individual lives and the decisions associated with them,"[3] women involved in income-generating activities are differentiated by their marital status. Jobs and workplaces are culturally defined as appropriate or inappropriate to a particular marital status. Young unmarried women are permitted to engage in extra-domestic salaried work. Spinsters, widows, and the abandoned (all viewed as exceptional instances of women without men) may also do this type of work, but married women's place is considered to be in the home. These distinctions by marital status throw into greater relief the renegotiation of the web of obligations of family members toward one another now under way in peasant households.

By following different generations of women through their courtship, marriage, childbearing, and child-rearing periods, I will show that women's nondomestic wage labor—in conjunction with other trends—has led to incipient sociocultural change in nuptiality, fertility, postmarital residential arrangements, intergenerational relationships, gender roles, and domestic power. Thus, this apparently narrow case study raises issues of vital importance to our understanding of the changing places and spaces of rural Mexican women.

The Setting

Quiringüicharo is an agriculturally based mestizo community of some three thousand persons located between two regional agroindustrial centers (Zamora and La Piedad) in the state of Michoacán in western Mexico. Since the 1960s, in addition to women's paid employment in the strawberry-packing plants, which I will analyze in detail below, the villagers have witnessed and participated in two other key processes that have changed not only their forms of livelihood but the very fabric of social interaction.[4]

The first process is male wage-labor migration to the United States. Quiringüicharo is located in the very heart of the principal migrant region of Mexico, and the departure of its able-bodied men has become a veritable exodus since the 1960s. Discouraged by the vagaries of rain-fed agriculture and encouraged by the prospect of building a nest egg of dollar earnings, the first migrants were adult men who left their families behind to take seasonal agricultural jobs in California. Especially since the 1980s, however, the flow has increasingly comprised more and more young single males who prefer service jobs in Chicago's periphery. Currently, one-sixth of the village's population shuttles back and forth between the United States and Mexico, sending remittances back to Mexico to support the family or to finance house construction or improvement.

Second, the drilling of irrigation wells in Quiringüicharo during the 1980s increased the trend toward mechanization and commercialization of its agriculture. Cash crops such as tomatoes, wheat, and sorghum now link farmers to regional markets, although in a disadvantageous position vis-à-vis large-scale merchants. Basically in the hands of older former migrants, the agricultural sector—now capable of producing two cash crops per year—nevertheless remains a risky business, and not all are willing or able to invest in it. Roughly one-third of the village's 607 families have access to *ejido* land; some others farm privately owned land. Landless families generally resort to emigration and regional wage labor.

To fully appreciate the extent of the changes under way in male and female roles and spaces, it is necessary to look back at the patterns that prevailed until approximately one generation ago.

Traditional Gender Roles in Quiringüicharo

Until the 1960s the lives of the peasants of Quiringüicharo were governed by clear-cut spatial and temporal rules regarding male and female activities as well as parental and filial rights and obligations. Men were the undisputed patriarchs of family life, responsible for adequately supporting large families with their work in the fields as day laborers, *ejidatarios,* or private landholders. For help with the farming and livestock raising they counted on their oldest sons, the heirs who would one day head the family holdings. In turn, children (particularly sons) felt responsible for providing for aging parents.

Women's realm was the domestic, and in the absence of running water and grinding mills for corn, household chores were extremely time-consuming. Daughters remained cloistered in the house, emerging only for such tasks as fetching water or washing clothes in the river. Courting was rigidly restricted by parents, forcing couples to resort to surreptitious love letters or whispering to each other through holes in the wall under cover of darkness. Such vigilance of marriageable women was deemed necessary because violent abductions and forced unions with virtual strangers were not uncommon. Potential marriage partners were drawn from the village or within a small radius of surrounding communities, and brides were as young as thirteen or fourteen. Sexuality and marital relations were largely taboo topics in this peasant society, even between mother and daughter.

Once married, the daughter moved physically and socially under the tutelage of her mother-in-law, whom she served, literally, until the new couple was able to establish some degree of independence. This often took many years, and even then she and her husband generally still lived within the husband's paternal household compound. A bride thus severed most ties with her own parents' household in terms of claims on her labor and received no inheritance from them. Her married life was marked by frequent childbirth, and in some cases by periods of absence of her migrant husband.

Women without men had few alternatives for supporting themselves and their families. Widows and those abandoned by a migrant husband generally eked out a living by resorting to extensions of the domestic role—washing and ironing clothes or grinding corn and making tortillas for the better-off villagers. A few were seamstresses; others were involved in petty commerce of eggs, groceries, or prepared food. Spinsters, on the other hand, generally lived with aging parents and, theoretically, were supported by their married brothers. A spinster daughter normally received some type of inheritance (e.g., a house, livestock, or land) in gratitude for the succor she afforded her parents in their old age.

Renegotiating Gender Roles

The entry of women into salaried work outside the village beginning in 1965—in conjunction with the development of transnational migrant circuits, the commercialization of agriculture, and other broad processes of change at work in the region—challenged the traditional gendered organization of this peasant society. The following comparison of the diverging work experiences of women of different marital statuses (single, never married; unmarried; and married) will point out the extent to which roles are specific with respect both to gender and to a woman's place along the expected path from single to married life. Each case will be exemplified with a vignette describing a real-life experience drawn from extensive interviews with villagers.

WORKING DAUGHTERS: THE FIRST FRESERAS

Overwhelmingly young and single, Quiringüicharo's initial strawberry workers (known as *freseras*) tended to come from large, landless families whose day-laborer fathers struggled to support them. Most had had little or no schooling, but the job required none; basically, only manual dexterity was important. There were two types of jobs in the packing plants. The majority of the workers stood all day long in front of crates of strawberries and removed the stems. This task (known as the *despate*) was paid at a piece rate per crate, so a woman earned according to the number of crates she completed. Dexterous *despatadoras* earned more than the average agricultural day laborer. The other workers (called *revisadoras* or *canaleras*) stood in front of moving belts and selected the destemmed strawberries according to size and consistency to be either frozen for export or ground into strawberry jelly. Many women from Quiringüicharo were promoted to this category, which paid by the hour. A few years after the plants opened, workers gained access to the state's system of socialized medicine; other benefits such as provision of uniforms, transportation, and profit sharing varied greatly from one plant to the next. Although a few men were hired to work in the freezers, maintain machinery, and transport products, the packing plant has always been predominantly a feminine workplace.

Confronting Male Opposition. The crux of men's opposition to women working in the packing plants was that it challenged their manhood on two counts: their ability to support the family, and their ability to control "their" women's movements. Common reactions of husbands and fathers were, "Why do you want to work? What needs of yours do I not fulfill?" Innuendo suggested that away from the watchful eye of the male guardians of their honor, women would turn to illicit liaisons with strangers. Boyfriends told their sweethearts: "If you go to work in the plant, you can forget about us." In the face of such visceral reactions, the acceptance of the plant workers as respectable persons who contributed to their family's well-being through their earnings had to be based on the dissipation of such fears and the gradual molding of new gender relations.

For their part, the packing plants began selecting women recruiters from the village. Generally somewhat older than the majority of workers and well known to the local populace, the recruiters served almost as chaperons who reassured parents that their daughters behaved properly on the job as well as en route to and from the plant. With few exceptions, the young workers demonstrated that they were capable of upholding the family honor while channeling much-needed cash into the family coffers. Until this opportunity for female salaried work emerged, parents expected more in the way of financial aid from their sons than their daughters. But having a daughter or daughters earning a salary (even in this notoriously low-paying sector) was a valuable asset to a peasant family with ten or twelve mouths to feed. With the availability of electricity, running water, and wells for drinking water by 1970, the domestic chores became less onerous and mothers could more readily forgo their daughters' assistance during the six-month strawberry season. Typically, one daughter remained at home to help with the domestic tasks, from which the freseras were excused.

As women generated monetary income to supplement the goods and income produced by the male head of household and other male family members, the balance of domestic power was called into question. Their spatial mobility may have increased, but young women had limited control of their income and little to say about how it was spent. Most of the first freseras turned over their entire earnings to their mothers. Others channeled resources directly into the family's greatest needs, such as food, in some cases conscientiously circumventing the siphoning of hard-earned resources into male vices (such as alcohol). The formation of mother-daughter alliances against irresponsible and physically abusive husbands/fathers constituted a form of female resistance to a society molded by patriarchy. In families with other sources of income (e.g., migrant remittances), the daughters' income was used to finance everyday needs, thus setting the stage for a more rapid building of family patrimony in terms of land, agricultural machinery, livestock, and so on.

> Tomasa, the daughter of a landless peasant family, had virtually no schooling; her family of eleven was too poor. When Tomasa was eighteen, she and another sister were among the first handful of women from Quiringüicharo to stand for two days in a row in the hot sun to enter the packing plant. Initially, no bus service was available for the workers to commute; they had to stay overnight with relatives or friends in the urban center until such time as they themselves arranged to pay for private transportation from the village to the plant. After only two months as a despatadora, Tomasa was promoted to the position of revisadora, where she earned nearly twice as much and came into contact with women from other villages for the first time. Tomasa handed her salary over to her mother, who in turn gave her bus money and bought her clothing. Eventually, four sisters from this family worked simultaneously in the packing plants while the mother and younger sisters did all the housework. By putting aside savings from the earnings of her four daughters, the mother was able to purchase some furniture for their home.

WORKING WOMEN WITHOUT MEN: SPINSTERS, WIDOWS,
AND THE ABANDONED

Mature women without male partners are of particular interest to the extent that, being in limbo between "not yet married" and "married," or between "married" and "no longer married," they are allowed to bend, to a certain degree, the norms regarding gender roles. Moreover, in a setting of massive male emigration and local violence (at least through the 1950s), the number of permanent spinsters was striking, and widowhood was not an uncommon (or necessarily a transient) experience for women.

The opening of the packing plants marked a new role for these unmarried women. Women who (out of personal preference or parental opposition) did not marry, as well as those unfortunate enough to have lost their spouses, could legitimately engage in salaried work. Although the pay was low and seasonal, it meant much-needed cash for their families and was perhaps less demeaning than performing domestic tasks for others. In fact, some former strawberry workers in this category were able to use their savings to start small business ventures in the village.

Elena, one of the youngest daughters in a landless family whose migrant father abandoned them for eight years, began to work in the packing plant at the age of twenty. First a recruiter for a new plant that opened in 1969, she rose to the post of supervisor of revisadoras. Although she had two serious suitors, her prospects of marrying were diminished by her family's move to a neighboring village during her courtship years and her dedication to her work. From the time of their father's death in 1975, she and her younger sister (also a spinster) have proudly provided for their aging mother and themselves without any assistance from their siblings. Elena bought a plot of land and built a house for the three women. When she was given a newborn baby to raise in 1984, she left the packing plant after nearly two decades of work and began to support her family by selling clothing. She hires a woman to help her octogenarian mother with household chores while she sells fruit and candy in the main square.

The men in Elena's family are largely absent figures. The father proved to be a poor provider whether present in the village or absent in California, and her two brothers emigrated to distant southeastern Mexico. Unlike her two older sisters, who followed the more traditional trajectory of early marriage (paving the way for their offspring to be caught up in the fever of migration and strawberry plant), Elena and her younger sister postponed marriage indefinitely and assumed roles as breadwinners that in other historical circumstances would have fallen to their brothers. As a spinster who raises an adopted child and supports her widowed mother, Elena has forged an alternative path to marriage and childbirth.

Lupe, a mother of four in her late thirties, was widowed in 1970; her husband left her a small house, a plot of land, and four children to raise. Leaving her youngest in the care of her daughter-in-law, who shared their small house and had young children of her own, Lupe turned to work in the packing plant to support her family. She did so for some eighteen years, joined by her elder daughter at one point, while her two sons migrated to the United States. Although she stopped working when her younger daughter reached the age of thirteen, Lupe continues to participate in union watches at her striking plant in hopes of being rewarded with an indemnization. Reflecting on her years as a strawberry worker and her childhood as the daughter of a schoolteacher forced to moonlight in order to make ends meet, Lupe remarks: "I wish that there had been opportunities for women to work in my youth so that I could have helped out my father. But in those days, women didn't go out— they stayed in their houses."

WORKING WIVES

Some wives and mothers also joined the ranks of the first freseras, although they were a minority. Invariably their husbands were agricultural day laborers and initially opposed to the idea. But the women argued that the household head's salary was insufficient to support the family, and they would be helping the children eat and dress better. One mother accompanied her eldest daughter to the factory, leaving remaining daughters in charge of the youngest siblings. Another wife eventually got a job for her husband in the plant. Some mothers worked until the eldest daughter reached the age of thirteen or so and was able to replace her as a wage earner.

> Eva, a mother in her late forties when the packing plants opened, was married to a day laborer. When one of her daughters asked for her father's permission to work in 1967, he referred the decision to his wife. Eva, who had seen her own widowed mother support her children by performing domestic tasks for others, decided to allow her daughter to go, but only if she herself accompanied her: "I wanted to know what it would be like to work in the packing plant. Many women from the village were working there and had told me about it." Entrusting the younger children to her mother, Eva and her daughter began to work "in order for the family to eat better." They faced criticism from Eva's brothers, who said that they had given her away to be supported by her husband, not to support *him*! Although she had never learned to read and write, Eva, like many other women, learned to write her name to claim her pay in the packing plant. She worked the day shift and did housework and made tortillas at night or early in the morning.
>
> "I felt like a bird out of its cage" is how she describes her contentment on the job. "At home one is always thinking about things to be done, worrying about the children, being very busy. In the plant one is just destemming. I didn't even think about the house. I felt free from worries." Over the course of more than two decades, she moved from plant to plant, joined by other daughters and sometimes a son. Mostly

she destemmed strawberries; for a time she was a supervisor, but her support of a fellow worker unjustly fired by the union leader caused her to descend the ladder once again to despatadora. A few years ago, she was injured in an on-the-job accident, but the same union leader covered up the matter and Eva received no compensation. She continued to be employed in a physically nondemanding position (handing out toilet paper in the bathroom) until 1990, when she turned seventy. She was unable to retire, since according to the official records she had not accumulated sufficient weeks of employment to qualify. Now at home with her husband, Eva depends on assistance from her married daughters and the harvest of a plot of land sharecropped by her son. "These last few months I haven't gone to work because I am ill. But I don't feel right at home. I like to work."

NEW ROLES: WIVES OF MIGRANTS AND MIGRANT WIVES

When the emigration of married males became increasingly common in the 1960s, wives were called on to assume new roles as de facto household heads during their husbands' absence.[5] They learned the management skills necessary to handle the remittances sent home by their migrant husbands, including banking, buying materials for house construction, and supervising land cultivation. With their husbands away for most of the year, and sometimes longer, women "lived as widows," often carrying single-handed the burden of raising children, attending to family holdings (land, animals, etc.), and making ends meet when remittances were not forthcoming. One way of making ends meet was working as a fresera, sometimes without the husband's permission or knowledge. While the proportion of married freseras is somewhat higher today than it was in the early years, they are still a minority.

Traditionally, married male migrants have preferred to leave their wives behind for two reasons: to maximize earning power, since the cost of raising a family in the United States is considerably higher than in Mexico; and because they do not want their wives and children to be exposed to what they consider the corrupting effects of U.S. society. Relatively few married women have joined their husbands in Chicago or California, and those who have come must negotiate with their spouses to be able to work outside the home. Recent interviews with young male migrants on the outskirts of Chicago indicate that on the whole they continue to share this view: the majority are opposed to the idea of Mexican women coming to work in the United States, although some have called for their wives to accompany them.

Recently, however, a few single women from Quiringüicharo have migrated to the United States to work, generally settling in with older siblings.

María and Julia, two sisters in their twenties, came to Chicago in 1990. Both former strawberry workers, they are the eldest children of an eleven-member peasant family with a plot of rain-fed land. As such, they feel a strong obligation to send as much of their earnings as possible to their parents and siblings in Mexico: "We came to help our family get ahead. Unlike other families in Quiringüicharo, we don't have irrigated land and we women are the oldest." They joined a brother and neighbors in Chicago, where, thanks to migrant employment networks, they obtained jobs as hotel maids. In Chicago, María met a man from Guadalajara, and she returned to her village to marry him in a traditional church wedding. Comparing her courtship in Chicago with courtship in her village, she says, "My courtship days in the village were nice, but there the boys tend to be *machista*. I'm not the type of girl who likes that attitude. They only want to do what they think. My husband is more understanding. He values me as a woman." Though she would like to work longer before having children, her husband's opposition and the downturn in Chicago hotel business over the winter months account for her present unemployment. Her younger sister, a junior high school graduate who was unable to continue her studies for lack of funds, holds down two jobs in order to help the family back home in Mexico. Outspoken and self-confident, both sisters feel that they have learned responsibility and self-reliance as a result of their emigration.

WORKING DAUGHTERS TODAY

Today, having lost much of their perceived danger as unfamiliar territory, the packing plants are widely deemed to be appropriate workplaces for the young women of Quiringüicharo. The number of workers from the village now surpasses two hundred, and they come from all social sectors. In fact, this work has become a rite of passage for girls, much as going north is for young males.[6] While neither form of work has lost its primarily economic motivation, they have become so ingrained in youth's experience that they constitute the natural thing to do, regardless of family status. In the words of one teenager, "All my friends were going to the packing plant; only I was staying behind. So I decided to go to work, too." Although most young people finish elementary school, they prefer the life of a wage earner to that of a secondary school student. Such disillusionment with higher education as a way to get ahead is widespread now in rural Mexico, unlike a few years ago, when giving their children a profession was a goal many families sacrificed to achieve. Youngsters today point to the many well-educated villagers who work in the United States in menial jobs alongside the uneducated. Yet, clearly, the motivation to go north—or to work in the packing plant—is more than economic. For young men, going north is an adventure and an opportunity to gain independence from the family and live among peers. For young women, working as a fresera represents an escape from the drudgery of household chores and the monotony of village life, a chance to meet new people and expand horizons, as well as an opportunity to earn and spend money.

Over the course of one generation, the perception—on the part of both workers and their parents—of the obligation to hand over earnings to the family has changed dramatically. While some do contribute as much as one-half of their salary directly to their household, others spend it entirely at their own discretion, usually on clothing and makeup. In a very real sense, this type of expenditure by a young woman constitutes an investment in her future by allowing her to more effectively enter an increasingly competitive marriage market. Mothers (many of them former workers themselves) tend to support such use of income, favoring their daughters' immediate enjoyment of the fruits of their labor, in sharp contrast with their own experience of contributing to the building of a family patrimony in which they—as members who married out—did not share. A sort of complicity is forged between mothers and daughters who share the packing plant experience, similar to that between fathers and sons regarding migration to the United States.

Clara, Fátima, and Ema are teenaged sisters whose father died in 1988. The family of seven was left with little more than their home and a small plot of land. Initially, the widow received financial assistance from migrant nephews. Soon afterward, like their mother and aunts before them, the two elder daughters (then only fourteen and fifteen) began to work in the packing plant to supplement what little income their widowed mother could earn at odd jobs (doing laundry for neighbors, selling prepared food). Ema, who had shown some intellectual promise, was encouraged by the others to continue in secondary school, but she soon succumbed to the lure of earning her own money. The three daughters contribute approximately half of their earnings to the family's income and spend the rest on clothes. When the strawberry season draws to a close at the onset of the rainy season, the three sisters turn to agricultural fieldwork. Though picking is physically more demanding than their factory jobs, they earn more picking tomatoes, in less time, than they make at the packing plant. Often they work for relatives, but they receive the same wages as nonrelatives.

The three sisters' combination of factory and agricultural work reflects the opening up of yet another "male" space to women. Due to the village's shortage of males, caused by emigration, it is also part of a larger trend toward an increasing proportion of female day laborers in the region. Such role overlap—women doing work traditionally considered men's—is on the rise throughout western Mexico.[7]

Women Crossing Boundaries

As the strawberry workers commuted daily from rural to urban areas, moving into and out of agroindustrial wage labor while residing in households dependent on agriculture and belonging to a peasant society unevenly swept up in capitalist relations, they crossed a number of boundaries, which Rhoda Halperin has labeled spatial, institutional, and cultural.[8] Let us examine each type of boundary in turn.

Young women—particularly those of courting age—moved outside the house and into unknown environments beyond the vigilant eyes of their parents. The breakdown of traditional *spatial* barriers was aptly summed up by an old-timer who complained, "It used to be that pigs roamed the streets while women stayed at home. Nowadays women roam the streets while pigs are penned up at home." Despite the increased mobility of women of all ages, their whereabouts continue to be more strictly monitored than those of male counterparts. Wives of migrants are particularly aware of the village's watchful eye, for gossip (whether warranted or not) is sure to travel quickly north to their spouses.

The workers' daily departure from the household to the plant implied a second type of boundary crossing: an *institutional* or organizational one. In other words, new types of relationships organizing social interaction emerged. Unlike the home, founded on a patriarchal organization that confined women to the domestic realm and subjected them to male authority, the workplace was a public, feminine domain where village women met and worked side by side with women from other communities and under the protective, maternalistic wing of female supervisors and union leaders. Women designated as recruiters for their village determined who would be offered employment and who would be recommended for the better-paying, more coveted work stations. These instances of women wielding power and occupying decision-making positions in the public sphere (even though high-level plant decisions were still made by male managers) were new experiences in institutional terms. At the same time, these rural women became acquainted for the first time with an industrial workplace organized along U.S. standards imported along with the American owners. For example, unlike the destemmers, who chatted and even sang as they worked, those who selected the strawberries from the moving belt had to work silently in order to concentrate on their task. Their willingness to comply with this type of industrial discipline was perhaps facilitated by the women's upbringing of obedience to elders and figures of authority; yet, even today, some workers state a preference for a particular plant where the pay is lower but disciplinary measures are not as strict and they can enjoy working more. As we have seen, women from Quiringüicharo earned a reputation as "good workers" (i.e., efficient and disciplined), and many were rewarded with promotions. They nevertheless participated in plant strikes and, as we have seen, on occasion confronted corruption on the part of union leaders.

Third, the women workers crossed a *cultural* boundary closely linked to the spatial and institutional ones. The forty-minute bus ride between village and plant implied a quantitative leap that led them to experience new cultural meanings. How they responded to these meanings is a measure of the clash of values and beliefs into which salaried work catapulted them. A female union leader from Zamora paints the following (almost humorous) picture of the first freseras of rural background, their heads covered by shawls, entering the packing plant where U.S. standards of hygiene in food processing required them to wear white caps over their hair. Rather than doff their rebozos, without which they felt naked, they put the caps on over them. Confronted for the first time with flush toilets—the union leader explains—rural workers stood atop the seats of the fearful contraptions. Many of the first workers related a certain feeling of displacement, of being looked down on by their more urbanized counterparts. Yet, on a deeper level, the strawberry workers gained a sense of self-worth and legitimacy as breadwinners for their families that the vignettes included in this essay clearly portray. In retrospect, the vast majority of workers insist that they worked to aid their families. Perhaps, like many of today's working women in Mexico, they legitimate their entry into the labor force in terms of economic necessity.

Of course, Quiringüicharo's migrants to the United States cross not only these boundaries but a very real international border as well. Interestingly enough, both men and women are aware of the fundamental differences in gender roles in the two extremes of the transnational migrant circuits in which they are involved.[9] Both accept the fact that while she is in the village, a married woman's place is in the home. Most men strongly disapprove of American values and perceive as particularly menacing a society where—in their eyes—women rule the roost and parents have no authority over their children.

Clearly, the crossing of these three types of boundaries—brought about largely by female salaried work, massive male emigration, and the commercialization of agriculture—has had broader implications for villagers' lives. Let us now turn to a discussion of emerging roles and spaces for rural Mexican women, as reflected in the important changes under way in patterns of family formation, residential arrangements, and intergenerational relationships. Though these changes are only incipient in Quiringüicharo, they appear to follow the nation's overall demographic trends and have been instrumental in the reshaping of gender roles in this setting.

Family Formation: Courtship, Marriage, and Childbearing

Largely as a result of migrants' exposure to U.S. culture and the freseras' increased contact with nonvillagers, courting patterns in Quiringüicharo have become much more open: couples now have ample opportunities to meet and get to know one another. They may meet in the plaza and talk at the gate to the girl's home. Dances and parties are daily occurrences at year's end, when the migrants return and matches are made and cemented in marriage. Although fathers seem to be having a difficult time accepting the new mores, mothers tend to consider such openness preferable to the surreptitious meetings of their own courting days and the frequent elopements necessary to circumvent parental disapproval. Mothers also see the increased communication with their daughters on matters of sexuality as a positive change.

The age at first marriage is increasing. Whereas previous generations of women were wed as early as fourteen or fifteen, today's brides are more likely to be nineteen or twenty. Apparently, youthful goals (attaining a higher level of education followed by a stint as a wage earner) as well as parental and church pressure to wait are responsible for this trend. Increased opportunities to meet potential partners from other places means that exogamy is also spreading, although most villagers continue to select spouses from the same village.

In concert with the dramatic overall reduction in Mexico's fertility rates since the 1970s, family size in Quiringüicharo is declining. Despite the Catholic church's continued opposition to contraceptives, many women agree on the need to limit family size to three or four children. Contraceptives and counseling in their use are available at local health clinics, and according to 1991 records, slightly more than half of married women of child-bearing age use them, especially young mothers.

RESIDENTIAL ARRANGEMENTS

Two forces have contributed to the trend toward neolocality among newly married couples. First, many single male migrants' goal is to own a home before marriage, and they earmark their remittances for that purpose. This is particularly true in the case of younger sons whose older migrant brothers have already contributed substantially to improving the parents' abode and standard of living in general. Interestingly, women do not contribute to their future home before they are married. For example, furnishings purchased by a single fresera remain in her parents' house when she marries.

Second, the successive subdivision of family compounds to accommo-
date married sons has nearly reached its limit. Given population growth and
the increasing attractiveness of land for growing cash crops (if it can be
irrigated), the village has little room to expand its residential area.

For the young wife, the trend toward neolocality means that the period
during which she would, by tradition, have lived with and "served" her
parents-in-law has been either drastically shortened or eliminated altogether. Neolocality seems to be facilitating the redefinition of intergenerational relationships; more and more conjugal decisions are made without
consulting the in-laws. Yet, ironically, if the husband migrates, the new bride
may move in with her parents-in-law or return to her own parents' household to avoid gossip and prevent placing herself in a dangerous situation as a
woman alone. Fears of infidelity run rampant in migrant communities.

INTERGENERATIONAL RELATIONSHIPS

Increased control over monetary resources by young persons of both sexes
has definitely influenced the traditional hierarchy of power and authority
within the family unit, weakening the claims parents can make for filial
support. This trend is, of course, closely linked to the widening of differences between the goals of the two generations.[10] Cases of migrants or
strawberry workers who make no contribution to family income where
there is a clear need spark criticism from parents and other family members,
but little pressure is placed on such offspring by the family to comply with
their perceived filial duties.

Kinship ties have by no means lost their significance. Many older siblings
continue to ease the way for younger ones (e.g., by paying for their education) and support parents in their old age. In this particular context, however, the web of obligations of family members toward each other (especially
children toward parents and brothers toward sisters) is undergoing a lengthy
process of redefinition.

Conclusions: The Redefinition of Gendered Roles and Spaces

In Quiringüicharo, traditional gender roles and gendered spaces were challenged by the confluence of several processes of change, notably the availability of salaried work for women and men's large-scale emigration. Men
struggled to retain their image as sole providers for the family, largely by
emigrating and sending home dollars, but they soon realized the advantage
of women working in the packing plants to improve the family's lot. The
resulting redefinition of long-standing gender roles and spatial schemes was
surprisingly swift for a peasant society.[11] By limiting such employment to

the years before marriage, the society attempted to retain the basic gendered division of public and private spaces within married life.

As women began to meet outside traditional village confines (e.g., church, corn-grinding mill, creek, afternoon embroidery sessions), they came into contact with persons from a broader range of backgrounds and witnessed females holding positions of power in the workplace. Strawberry workers from Quiringüicharo have themselves risen to supervisory posts, and they have doggedly participated in the drawn-out fight for rights to profit sharing in one plant that became a cooperative, and in a lengthy strike in another. Their trade union experience taught them new organizing skills while making them aware of corruption and politics in the workplace—abuses perpetrated by women as well as by men.

Tomasa, herself one of the first freseras and now a mother of freseras, aptly sums up the changes wrought in women's self-esteem and behavior over the years of factory work: "Things have changed since women started to work in the plants. The village has progressed. Before we didn't have enough to eat. Now families can buy food and clothing. The girls have changed, too: they are not afraid to go out alone; they go wherever they want. It used to be that we didn't even know what the nearby town was like and we didn't talk to anyone who wasn't from the village. Now the girls have girlfriends and boyfriends—why, some even marry boys from other places whom they meet in the packing plants!"

The experience gained through generations of salaried labor has spilled over into home and community life, affording today's women a wider range of action and an embryonic sense of empowerment. As for the power relationship underlying gender roles, there is increased participation of wives and daughters in family decision making (regarding, for example, labor force participation, marriage, childbearing, or migration of a family member). Middle-aged women compare their daughters' more equitable relationships with their spouses with their own sense of powerlessness in the early days of marriage: the mistreatment and humiliation by in-laws, the need to pressure the husband to found an independent household in which they could make decisions without the extended family's constant interference. Clearly, most young wives today are not willing to adopt a submissive role when faced with physical abuse or adultery on the part of their husbands. Young girls are adamant in their views, and they reject being victimized: "I don't think like my mother did that one must put up with whatever kind of husband one might happen to marry."

Yet, a period like this one of redefinition of gender roles and gendered spaces is a time of turmoil. Changes do not flow in a unilinear fashion, as in an elegant model, from female subservience to emancipation. Ambivalence and contradiction abound. Some villagers interpret women's mobility and the growing input from wives and daughters in household decisions as signs of loss of respect: of children for parents, and wives for husbands. Nevertheless, a reshaping of gender roles and spaces is undeniably under way in Quiringüicharo. As in other historical times and places, it is a product of the combined impact of structure and agency, of women and men seizing opportunities created by broad processes of socioeconomic change. To that extent, the rural Mexican women I have focused on here crossed boundaries and created new spaces for themselves both in the workplace and in the household.

NOTES

I gratefully acknowledge the support of El Colegio de Michoacán, the institution in which my project was conducted, as well as the financial assistance of the Asociación Mexicana de Población. A 1991–92 visiting research fellowship at the Center for U.S.–Mexican Studies of the University of California at San Diego afforded the opportunity to write up my research. Finally, the central argument was honed thanks to critical remarks from Sergio Zendejas.

1. My six-month field study, conducted in 1991, included a village census, a family-level survey of household structure and organization, and in-depth interviews and observations on topics such as family division of labor, decision making, budgeting, residential patterns, and inheritance practices. Interviews were also conducted in 1991–92 with migrants in Chicago and in California.

2. I adopt Jean Lipman-Blumen's notion of gender roles as "all those cultural expectations associated with masculinity or femininity that go beyond biological sex differences"; see *Gender Roles and Power* (Englewood Cliffs, N.J.: Prentice-Hall, 1984), 3.

3. George Alter, *Family and the Female Life Course. The Women of Verviers, Belgium, 1849–1880* (Madison: University of Wisconsin Press, 1988), 10.

4. Undeniably, other, broader processes are also at work in Quiringüicharo. Foremost among them are the rising level of education of rural Mexicans and the role of television in making rural folk aware of events beyond the local sphere and exposing them to alternative cultural models. Acquiring a complete elementary education in the village has been possible since 1971, and a secondary school was constructed on its outskirts in 1986. Therefore, while I will focus on the three processes considered to be crucial by the actors themselves, one should not lose sight of the possible impact of other factors.

5. I discuss these new roles for migrants' wives (as well as for women migrants) in greater detail in Mummert, "Mujeres de migrantes y mujeres migrantes de Michoacán: Nuevos papeles para las que se quedan y para las que se van," in *Movimientos de población en el occidente de México*, ed. Gustavo López Castro and Thomas Calvo (Mexico City: El Colegio de Michoacán, Centre d'Etudes Mexicaines et Centraméricaines, 1988), 281–97.

6. The identification of the packing plant with the feminine role is illustrated by the oft-heard remark at the birth of a daughter: "You had a fresera."

7. Also see Patricia Arias and Gail Mummert, "Familia, mercados de trabajo y migración en el centro-occidente de México," *Nueva Antropología* 9.32 (1987):105–27.

8. Rhoda Halperin, *The Livelihood of Kin. Making Ends Meet "the Kentucky Way"* (Austin: University of Texas Press, 1990), 139.

9. Here I draw on Roger C. Rouse's concept, which he defines as the constant circulation of people, money, goods, and information between settlements that have become so closely linked as to form a single community spanning a variety of sites on both sides of the border; see his "Mexican Migration to the United States: Family Relations in the Development of a Transnational Migrant Circuit" (Ph.D. diss., Stanford University, 1989), 2–3.

10. Rouse analyzes such a generational divergence of life projects in an immigrant community: migrant sons were not willing to sacrifice their ambitions in obedience to parents' wishes; see "Mexican Migration to the United States," chap. 4.

11. The swiftness of the change can be appreciated in the fact that younger sisters were granted permission to work in the packing plants while this was denied to older sisters only a few years earlier.

12

Changes in Rural Society and Domestic Labor in Atlixco, Puebla, 1940–1990

Maria da Glória Marroni de Velázquez

*T*he reconstruction of women's participation in historical and social processes involves a critique of traditional paradigms. Historians have habitually constructed a history of men which ignores the presence of women or focuses on a heroine who plays a masculine role in the execution of "important" deeds. These conceptualizations are not the result of a misogynist conspiracy. Rather, they reflect a philosophy underlying the construction of knowledge which privileges the macro, the structural, the economic and political; monumental events and great currents; the formal and objectively demonstrable, which is almost invariably associated with written documents and statistical truth—in synthesis, the public world. In consequence, the social, the micro, the little currents, the informal oral tradition, the subjective, and the spaces of everyday life are made to seem secondary and inconsequential.

This methodology fosters the historical absence of women. When we look for them in male spaces, we cannot find them. "Things outside belong to him, those within are yours," Diderot counseled his married daughter.[1] If we search for women in the spaces where they can be visualized—the private sphere—we seem to be accepting the discourse dividing reality into two artificial, oppositional, and mutually exclusive spheres: the public and the private. Through examining the spaces to which women have been culturally and epistemologically relegated, however—the private world—we may discover their presence in the public world, demonstrate their integrated roles in both spheres, and describe a dialectical social division of labor in which both sexes participate. This essay considers the private space of women in intimate connection and interaction with the public world. Rural households demonstrate this integration well. The campesino family unit synthesizes the confluence of public and private worlds and requires the participation of women in both.

My examination of campesino agriculture in the valley of Atlixco in the state of Puebla is based on written sources, both historical and statistical, and three years of extensive fieldwork and interviews.[2] In this essay I will show how technological change and the pressures of capitalist development on small-scale agriculture render the dichotomy of public and private spheres useless for understanding women's work. A series of technological and infrastructural changes have enabled women to combine reproductive tasks with productive work, an ability increasingly demanded by economic conditions. At the same time, women's reproductive work extends into the public sphere. The resulting heterogeneity in women's work across spheres is not as readily complemented by a similar tendency among men, who are reluctant to assume tasks in the reproductive-domestic sphere. Men are much more bound in their labor practices to a separation between private and public. Further, both men and women approach technological changes that affect women's work with ambivalence, especially when these threaten socially constructed notions of gender identity.

Structural Change in Four Atlixco Communities

During the sixteenth century, the valley of Atlixco, an important indigenous region, served as New Spain's granary. At the end of the nineteenth century, during the Porfiriato, agriculture expanded here in response to urbanization and the opening of new markets. The expansion was based on a structure of land tenure formed by haciendas, ranchos, and villages with access to land. The haciendas, dedicated to wheat and sugar production, controlled the best lands and most of the water. During the revolutionary period (1910–17), the zone became involved in agrarian struggle, partly because of its proximity to Morelos, the cradle of Zapatista agrarianism. The division of the haciendas was accomplished soon after the Revolution: 80 percent of the *ejidos* were awarded between 1925 and 1930.[3]

Sociocultural change since 1940 and its impact on rural women in the valley are examined here in four representative communities: Huaquechula, San Juan Tejaluca, San Pedro Benito Juárez, and Tezonteopan de Bonilla. The first important change occurred in the 1920s when agrarian reform, or ejidalization, created the basis for renewed campesino production. Subsequent changes in crop patterns occurred in the 1940s and 1950s when water resources were redistributed. In Tejaluca, intensive cultivation of vegetables, fruit, and flowers replaced wheat growing. In Bonilla, the same products substituted for sugar cultivation. Huaquechula lost its rights to water and entered a period of agricultural decline. Although ejidatarios and small property owners there still produce and market corn, beans, vegetables, and peanuts, the town now depends on urban employment and emigration. Productive processes hardly changed in San Pedro, which remains an area of subsistence agriculture and livestock grazing combined with exploitation of the forests in the folds of the volcano Popocatepetl. In all the towns, women market the small livestock and fruit they produce in their small gardens.

The valley of Atlixco yields a diversity of crops not frequently encountered in small regions. On the ten thousand irrigated hectares in the valley, crops such as onions, squash, cucumbers, coriander, and avocados are grown, along with flowers; corn, beans, and peanuts predominate on the nonirrigated land. Overall, the villages maintain family agriculture that, broadly speaking, is commercially oriented, diversified, and minifundista. Patterns of production differ within and between villages, as does the use of nonfamily labor. Modern technology is used selectively, and the zone remains distant from modern agriculture in the sense that water resources are poorly managed, property is excessively fragmented, and traditional practices of productive organization and commerce prevail.

Social differentiation is pronounced. A small group controls the resources (capital, transportation, channels for marketing, property, and public office) in each community. Beyond this privileged group, social structures are diverse. San Pedro has a homogeneous mass of impoverished campesinos. Bonilla's majority is closer to the middle strata. Tejaluca's population is divided into ejidatarios with access to irrigation and a landless, impoverished group. Huaquechula has the most diversified social structure, the result of nonagricultural sources of income.

Families in all the villages rely increasingly on nonagricultural external income from regional wage labor and migration to Mexico City and, especially, the United States. Young single women may go to Puebla or Mexico City to enter domestic service. Young men, single and married, and a growing number of women, also single and married, work in the service sector in New York City. The trip to New York is costly, so migration is not a function of poverty. In prosperous agricultural families, emigration of family members may form part of a strategy of accumulation, with remittances used to improve the productive infrastructure at home. In less-well-off families, remittances are used to meet immediate consumption needs.

Since the 1940s, infrastructural transformations in communications, energy sources, and urban services have affected women's work in the four communities. Between 1940 and 1950, mechanized transportation (buses and trucks) was introduced and gas-driven corn grinders (*molinos de nixtamal*) came into use. At the end of the 1960s, electricity was installed. In the late 1980s, domestic gas began to replace wood and charcoal. Roads were paved, and transportation services to Atlixco improved. Telephones, drainage, and bathrooms made an appearance.

Services are unevenly distributed within and between the communities. Huaquechula and Bonilla have the most complete and best-distributed services. Huaquechula is a municipal seat located twenty-seven kilometers from Atlixco and linked to the Atlixco-Matamoros highway by a paved road. Bonilla, the agricultural center that has prospered most, is located close to the Atlixco-Matamoros highway twenty-one kilometers from Atlixco. By contrast, San Pedro Benito Juárez, seventeen kilometers from Atlixco, is linked to the city by unpaved roads and lacks public lighting and drainage. Only 20 percent of the families there use domestic gas. San Juan Tejaluca, just outside of Atlixco, has easy access to the city but lacks drainage. There is a distinct difference between the services enjoyed by the ejidatarios who occupy San Juan's center and the landless population on the periphery: homes in the center have electricity, wells, and gas; households on the periphery generally lack these. In all communities and most households, access to water is a problem, and this has important implications for women's lives. Even in urbanized Huaquechula, the system of wells providing water for domestic use is defective. In San Pedro Benito Juárez, only a few houses have their own wells.

Symbolizing the integration of the productive and the domestic, houses are generally situated on large plots of land where small livestock, fruit, vegetables, and herbs are raised and seeds and crops are stored and sometimes processed. A confluence of economic, social, and infrastructural factors has resulted in three types of houses, which can be classified as follows:

1. Houses built with local materials and consisting of one room or two separate buildings. Houses of this type lack windows and have a dirt floor and a palm or laminate roof. Family belongings consist of sleeping mats (*petates*) or a wooden platform that serves as a bed; some bedclothes; clothing, which is hung on the walls; small benches; a table and/or chairs; clay, metal, or plastic utensils; a calendar; a portrait of the Virgin; some photographs, a radio, an electrical appliance or two, and a variety of small animals. These are concentrated in a single space where the family both sleeps and lives. Almost always there is another, partially closed, space that functions as a kitchen around the *tlacuil*, the earthen hearth.[4]

2. Houses with a similar exterior but larger, with covered floors and roof, and more divisions in the internal spaces. The principal room serves as dormitory, living room, and sometimes kitchen. It contains double beds

with sheets and mattresses, cupboards, electrical appliances, utensils of china and plastic, a calendar, framed photographs, and religious portraits, many of them mounted on a flower-bedecked altar.

3. Houses with an urban, popular design, painted, with various rooms, mosaic or cement floors, and windows of glass and iron. The rooms are differentiated by their functions, making this a "modern" house. The living room has chairs. The beds are in a separate room. The utensils and decorations are diversified and ratify the passage to modernity. There are water faucets and sinks, gas heaters, and ventilators. Rustic installations housing the animals and work instruments are in the backyard. Sanitary spaces are behind them.

The types of houses present in the community depends to a degree on the socioeconomic strata present. Huaquechula and Bonilla have the most diversified housing. San Pedro Benito Juárez has primarily rustic and deteriorated housing. Differences between houses and the items they contain also depend on cultural approaches to income management, priorities in spending and investment, and, above all, on the influence of migration. Migrants always include electrical appliances in their remittances.

Women's Work and the Sexual Division of Labor

Women's work in the valley of Atlixco shows remarkable similarities at the macroregional level of analysis and across communities. Increasingly, women's work takes place in both public and private spheres and involves both productive and reproductive work. Men, on the other hand, more strictly guard the sexual division of labor and seldom enter the so-called private, domestic, reproductive sphere of work. However, there are important differences in women's work according to the social stratum or class. These differences relate to the degree and frequency with which women are incorporated into the wage labor force; that is, the level of impoverishment of landless families and, in the case of the most prosperous producers, the degree to which wives manage and supervise agricultural activities.

Despite the ideological construction relegating women to the reproductive, domestic sphere, Atlixco women have traditionally participated in production. In their household patios they cultivate fruit and small livestock. They generally help cultivate the family parcel as well, although this is considered a public space. Under the rubric of *ayuda* (assistance) women intensify their participation according to the agricultural cycle. The degree of surplus generated by the family unit helps to determine women's participation in agricultural work, dictating whether women can confine their productive work to the family unit, retire from it to confine themselves to the domestic sphere, or are forced to look for income from other sources. The most prosperous families generate a surplus which requires hiring wage labor and sometimes results in the wife leaving the fields—an act that improves her status—although a surplus can also increase the wife's participation as she must supervise and attend to the wage workers.[5]

Women in very impoverished families are often obliged to seek wage work. Intensive vegetable and flower production in the Atlixco Valley has stimulated the growth of a regional labor market, which has become feminized. Flowers and vegetables are considered delicate "feminine" crops that require "meticulous care." Men prefer migration to work that has been defined as female.[6] Although in some regions of Mexico the wives of migrant husbands do not work outside the household, wives in Atlixco may work in horticulture outside the family holdings.[7]

True to long-standing indigenous traditions, women also participate in market trade. A woman's commercial activities are economically important and have implications for her position in the family. Her contact with the public world, her freedom of movement, and the interregional mobility implicit in these activities can provide her with some autonomy in certain spheres and under specific conditions. Her participation in commerce projects her into the public world of business. More than simply wives of producers, many women are wholesalers and retailers of family produce. They interact with Atlixco merchants and with municipal officials responsible for the administration of commerce. There does, however, appear to be an inverse relationship between the volume of commercialized family production and women's market participation: women tend to manage the small surpluses, whereas men manipulate the large ones.

Women's work in the public and private spheres is intertwined with the organization of family life, which reflects campesinos' transition from subsistence agriculture to other sources of income. The patrivirilocal system of residence, centered on mechanisms of patrilineal inheritance, remains the point of departure for new couples and is the basis for a familial division of labor sustained by the presence of several women in the household—the mother-in-law and her daughters-in-law as well as young daughters and single adult women. A rigid sexual division of labor is complemented by flexibility in work tasks among women of distinct generations and situations. In addition to their remunerated and productive work, women are responsible for domestic tasks. Men are insulted at the idea that they might do domestic work. Women asked about this option respond with surprise and irony, mixing resentment, resignation, and fatalistic acceptance of a role they consider determined by their biological condition as women.

Obscured in this discourse, however, are a few signs of men's hidden participation in "feminine" work—not in the care of clothing, cooking, or direct attention given to small children, but, for instance, in the carrying of water and wood, usually considered women's work. Women's activities in marketing, and their resultant absence from the home, sometimes create situations in which men have to undertake "women's" functions, although this is almost always done in a sense of emergency because the woman is not available.

Some men temper their demands on women when the latter are integrated into productive activities—during periods of intense fieldwork, for example. In such situations, women also demand less of themselves in relation to their domestic work. This is not a generalized norm, however, and in most cases women must reconcile their diverse public and private tasks.

The Integration of Public and Private Spheres, and the Division of Labor Among Women

A brief description of women's reproductive work makes it apparent how this work and its organization intersect with the so-called public world. The performance of reproductive tasks is organized within the context of a division of labor among women in the household.

Domestic tasks and socioaffective reproductive work are at the heart of women's relentless daily routine. Of the first, the most obvious are cleaning the house, washing and ironing clothes, mending and sewing, and food preparation. Today, most households purchase their clothing, and women are no longer required to make clothes for everyone in the house. Laundering, which can involve carrying water or going to its source, is a major effort. Some women use nearby wells or springs; others have wells in their yards; a few lucky ones have tubs with running water in their yards or patios. In the interviews, women identified walking long distances to do laundry as one of the greatest difficulties of domestic life. Women have been active in struggles to obtain water services and are almost always responsible for solving this problem for the family.

Of the socioaffective tasks in family maintenance, the most important are health care, care of the old, the socialization of children, and a series of activities linking sociability with specific functions (the organization of fiestas, participation in religious activities and group activities to solve community problems, and communal labor in the village). Women are responsible for the family's health. The prevailing combination of traditional indigenous medicine and modern medicine demands intense participation. Women devise strategies for preventing and controlling particular illnesses. In the past they relied on ancestral knowledge and native cures to control common respiratory and gastrointestinal infections, but they are turning increasingly, although reluctantly, to modern medicine. For muscular and bone problems, local *hueseros* (literally, "bone experts") continue to enjoy prestige, and although the data are imprecise on this point, most women seem to continue to use local midwives and traditional methods of childbirth.

Women are decisive in the socialization of children, above all in their schooling. Taking them to school, participating in school activities, and meeting with teachers are all women's work. The school's role as a dynamic center for the expression of communal sociability and issues has diminished in recent decades. The school has increasingly become a space for instruction and formal training separate from the "pueblo." Teachers no longer necessarily live in the village, and their links with the community have decreased as their work has become professionalized, demystified, and modernized. This transition makes new demands on women. There is a consensus that education is a resource for social mobility, or at least a necessary weapon for confronting life. It is not enough that children attend school. The family must help in the children's scholarly success. Women provide this support in areas such as helping with homework, even though they may lack the necessary preparation.

Acceptance of girls' schooling has generated changes in the organization of family labor. The oldest daughters are now exempt from domestic chores, and the workloads of the adult women have increased proportionally. Before, the oldest daughters took care of their younger siblings so their mother could more easily assume her functions outside. This organizational scheme has not been entirely lost, however, because not all girls attend secondary school.

Finally, women work in a variety of communal social contexts. Along with men they perform *cumplimientos,* community tasks decided upon consensually and generally involving public works. Religious or lay festivals are basic forms of sociability and enjoyment, and they are almost the only forms of entertainment permitted to women besides television and radio. Women's participation in festivals is governed by rules of gender separation. They decorate the church and provide costumes and food, while the men arrange for music and drinks and make speeches.

Although there is little tolerance for other pleasurable activities, especially when this implies mobility outside the community, there are accepted ways for women to subvert this socially constructed rigidity. Young women, for instance, are allowed to go to Atlixco and spend the whole day in search of work, without this work's being defined or made explicit. The Atlixco market is the window of opportunity for married women. There they escape the closed, everyday world. They talk with each other, exercise their assertive skills, and enjoy themselves over a fruit cocktail or some other pleasure they can purchase and savor with friends.

Domestic work is distributed among women of the family in consonance with the work requirements of the entire productive unit. The distribution is flexible and specific to family strategies, which balance macrostructural constraints and opportunities with microfactors such as the socioeconomic level of the family, their aspirations, the family size, and the ages of the women and their individual characteristics. I focus here on the variables of age, individual characteristics, and socioeconomic level.

Although young single women appear to have two concrete alternatives—study or wage labor—most go through a period between the ages of thirteen and sixteen when they have finished with school, are not engaged to be married, and have not embarked on the "adventure" of migration. They find this situation uncomfortably indefinite, and they and their families try to correct the matter through accepted channels: marriage, emigration, or, rarely, stable work in the community.

The young woman who opts for marriage begins her married life living in her husband's home. The care of children is the responsibility of the adult women of the family. Because of the early age of marriage, mothers-in-law and daughters-in-law may have young children at the same time. In this situation one of the women may take care of all the children, freeing the other or others for different activities. In any case, women in their reproductive years concentrate on activities related to child care, without abandoning the necessary productive activities.

Women beyond their reproductive years have greater autonomy outside the home and participate more in family decision making, depending on factors of class and income. Wives of producers with profitable holdings seem to enjoy more autonomy. They may intervene in activities related to the family parcel by dealing with hired laborers and marketing the crops. But there is a large group of older women, married or alone, whose extreme poverty reduces their possibilities for autonomy.

Women's personal characteristics influence their functions in the family. Individual talents are mobilized and used for the group's interests. This is clear in marketing. In principle, marketing is the responsibility of older women because they are more experienced in dealing with the public world, but the family also selects the most competent of its young women to train for this activity.

Among the recent changes that have affected the distribution of work among women in the family are alterations in the patrivirilocal system of residence, most commonly a shortening of the period of cohabitation with the husband's parents. Living with one's mother-in-law is not a gratifying experience. "Mothers-in-law are nasty" and "He who marries in his own home will leave it" are typical negative observations. Even older women, the privileged mothers-in-law, favor changing the practice and encourage young couples to establish their own households. As land loses its importance to family survival, the traditional residential pattern is changing. Young couples move out when they are capable of sustaining their own households. If the husband enlists in the army or the police, his wife and family follow him to his post.

Changes in patrivirilocal residence can alter the division of labor among women in the household over time. Ideologically, the abandonment of the old premise that the daughter-in-law must serve the mother-in-law increases the decision-making capacity of the daughter-in-law and terminates the hegemony of the mother-in-law. Economically, the absence of numerous women of at least two generations can reduce flexibility in the organization and performance of domestic work. It is not possible to generalize about these changes, however, because, on the one hand, they are gradual, and, on the other, the extended family is often reinforced through men's emigration because the wives of absent men stay in the households of their in-laws.

The Kitchen: The Generic Space of Transformation and Tradition

In campesino communities, the house captures the complex relation between new and old, between modernization and tradition. The logic that new goods ought to be consumed—used, repaired, and replaced—has not yet penetrated community beliefs. As old parts of the home deteriorate, even well-off families continue to use them. An informant from San Pedro, the community least integrated into consumption, affirmed that purchased items are protected rather than used. This tendency is a widely accepted norm in impoverished and prosperous households alike: what is new is used less. Customarily, strangers are received in the traditional spaces, not the new ones. This might be interpreted as a natural form of defense against outsiders, but even when people know each other, the "best" areas of the house may be off-limits in order to preserve them.

The house is the woman's dominion, and her attitude determines the use, consumption, conservation, and recomposition of domestically used goods. It is she who adopts, or does not adopt, new household technologies or new forms of organization. Changes are not easy to perceive. Technologies are slow to be adopted and do not seem to affect women's lives significantly in immediate terms. Rather than discussing the domestic innovations that have modified their lives, women tend to historicize them. Their measure of time surpasses their personal space to locate transformations in generational terms and in long-term processes. "When my grandmother was little . . ." "When my mother was a child . . ." are expressions women use to describe change. They say that the most important transformative processes of the last forty years are the introduction of domestic gas, the molino de nixtamal, and more accessible water.

The essential nucleus of a woman's life in the private sphere is her responsibility for feeding the family, especially when the family lives close to the subsistence level and she must dedicate much energy and time to the task. Feeding the family involves a gender division of labor permeated by socio-affective relations and dictated by the organization of domestic life. Several factors enter into play, including eating customs, patterns of consumption, disposable income, costs in human energy, the adoption of or resistance to new technologies and their availability, and the insertion of this activity into the daily life of the family.

Daily food preparation requires addressing three problems: (1) obtaining wood, charcoal, gas, and/or water; (2) making tortillas and preparing other foods; and (3) taking the food (*comida*) to the husband in the field. Women always bring meals to the husband and other family members working in the fields; it is an unquestioned practice. If the land is located some distance from the house, transporting the comida may require a big investment of energy and time—up to two hours daily.

The physical space of the kitchen is the material expression of the socio-affective relations linked to food. It is also the generic space in which tradi-tion is transformed or maintained. By the 1980s, two spaces were often used to prepare food, representing the interconnection between the old and the new. The traditional kitchen has an earthen floor. In it is the hearth, or tlacuil, over which the *comal*, a flat pan, is laid for cooking tortillas. Clay or metal utensils are stored on the floor or hung on the walls. Low wooden benches or stools make up the furnishings. Often, this kitchen is partially open to the outside and has a thatched or laminate roof. The modern kitchen has a gas stove, a table with chairs, a cupboard, and electrical ap-pliances. In the urban-type houses owned by prosperous families, walls separate the combined kitchen and living room from the bedrooms; in other houses there are no walls dividing the modern kitchen from the sleeping quarters.

This combination of modernity and tradition is the concrete expression in women's lives of the transformations they have experienced and are expe-riencing. Although there are differences according to class and community, women generally spend more time in the old kitchen. They seem better able to identify with utensils they manage with ancestral knowledge than with new appliances and sources of energy. This resistance does not mean that women reject the new technologies; on the contrary, these are increasingly incorporated. Rather, it reveals a reluctance to abandon ancestral ways. Two sets of ideological factors are at work here: a fear of managing new tech-nologies such as gas stoves, and the feeling that this technology ought not replace women's skills, knowledge, and functions.

The humble tortilla represents this ambivalent mentality. Not without reason, Mexican culture has been called the culture of corn. Daily reproduction of campesino life is permeated by this grain, which, in the form of the tortilla, is the basic food in the three daily meals. In the Atlixco Valley tortillas are eaten with salsa and beans, a vegetable, avocado, herbs, and sometimes eggs. Other elements of the diet are *atole* (a corn beverage), tea, coffee, chocolate, soda pop, beer and *pulque* (alcoholic beverages drunk in great quantities), pasta, rice, bread, and fruit. Better-off families diversify the diet, but not much.

The technological innovations in tortilla making epitomize the modifications in women's domestic work. First came grinding mills fueled by gas, introduced between the 1930s and 1950s. In the 1960s electric mills came into use. The mills save time and energy for women by eliminating manual grinding, which is remembered as one of the most burdensome of women's tasks. Women had to begin grinding at four o'clock in the morning in order to have tortillas ready for breakfast. Oral testimonies, however, indicate that the grinding mills were not immediately accepted by all. Many women continued to grind by hand out of attachment to traditional ways and skills.

The introduction of the mills not only saved time, it represented a form of transition in women's domestic tasks from isolated household work to collective activity. Going to the mill became not only a daily task but a new form of sociability. Today, campesina women begin their descriptions of work by saying, "I go to the mill to grind the nixtamal and come home to make tortillas."

Only small improvements in tortilla-making technology occurred after the 1960s. Innovations in food preparation brought about by the introduction of domestic gas and new appliances such as the electric blender were gradually integrated and superimposed over older methods. The two kitchens syncretized the process of transition. Complete conversion to gas cooking was inhibited by the tradition of making tortillas on the comal over the tlacuil.

I believe that the persistence of manual methods of preparing tortillas indicates women's refusal to abandon traditional forms of gender identity in situations of accelerated change. Most women resist purchasing tortillas in the new *tortillerías*. Preparing tortillas requires an hour or more of work every day, depending on the quantity made. The craft is part of women's experience, duty, and social gratification, even when the amount of time they invest is increasingly in contradiction to their new roles.

As with all technological innovations, cultural factors interrelate with structural ones. Jaime Aboites argues that the adoption of the technology for producing machine-made tortillas has various requirements that the rural sector finds it difficult to meet.[8] There must be a high, concentrated, and constant demand for the product, but campesinos tend to use home-grown corn for their own consumption.

The following reflections on tortillas articulated by Señor Fer, an eighty-one-year-old ejidatario, and his fifty-four-year-old daughter, Señora Da, both relatively well off, are illustrative.

Interviewer: You do not buy tortillas?

Da: No, because we don't like them.

Fer: They are not cooked. They are raw and stick together.

Da: We don't like them, and what we don't like we never buy.

Fer: We make them to suit our taste.

Da: And then we know how they are made. You buy tortillas and then you have to separate them. I never got used to buying them. I have to make tortillas because that's correct.

Interviewer: You don't remember the time they ground corn by hand?

Da: Yes, my mother did it. I remember when the mill opened. Many people went there but others did not. They didn't like the *masa* ground that way. My mother ground her own masa. Things are easier now. At least there is the blender. Before we had to grind chile, tomatoes, everything at the *metate.* Now, we use the blender, which is much easier. Most people use the blender now. We don't have the customs we used to. People are getting civilized. If people don't buy the new things, it is because they don't have the money.

How does this process of "getting civilized" interfere with gender relations? Empirical observations make it clear that distinct social and age groups and the two sexes have very different views of modernization's effect on women's lives. The following extract from an interview with Señor T. A., a seventy-six-year-old campesino, is illustrative:

Señor T. A.: In work, women have gotten used to bad habits, to being lazy. . . . They leave the house, the house the man supports. A woman rarely thinks about helping her husband prosper.

Interviewer: What changes have benefited men?

Señor T. A.: In the same way I have just told you . . . now the woman, pardon me for saying this among you women, buys everything for the man already made, even his underpants.

Interviewer: Who benefits?

Señor T. A.: Industry . . . but women benefit too. For example, if the man says, "I want chocolate," she answers, "I'll go to the store and buy it and then I'll come home and prepare it." Before, she ground chocolate and coffee in the house. Now in what house here do women make atole every day? These changes benefit women but men get treated badly. "The party's over" is the first thing the woman tells the man.

Despite the considerable subjectivity in the interviews, it is possible that Señor T. A.'s affirmations condense the memory of a whole generation of men who see modernity as a threat to their domination. For them, the commercialization of goods previously produced by women confined in the home does not represent liberation from arduous work but a rupture in the form of the relations that guarantee male dominance. Women themselves may not perceive it as liberation, especially when they weigh their work against the men's. Señora Licha, a forty-two-year-old campesina married to a well-off ejidatario and the mother of six children, was asked the question, What do women do here?

> *Señora Licha:* What do we do? We make tortillas and go to the fields. In March, we sow. After May, we begin to work the milpa: women weed. When the harvest is ready, we raise it. We make tortillas and go to the fields to pick.
> *Interviewer:* What work do men do in the house and in the fields?
> *Señora Licha:* Here in the house, they don't work. When they get up, they feed their animals and go to the fields, and when they return, they don't do anything. With us it is different because we go to the fields and when we come back we have to make dinner. The men don't do anything in the afternoon. What would they do?

Conclusion

The private sphere has been ideologically constructed as women's reduced space; it is also the most internal dimension of social life. Counterposing this space with the public world results in cosmovisions that reinforce relations of gender inequality. The private world is the world of permanence, of immobility—the world "against change." The great transformations are related to macroprocesses and are attributed to men as the agents appropriating nature and constructing society. Women are assigned no more than a passive, conservative role perpetuating tradition in its most negative sense. Confining women to the private sphere guarantees masculine domination on the basis of the formulation public-active-modern versus private-passive-traditional.

These cosmovisions create an artificial separation, however, and a Manichean vision of the world, which requires revision. The brief description above of the domestic sphere of Atlixco campesina women demonstrates the inadequacy of this construction. The campesino family unit's productive functioning involves an organization that blurs the limits between domestic and productive activities. Increasingly, the conditions of rural life diminish the separation. On the one hand, women are engaged in productive, remunerative activities; on the other, the performance of traditional reproductive functions draws them into the public sphere. Survival requires women to create a strong link with the public world. Women often stimulate change because they propose and participate in the transformations of their communities. But they are not always direct agents of change. Innovations that may benefit women in the long run are not necessarily proposed or readily accepted by them. Women may be especially ambivalent when innovation threatens socially constructed notions of gender identity.

NOTES

I am grateful to Mary Kay Vaughan for her comments and for translating the Spanish version of this essay.

1. Cited in Elizabeth Badinter, *O que e uma mulher?* (Rio de Janeiro: Nueva Fronteira, 1989), 17.

2. The research described in this essay is part of a wider project about rural societies that I am carrying out at the Universidad Autónoma de Puebla.

3. See *Catalogo de la Propiedad Definitiva Ejidal y Comunal* (Puebla: Gobierno del Estado de Puebla, Secretaría de Reforma Agraria, 1984). Today, there are seventy-five ejidos and 8,965 ejidatarios, plus some small private properties and various mechanisms of land use, including rental. See *Encuesta Nacional Ejidal 1988* (Aguascalientes: Instituto Nacional de Estadística, Geografía, e Informática, 1990).

4. The *tlacuil* is the traditional hearth used since pre-Hispanic times. It consists of three stones placed in a triangle around a fire on the ground.

5. See Gloria Marroni de Velázquez, "Trabajo rural femenino y relaciones genericas. Informe de investigación" (Programa Interdisciplinario de Estudios sobre la Mujer, Colegio de México, 1991).

6. Ibid.

7. For the opposite case, see Patricia Arias's essay in this volume.

8. Jaime Aboites, *Breve historia de un invento olvidado: Las máquinas tortilladoras en México* (Mexico City: Universidad Autónoma Metropolitana, 1989), 48.

13

Antagonisms of Gender
and Class in Morelos

JoAnn Martin

*I*n 1977 Mexico's ruling Institutional Revolutionary party (PRI) attempted to install an outsider—someone not born in Buena Vista, Morelos—as mayor.[1] In so doing the PRI violated a time-honored tradition: the mayor must be someone Buena Vistans "know." (His family, which dates back generations in the community, can be placed in the landscape of enduring political conflicts.) Buena Vistan men held nightly meetings to discuss the matter. The women understood that they, too, had to become involved because they are *mas astuto* (more astute) in such matters.

Doña Juana explained, "I said to my *comadre*, 'Let's go and see what is going on.' We got three more women together. [She leaned forward, eyes widening.] My comadre said, 'We are going to go in the night,' and I said 'yes'; so we went with our shawls wrapped around our heads [reliving the experience she pulls her shawl around her head, covering her face almost completely] and with our flashlights."

After the women arrived, they listened from behind the bushes before making their presence known. Finally, they walked to the center of the group of males and announced that they wanted to help organize. The men applauded. The women began organizing other women, and when the town's inhabitants marched to the state capital, the women marched in front. On election day the townspeople occupied the municipal building in order to count their own votes and declare the winner. When the army surrounded the building in an attempt to frighten them, the women offered the soldiers food and drink.

So goes the story of how Buena Vistan women became involved in politics, a domain that they say was previously restricted to men. In the story women draw on gender images from historical events to place themselves at the center of politics. Their journey into the night acknowledges the subtle violation of cultural norms. La Llorona, the ghost of a women burdened with guilt for having killed her children, also roams in the night. Clearly, the night is not a place for "good" mothers and wives.[2]

By building their politics on existing cultural themes women effectively established themselves as *both* astute political actors and newcomers to the political scene. Even men acknowledged women's experience and skill in mothering, and the women themselves connected motherhood to political issues such as corruption, community development, and resource distribution. A leader of the Buena Vistan Women put it very clearly in a speech to that group: "This [communal land][3] is a very important issue for women because this is the land that our children will use and that our grandchildren will use. Men will think of going other places. It is up to us to make sure that they have enough land to farm."

In 1984, when I first began my research in Buena Vista, these carefully crafted assertions of women's place in politics seemed to be the cornerstone of a developing "women's culture of politics."[4] Charges of corruption and abuse of power were leveled against those in authority, and because men dominated in these positions, women linked corruption to gender. Moreover, men's inability to support their families during the economic crisis became, in the discourse of the Buena Vistan Women, one with their failure to defend the community. The suffering mother fighting for her family's future seemed an apt metaphor for women's role in politics.

In 1984, between ten and twenty women attended each meeting of the Buena Vistan Women. Every evening during the week the women gathered in the plaza or in the courtyard in front of the church. Standing in small clusters of four or five, women exchanged information on the latest illegal land sales, water shortages, and injustices wrought by the corrupt bureaucracy. Later, when the *maestra* (teacher) appeared, the clusters gave way to a circle, the maestra in the middle. Some women toted young children, but most of the women had children old enough to watch their younger siblings at home. One impoverished woman, her clothes in shreds, her feet flapping in oversized men's sneakers, arrived every day with her dog. Doña Rosa, who boasted that she was still politically active at eighty years old, shuffled slowly into the meetings, greeting everyone with a wide smile, anticipating the latest political intrigues.

The group included mestizo women of different class backgrounds, most of whom hoped that in addition to helping the community the group would benefit their families. Four of the women owned small businesses (restaurants and corn mills), and the rest engaged in a variety of income-generating activities, from selling handicrafts to working as maids for foreigners and outsiders. Occasionally the group pooled money to help someone start a business or to send a member to the doctor. The poorer women looked forward to using the network of personal ties the group provided to find work for themselves or a child. But always, these elements of self-help were the subtle undercurrents in a discourse that emphasized women's care and love for their community.

In 1988 I returned to Buena Vista. Nervously, I disembarked from the bus. The plaza was unusually full even for the early evening. In the distance I spied a gathering of about a hundred people around the municipal building. As I mounted the steps to the building my friends-informants from the Buena Vistan Women surrounded me. In between hugs a vague but familiar tale began to emerge. "Pigs" had been elected to the presidency—perhaps through corruption—and they were going to destroy the town if they were allowed to take over. "Which pigs?" I asked. "The people from the Office of Communal Resources, those people that you were with when you were here last time."

For eleven days the women occupied the municipal offices. They entertained the crowd with traditional Nahuatl music and dance and provided refreshments and food for those who joined them. Proclaiming themselves the authentic Buena Vistans, they spoke to the crowds of their commitment to the community; they resolved to keep the office out of the hands of people who would hurt the town. After eleven days the governor intervened to form a coalition town government. The coalition included the male candidate whom the women supported as treasurer and the candidate of the Office of Communal Resources as mayor.

The contested election marked a shift in women's politics in Buena Vista. Prior to the election, and in more pronounced form after it, several of the women who did not own businesses in the center of the town left the group. Many joined an organization whose roots lay in the Committee to Defend Communal Land (Comité para la Defensa de Tierra, CDT), a group whose rhetoric was as decidedly class focused as the Buena Vistan Women's was community focused. In 1991 I again returned to Buena Vista. Doña Juana proudly showed me a picture of the group, nine women, all nicely dressed, with the governor in the center. I recognized the faces of Buena Vista's small-scale entrepreneurs, women who owned restaurants and stores in town. The group's rhetoric still emphasized motherhood and protecting the community, but those who had left the group claimed that the Buena Vistan Women were really only for themselves.

How can we interpret this shift in political alignments? Had the women exchanged a gender-based political identity for a class-based identity, and if so, can we understand either of these to be a more accurate reflection of their interests? Can the whole story be told through manipulating only these two categories? In raising these questions I intend to explore the seemingly antagonistic relation between the instability of identity and the demands of political participation.

Theoretical Interventions

The events that occurred in Buena Vista between 1984 and 1988 cannot be understood within a framework that assumes a split between the "ideal" and the "material" worlds, making the semiotic a mere epiphenomenon of political and economic processes. In this essay I view the semiotic as part of the material, productive realm of human activity so that meanings constituting activities can be viewed as having their own independent effects in the world.[5] My goal is to map emerging discursive formations and their roles as new objects of concern and reflection.

Consistent with this view of discourse, I distinguish between class as the economic processes "associated with production, appropriation and distribution of surplus labor" and class as a semiological system deployed in the political arena.[6] The latter can assume a multiplicity of meanings vaguely or not at all related to class as an economic process. Buena Vistans index "class" divisions in their relations to capital and land, but there is considerable slippage. A person may be labeled as either rich or poor according to the role of his or her family in local conflicts. Likewise, when I address the connection between motherhood and women's power I am not claiming any "natural" connection between women's position in the society and their role in rearing children. Rather, in the setting of Buena Vista, where women assume primary responsibility for child care, women's roles *appear* to them as biologically determined.

I came to appreciate the productivity of the semiotic when I discovered that I could not make sense of the dynamics of Buena Vistan political identities without taking seriously the role of language in producing the world. Taking language seriously meant following the identity claims of individuals and groups without demanding that those claims be grounded in a more stable political or economic analysis. Thus I became concerned with how discursive practices (narrative, political speeches, and folklore) and nondiscursive practices (the activities of work, family life, and politics) produce the experience of identity. Such an approach challenges us to incorporate the flexibility and fluidity of identity claims into an analysis of political movements.

With rare exceptions, scholars who become concerned with the social construction of identity tend to emphasize resistance rather than collective social movements as the site of politics. But the focus on resistance is problematic: If subjects are socially and discursively constructed, why and what are they resisting? One can argue that their resistance is enabled by the fact that as subjects they are located at the intersection of multiple relations of power that are expressed through competing discursive formations. But that answer begs the important question of what constitutes *competing* discursive formations. For example, what happened in Buena Vista between 1984 and 1988 to make it necessary for women to choose between the Buena Vistan Women and the Committee to Defend Communal Land? In order to answer that question we must understand social movements as at least one of the many institutional frameworks in which identity is produced.

Subjects are formed not only in individual or collective opposition; they come together in groups that reconstitute shifting identities as they try to develop a coherent project together. The multiple discourses that construct individual subjectivity at times threaten the coherence of group identity, particularly when political discourse pits aspects of identity against one another. Thus, the signifiers that emerge in political discourse are no more stable than those that shape the formation of individual identity.

In what follows I begin by illustrating the relationship between the discourse of women's politics in 1984 and adult women's roles in the household. This section situates motherhood discourses in the setting of potential conflicts over money and female morality within the household. It illustrates the contradictory place of women's political discourse in 1984 as part of an overall structure of household power in which older women attempted to maintain control over their daughters and, to a more limited extent, their husbands, but at considerable costs to themselves. In the next section I show how the discourse of the self-sacrificing mother when extended into the political arena subverts male power. The discussion of the Committee to Defend Communal Land sets the tone for analyzing the transitions that took place in both groups between 1984 and 1988.

Women's Labor and the Politics of Domesticity

In Buena Vista, income-generating activities center on the household division of labor, which places family members in distinct positions with respect to the flow of capital at the global and local levels. Wage labor is the province of young males and females; older family members engage in subsistence activities that compensate for the low wages the younger family members receive. The mother of the household manages the division of labor and tries to control expenses. Concerns about female morality constrain household strategies, and where there is a male head of the household (husband, father, or brother) the mother's management is subordinated to his needs and demands.

The outsiders (Mexican nationals and foreigners) who have settled in Buena Vista to enjoy the tranquil setting and the tourists who come in steady streams provide the primary source of cash and create opportunities for female employment. The effects of domestic labor opportunities for women within the community blunt some of the more "progressive" effects of wage labor noted in studies of female factory workers.[7] Domestic work places Buena Vistans in intimate contact with foreign employers and distances them from other workers. And these employers try to intervene in what they see as the less admirable aspects of local culture. They admonish their domestic workers not to marry too soon, to use birth control, and not to spend money on useless fiestas. They try to teach young women about "proper" nutrition and to inculcate habits of personal hygiene and household cleanliness.

Buena Vistan families sanction this employer-employee relationship in a variety of ways. They describe domestic labor as "working for the *señora*" (the woman of the family), minimizing any encounters females might have during the work day with the men of the household. Viewing the employer-employee relation within the idiom of patron-client ties, families boast about how well the señora treats their daughter and how kind and helpful she has been to the family. Employers reinforce the patron-client idiom by recommending other members of the family to new residents looking for domestic help. Over time the Buena Vistan family and the employer form a long-term relationship in which the family's pride as well as its income is shaped in relation to the status of their foreign employer.

At home, adult women preside over the household, setting an example for their daughters with their unending hard work and innovative income-generating activities. Most women wake up at five in the morning to walk to the corn mills in the center of town. Upon their return they begin household chores that are more easily performed while the family sleeps: washing floors, cleaning bathrooms (if there is an indoor bathroom), and preparing breakfast. After breakfast, mothers send children to school and other members of the household to work before they begin their own income-generating activities: making handicrafts to sell in the market, working as domestics, or managing restaurants or small stores. By nightfall they are once again doing household chores, often working past eleven o'clock. Daughters who are not in school help with these tasks, but the mother's exceptional skill and efficiency is widely acknowledged and praised by all members of the family.

The matrix of income-generating activities in which women engage means that there is no single definable site in which to locate the disciplining techniques of the labor process.[8] Adult women's identity is shaped by the devotion and self-sacrifice they bring to all their work, be it for the family, in wage labor, or in petty commodity production. Women take pride in their skill and cunning in inventing new ways of making money, and the government, church groups, and foreign donors reinforce their abilities by sponsoring classes in sewing and other skills. Income from petty commodity production flows directly into the household budget; the woman does not use it to pay for personal expenses.

Age and marital status intersect in gender iconography to elevate the position of the mother and wife, conceding control over daughters and daughters-in-law and to a lesser extent, sons and sons-in-law. When husband, children, and children's spouses comply with the norm by handing their income to the wife and mother, they do so because her faithful adherence to gender norms proves that she will manage the money wisely, in the interest of the family. Women do not expect men to be as trustworthy; they assume that men and boys waste money. But even at an early age daughters show signs of conforming to the pattern of self-sacrifice and hard work.

Although women clearly recognize the inequity in the division of labor and complain about the burdens it poses, they also embrace the inequality as evidence of their love for their children. Indeed, women help to elaborate the discourse of the self-sacrificing mother and promote these beliefs, values, and attitudes among their daughters. It is therefore not surprising that women's politics in Buena Vista drew its metaphors from the arrangements of domestic life. And, as in the case of women's roles in the household, the moral authority of the self-sacrificing mother buttressed women's power in the political arena.

Women's Political Culture in Buena Vista

In order to comprehend the hold gender symbolism exerts over women's lives, it is necessary to understand how images of gender, class, and age provide overlapping and contradictory scripts for women's lives and how women transform those images into sources of power. Women are not simply victims of power. Paradoxically, they constitute their own power through the discursive formations that render their tireless work in the household meaningful.

In the iconography of gender, Latin American women are accorded exceptional and mystical power based on their reproductive capacity. A woman can transform a macho man into a vestige of his former self with a drop of menstrual blood in his tea.[9] In Mexican lore, an Indian woman, derogatorily termed La Malinche, bears responsibility for the conquest and for the emergence of the race of mestizos. Sold as a slave to Cortés, La Malinche served as a translator and guide for Cortés and bore his child.[10] Furthermore, the appearance of the dark-faced Virgin of Guadalupe to an Indian boy, Juan Diego, marked the spiritual beginning of the struggle for independence.[11]

The images of the Virgin and La Malinche (also known as Doña Marina), although contradictory, evoke gender-specific forms of power relations embedded in motherhood and notions of redemption. Many scholars have argued that the two images place Latin American women in a double bind: in order to reproduce they must have sex, but in having sex they become affiliated with the violation and betrayal represented by La Malinche.[12] But this binary logic needs to be analyzed in historical context. Bernal Díaz del Castillo attributed charm, bravery, and cunning to Doña Marina; the Tlaxcalans praised her for freeing the subjected people from the "evil" rule of the Aztecs.[13] The separation between the Virgin and Doña Marina was the work of Ignacio Ramírez, who made the comparison in his 1886 commemoration of Mexican independence.[14] But the importance in popular imagination of the separation and the dual images it produces may be exaggerated. Speaking of Tlayacapan, in Morelos, Ingham observes that "there are, then, two Eves: the innocent Eve and the Eve of the Fall, *although both are one*. These considerations may explain why young girls dress as Malinches for the fiesta of the Virgin de Guadalupe. . . . The practice implies that Malinche is identified with the Virgin and indeed 'Malinche' is the diminutive form of Mary."[15]

Taking a page from Tlayacapan, we might point to the similarities between the two images. Both unite the private and the public, the personal and the political, to bring about dramatic changes in the course of history. The power of both is imbued with the mystical forces of the female body, the same forces that are expressed in beliefs about the power of menstrual blood, the redemptive powers of childbirth, and men's fear of being betrayed by their wives.

That men would attempt to bring the power of the church, law, and custom to bear in order to discipline this mystical female power is no surprise. What has received less attention is the subtext built into the narrative of history and gender: that at points of crisis women may call on their extraordinary power to reshape the course of history. In other words, the discourse of women's politics draws women into a seductive logic of gender relations, which is powerful because it builds on, yet transforms, culturally significant themes. In this process of transformation women's politics evokes the more unruly dimensions of gender symbolism.

Buena Vistan women describe their entry into politics in 1977 as "the time in which the struggle for *el pueblo* began." The phrase also reflects women's response to the economic, political, and community crisis that Buena Vistans were experiencing in 1984. Food prices doubled nearly every day, and many men were underemployed or unemployed. Women responded by inventing ways of compensating for declining family incomes. But the political crisis, whose roots stretched deep into the fabric of the Mexican state, was more intractable. Since the Mexican state consolidated its power in the 1940s, it has used centralized control of resources to dictate municipal elections, to determine the fate of communities by imposing development projects, and to direct the demands of popular organizations. Viewed in the light of this history, the state's attempt to impose an "outsider" as mayor in 1977 was one more intolerable affront to the community.

The reach of the state deep into Buena Vistan life colors attitudes toward politics and influences relationships within families and between neighbors. Most Buena Vistans encounter the state through their interaction with the local bureaucrats who staff municipal offices. These people allocate teaching jobs, control access to land and water, and solve legal disputes. They are also friends, neighbors, and family members who must be placated to get children into good schools or to get a good plot of land. The deployment of these bureaucratic practices at the local level intruded on distinctions between community and state and community and family, and transformed the governmental legitimacy crises into a general crisis of social relations.

The political rhetoric of the Buena Vistan Women linked the mother's role in the family, with its implications of honest self-sacrifice, to the town's need for officials who could resist the temptation to rob the public coffers. Many women believed that they were the ones taking responsibility for the family during the economic crisis; if men could not be trusted to handle the family budget, why should they retain guardianship over the town's future? Moreover, for women, but not for men, politics was an obligation—a burden—that they assumed because of their love for their children and their community. Strictly speaking, the proliferation of corruption did not follow gender lines. But, buttressed by gender iconography, women claimed that men's politics was self-interested while theirs was family-centered. Women had become involved in politics because they understood the link between community and family welfare; men entered politics to profit from community resources.

In 1984, Maestra Maria led the Buena Vistan Women because, as one member explained, "ella tiene la palabra." The literal translation, "she has words," accurately captures the way Buena Vistans view "words." Having "words" means being able to move people with public speech and gives one the right and obligation to voice the people's fears and anxieties, to speak out against injustice. Doña Rosa explained that everyone was equal, but the maestra was the authority. Just as a student does not begin to teach a class if the teacher does not arrive, the women do not hold a meeting if the maestra is not there. But those who have words occupy a tenuous position because gossip about those in positions of political power is one of the major tools shaping the definition of what a political group "really" represents. The wise political leader anticipates sources of division and tries to heal them through the power of her words.

The subtle class differences that characterized the Buena Vistan Women became, in the maestra's skillful rhetoric, the bonds developed by a common biology and a universal experience of need. My field notes from May 11, 1984, record a discussion that took place when Doña Juana stopped coming to meetings because she was afraid that she would not have the money to contribute to the various causes the group took up:

> Juana started to cry and said that she was not going to feel shame in front of the group. "I will tell you I am going through a difficult time because I am having these problems with my kidneys and the doctor tells me that I have to buy this very expensive medicine." The Maestra replied, "We should never be afraid when we have need, if it is not need of money it is need of companionship or friendship, and we should help one another in this because we all go to church on Sunday and we all know that God said we should help one another." . . . Then the Maestra told the group, "When I had need—I remember my husband was participating in the election and that cost us a lot of money—we lost our store and we had no money, I would ask people for money, and they would say 'no,' that I had everything with my restaurant, with my store and with my job. But, they didn't know I was paying 500 pesos a month for lights, for the telephone . . ." The women sitting next to me replied, "Of course you had need."

To view this discourse of community unity only as a calculated disguise of obvious differences in wealth would be misleading. The claims to universal needs, positions, and powers, although only partial truths, did for a time shape women's experiences of the group and reconstitute individual and class interests into collective desires based on the responsibility of mothers.

The Buena Vistan Women crafted a view of community in which differences fit into an overall pattern of harmony.[16] Internal differences in wealth, occupation, and social status contributed in their eyes to the overall strength and importance of the group. In their ideal construction of community, differences in power and resources complemented disparities in need. In contrast with the view that emerges in social theory, community was not an epiphenomenon of an underlying similarity but rather a force *sui generis*. The women expected that "community" would intervene in differences among themselves and transform them into a source of strength.

The concept of community, in any form, lends itself to a form of idealization that can obscure points of tension, and the Buena Vistan Women were no exception. But the tensions among the women were not, strictly speaking, over differences in wealth and power but over the perceived unwillingness of some members to use their positions for the benefit of other members of the group. As will become apparent below when I talk about transitions, discussions of who had greater need were at the center of many debates within the group.

The power of the discourse of the Buena Vistan Women lay in its ability to present a model, inspired by the role of the mother in the family, for achieving the desired community unity. At issue is the productivity of motherhood as a "signifier." For example, in spite of the subordination of adult Buena Vistan women to their husbands, mothers enjoy considerable power over their daughters. At the same time, ideologies of motherhood reinforce a division of labor in which women, regardless of age, create the surplus value that helps to support men. But in politics, the ideology of motherhood shapes demands that challenge men's domination of political life. Motherhood links women to a powerful, God-given mission; to evoke this imagery in the political arena is to draw attention to women's exceptional power. In the end these multifarious forces intersect to redefine women's position and transform their identity.

The Committee to Defend Communal Land

On Tuesday, Thursday, and Saturday evenings a group met in a tiny office not far from where the women held their meetings. Peasants arrived at the office, mumbling "*Buenas tardes*" (good afternoon) as they passed into the room to take their places on the benches that lined the interior walls. Most sat silently, heads lowered. The CDT was the invention of a teacher, Maestro Estevan, well known in Buena Vista for his radical politics. Few Buena Vistans doubted that the CDT would bear the imprint of the maestro's left-wing class politics, but the maestro preferred to emphasize his desire to help the poor of the community. By 1984, he had organized peasants to monitor the town's communal land and to take back land that had been illegally sold or taken over by private property owners.

Members of the CDT explained that they learned two important things when they read law books with the maestro: first, that no one had the right to collect taxes on communal or ejidal property; second, that the authorities could not distribute land without the approval of an assembly of ejidatarios and *comuneros*. Assuming the rights and responsibilities of comuneros set forth in the agrarian law, the group constituted itself as the Comité de Vigilancia, a watchdog group, to protect themselves and their neighbors from corrupt bureaucrats and from the rapacious appetite of outsiders for land.

The CDT based its interpretation of land categories on a 1929 presidential resolution that declared that for the purposes of adjudication all the land within the boundaries of Buena Vista would be treated as communal land. The 1929 resolution seems to confirm the land reform that Zapata, leader of the revolutionary forces in Morelos, carried out during the revolution. "It is all communal land and we are all comuneros. Zapata declared it all communal land," the maestro reminded members of the committee repeatedly. This interpretation contradicted that of many of the "progressive" members of the community, some of them members of the Buena Vistan Women, who viewed the sale of land as a "natural" reaction to the need for capital. His interpretation also linked the class project of the maestro with the preservation of "tradition," thereby ensuring an important place for elders in the CDT.

Don José was a member of the CDT who had the "words." An eighty-three-year-old peasant, he had been involved in land struggles for most of his life and could talk for hours about every conflict the town has had with its neighbors and with *los ricos* (the rich). He claimed a series of seemingly conflicting identities: Marxist, preacher in the Seventh-Day Adventist church, traditional healer, and, proudly, once a gifted womanizer. As the vice commissioner of communal resources, he used his authority to lecture those who brought conflicts to the CDT on traditional family values: families should not fight like enemies, children should respect their mothers who had shown them the light of day, families disgraced themselves when they took cases to court. And he counseled younger members in the glories of the past, when "the people were united." According to Don José, before the formation of political parties the elders met to decide who should be mayor. When they presented the mayor to the people, everyone would applaud and begin working together. Now, he complained, with parties, people put their candidates forward and if their candidate loses they fold their arms and will do nothing.

Although interwoven with images of community unity, Don José's view, and that of many others on the committee, emphasized a community of peasants united in confrontations with rich *caciques*. An older member of the CDT explained, "The rich fight to defend what they have, their capital; we fight to defend what we have, which is our work, our land."

That statement speaks to a notion of class that emphasizes the collective interests of the poor in controlling land as a strategy of protecting against the uncertainties of wage labor and as a reflection of love for the land. Peasants who work for the rich are seasonal workers. They have learned that los ricos do not "take into account the needs of their workers." The rich pay poorly and often expect long hours of work. More important, Don José complained, was the younger generation's declining love for the land. "Soon we will be eating *tacos de billetes* [money sandwiches]," he joked. That statement captures the "life-sustaining" aspect of working the land and highlights the absurdity of viewing wage labor as a substitute for working one's own land.

As I pointed out earlier, it is a mistake to assume any essential connection between class as it is defined with respect to position in a capitalist mode of production and class as a signifier in political struggles. In the case of the CDT, "class" discourse indexed not only a position within a mode of production but also a style of life that promoted a particular relation between human beings and the land, a gender order, and a sense of place in history. The coherence between these different dimensions of life was captured in representations of the poor, humble peasant, always a male figure. Such a person works honestly on the land to produce life-sustaining food, not commodities. Bowing to a higher order dictated by timeless tradition, he is not tempted by the lure of consumption or the promise of political power. He commands the respect of his wife and children, and if they fail to grant him this respect he takes appropriate measures.

At the level of politics, then, class is defined as a defense of a lifestyle rather than a position in a mode of production. And the central significance of this defense is its oppositional relationship to the lifestyle of the ricos, an opposition Buena Vistan peasants recall as a long-standing one.

To an outsider, the relative wealth of Buena Vista's own ricos pales in comparison with that of foreigners and Mexican nationals who have purchased land in the town. But the corpses of past political and economic fights in which individual families established a reputation as either ricos or *pobres* (poor) are firmly lodged in the memories of Buena Vistans. Often, these struggles involved control of land. Although historians who have studied Morelos argue that the Revolution effectively destroyed the land base of the rich, the categories of struggle from that period (e.g., rich and poor, caciques and indios) continue to inform contemporary politics.

In 1984 only three women in addition to myself participated in the CDT; the other twenty to thirty members were men. All of the women were young, single, and therefore "available." When the committee went on long investigations, we made the sandwiches for the journey. Along the way we endured "good-natured" flirting and jokes about male leaders weakened from "drinking the water," a reference to the devastating power of menstrual blood. The four of us never spoke in meetings, but we did share our impressions with the maestro afterward.

The communal land disputes that structured most meetings of the CDT provided a forum for subtle clashes between tradition and changing gender roles. When a woman threatened with eviction by the relatives of her deceased common-law husband brought her case to the CDT, the maestro used the opportunity to instruct committee members on women's rights. After she left the office, the maestro explained that "in the past the law did nothing for women in that position but now the law does protect them. It's obvious that she had been living with the man—she has grown children by him— What more evidence do you need [said with obvious sarcasm]?"

In 1984 changing gender relations was not on the agenda of the CDT, but poverty forced many of the women who had assumed responsibility for their families during the economic crisis to turn to the CDT to request a plot of land. Often, the women who came before the committee did not have a spouse to represent them. In some cases their spouses were away searching for work; others had been abandoned by their spouses. Like the case of the woman cited above, many of the women had never married the men who fathered their children. Emphasizing poverty and need, the CDT threaded carefully across the delicate terrain of gender relations in handling these cases.

Transitions

Indications of the antagonism between the class-centered approach of the CDT and the community focus of the Buena Vistan Women surfaced early in interactions between the two groups. The women argued that communal land should be given only to people from Buena Vista who had need, including professionals, small entrepreneurs, and others with children who might *eventually* need land. In contrast, the CDT thought that land should also be given to individuals who had come to Buena Vista from other states and settled as squatters on the town's land. The CDT could not explicitly defend the rights of outsiders to the town's communal land—the political cost would have been too great—but privately most members of the committee privileged poverty over territory in determining rights to land.

Between 1984 and 1988 numerous interpersonal conflicts between members of the Buena Vistan Women became interpreted in local gossip as an indication of the class origins of the most powerful leaders of the group. One such conflict was ignited when Doña Rosa, the oldest women in the group, died in 1987. Although she had two daughters, Doña Rosa left all her land and her house to her daughter Teresa, a single mother who had raised her family on the not insubstantial income she received from a small store. Her other daughter, Celia, who depended on her husband's sporadic income as a carpenter, received nothing. Both daughters had been members of the Buena Vistan Women, but, angry at her mother's "betrayal," Celia left the group.

That was not the end of the conflict, however. Two years later, Celia's son became engaged to Maestro Estevan's daughter. When the couple tried to register their marriage, a member of the Buena Vistan Women, now in charge of the civil registry, claimed that the young man had made another local girl pregnant. Celia attributed the attack on her son's character to her sister's opposition to the maestro's political activities. She was furious that her sister would use her position in the Buena Vistan Women to hurt her, and she claimed that the group sided with her sister because she was also a businesswoman.

When people share their injustices with others, as Celia did in this case, gossip transforms personal conflicts into general commentaries on inequality that demonstrate the ways the rich—those with economic wealth as well as those with words—use their power to oppress the poor. More important, the gossip defines who is rich and who is poor. In this way the discourse of long-standing political conflicts between rich and poor intrudes into the space of other rhetorics such as those of gender and community. These intrusions do more than force individuals to choose between competing loyalties; they redefine the *group,* rendering certain choices impossible.

In 1988, actions taken by the Committee to Defend Communal Land gave disgruntled members of the Buena Vistan Women another avenue for political participation. The CDT joined with the ejidatarios to establish a new ejido in Buena Vista, and many Buena Vistans who had little or no land, and some who already had land, received small plots. But the pattern of distribution broke with the long-established system of patron-client relations by granting land to people who were not members of the CDT. Even women who had worked with the Buena Vistan Women, by that time a more direct rival of the CDT, received plots. One former member of the Buena Vistan Women explained, "They [the CDT] did not know me. I had never worked with them, but they gave me land because they knew that I was poor." It was on the heels of this massive redistribution that a candidate supported by the CDT won the 1988 mayoral election. It was a short-lived victory, however. The constant complaints of the Buena Vistan Women—now comprising female small business owners—about his administration led the governor to remove him from office after a little over a year.

The quality of class and community as a signifier informs the fit between politics and identification/identity. By creating a new group of ejidatarios, the land distribution redefined class boundaries, forming a class category out of a mosaic of economic positions. In other words, the act of receiving land repositioned the women who received it, transforming them from gender subjects to class subjects. With the CDT's achievement of an identity based on class, the meaning of the discourse of the Buena Vistan Women shifted. Aided by gossip—much of it based on personal conflicts—from disgruntled former members of the Buena Vistan Women, the women's group began to appear to protect only the interests of small business owners. Their role in opposing the mayor seemed to confirm this class interpretation. With the identity of both groups stabilized around issues of class, women no longer were choosing between gender-based and class-based organizations, because the former no longer existed. And in the CDT, in which women now outnumber men, identities are still being reworked.

In one of the CDT's recent battles with the state over a development project, a woman stood to make a fiery and passionate speech about the need to defend communal land. After describing the problem, she admonished the crowd, more than half of whom were women, "What we need is real men, men willing to shed their blood. Excuse me, we need men women who are willing to die for Buena Vista." I have resisted the temptation to punctuate "men women." She could have meant "men, women" or "men-women." If there were semantic cues in her delivery I missed them, but the ambiguity speaks to the complexities of the coalition now engaged in this new struggle.

The semiology of gender and power leads the female speaker into confusion. She constructs the task at hand as one that demands male power, as she must, given local political culture, but when she corrects herself, adding women to the formula, she complicates the images of female power. Within the framework of Buena Vistan gender iconography, women's power is located deep within the recesses of their bodies, where it eludes men, who remain so trapped in the ideology of reproduction that they fail to see how women could use their breasts and vaginas for political ends. Thus, women's power rests in their ability to simulate compliance with gender norms while subverting their intent. Men's power, in contrast, resides in their willingness to shed blood—their own and others'—in direct and open confrontation, as they did during the Mexican Revolution. But in the new group where both men and women engage in similar forms of political protest, power seems to escape the constraints of biology and gender. Once again, collective political action is challenging and reconstituting notions of identity.

Conclusions

The difficulties of theorizing the connection between constantly emerging identities and the development of social movements has led many scholars to deemphasize social movements in favor of examining the micropolitics of everyday resistance.[17] But in focusing exclusively on resistance we risk a premature dismissal of collective activity. Social movements continue to form, and we cannot possibly understand worker consciousness and subject constitution without looking at the movement of workers into and out of these social movements. More important, though, we need to realize that our concepts of social movements depend on the notion of a unified subject with clearly defined interests. In reality, most social movements are more complicated than the theories we use to understand them, just as most human beings are more complicated than the notion of a unified self. If we measure the success of a movement in relation to yet-to-be-deconstructed concepts of social movements, we will arrive at a gloomy assessment of their achievements.[18]

The political process involves a movement of persons among the competing discursive formations of political rhetoric as well as an attempt to stabilize the free-floating signifiers of political rhetoric. The latter process links discursive and nondiscursive practices, creating the possibility of momentary stabilization of groups around given projects. Politics needs to be thought about in terms of the simultaneity of these processes of shifting identities: individual and collective. The challenge facing political theory today is to account for the transitions between moments when identities seem clear and unproblematic, and times when fragmentation prevails.

NOTES

I thank Jonathan Diskin for his insightful comments on this essay and Jan Slagter for many hours of discussion about feminist theory and multiple identities. This essay also benefited from the suggestions of Mary Kay Vaughan and Heather Fowler-Salamini. My research was funded by the School of International Studies at the University of the Pacific and by Earlham College. The essay was written while I was on a leave from Earlham College, sponsored by the Joyce Foundation.

1. Buena Vista is a pseudonym for the highland Morelos community where I have been conducting research since 1984. Although some Buena Vistans can speak Mexicano, the local term for Nahuatl, Buena Vista is a mestizo community.

2. Norma Alarcon argues that Chicana feminists have appropriated and revised the "negative" images of a Manichaean system of thought rather than break entirely with their culture and community; see "Traddutora, Traditora: A Paradigmatic Figure of Chicana Feminism," *Cultural Critique* 13 (1989):57–87.

3. Buena Vistans recognize three types of landholding: private property, communal land, and ejido land. Neither communal land nor ejido land may be bought or sold, although use rights can be inherited. Communal land can be traced back to preconquest village landholdings; ejido land is a result of land reform after the Mexican Revolution. For a discussion of preconquest Morelos, see Robert Haskett, *Indigenous Rulers: An Ethnohistory of Town Government in Colonial Cuernavaca* (Albuquerque: University of New Mexico Press, 1991).

4. JoAnn Martin, "Motherhood and Power: The Production of a Women's Culture of Politics in a Mexican Community," *American Ethnologist* 17 (1990):400–490.

5. See Rosalind Coward and John Ellis, *Language and Materialism: Developments in Semiology and the Theory of the Subject* (London: Routledge and Kegan Paul, 1977).

6. H. Fraad, S. Resnick, and R. Wolff, "For Every Knight in Shining Armor, There's a Castle Waiting to Be Cleaned: A Marxist-Feminist Analysis of the Household," *Rethinking Marxism* 2 (1989):10–69.

7. María Patricia Fernández-Kelly, *For We Are Sold, I and My People: Women and Industry in Mexico's Frontier* (Albany: State University of New York Press, 1983).

8. I use the term *disciplining techniques* to emphasize that labor is not only a means of economic survival but also the way in which the sense of self and identity is shaped and controlled in relation to a larger cultural order.

9. Ruth Behar, "Sex and Sin, Witchcraft and the Devil in Late Colonial Mexico," *American Ethnologist* 14 (1987):34–54; Martin, "Motherhood and Power," 479; Lois Paul, "The Mastery of Work and the Mystery of Sex in a Guatemalan Village," in *Women, Culture and Society,* ed. Michelle Zimbalist Rosaldo and Louise Lamphere (Stanford: Stanford University Press, 1974), 281–300.

10. The name Malinche evokes images of a traitor and, in Octavio Paz's analysis, of symbolic rape; see Paz, *The Labyrinth of Solitude: Life and Thought in Mexico* (New York: Grove Press, 1961). Feminists attempting to escape from Paz's gloomy portrayal of this woman have tried to recover her name as well as elements of her history. Rachel Phillips calls her by her Christian name, Doña Marina; see "Marina/Malinche: Masks and Shadows," in *Women in Hispanic Literature: Icons and Fallen Idols,* ed. Beth Miller (Berkeley: University of California Press, 1983), 97–114. Alarcon recovers her Indian name, Malintzin, in "Traddutora, Traditora," 57–87.

11. Jacques LaFaye, *Quetzalcóatl and Guadalupe: The Formation of a Mexican National Consciousness, 1531–1813,* trans. Benjamin Keen (Chicago: University of Chicago Press, 1976).

12. J. L. Alegía, *Psicología de las mexicanas* (Mexico City: Ediciones ERA S.A., 1975).

13. Phillips, "Marina/Malinche", 104–5.

14. Ibid., 111.

15. John Ingham, *Mary, Michael and Lucifer: Folk Catholicism in Central Mexico* (Austin: University of Texas Press, 1986), 183; emphasis added.

16. For a discussion of harmony ideology and community in Mexico, see Laura Nader, *Harmony Ideology: Justice and Control in a Zapotec Mountain Village* (Stanford: Stanford University Press, 1990).

17. See, e.g., Jean Comaroff, *Body of Power, Spirit of Resistance: The Culture and History of a South African People* (Chicago: University of Chicago Press, 1985); Michel De Certeau, "On the Oppositional Practices of Everyday Life," *Social Text* 1 (1980):3–4; Aihwa Ong, *Spirits of Resistance and Capitalist Discipline: Factory Women in Malaysia* (Albany: State University of New York Press, 1987).

18. For an example of such a gloomy assessment, see Aihwa Ong, "The Gender and Labor of Postmodernity," *Annual Reviews of Anthropology* 20 (1991):279–310.

Contributors

PATRICIA ARIAS is a professor of anthropology at the Universidad de Guadalajara. Her publications include two monographs, *Guadalajara, la gran ciudad de la pequeña industria* (1985) and *Industria y estado en la vida de México* (1990) published by the Colegio de Michoacán. She recently published *La nueva rusticidad mexicana* (Conaculta, 1992), which deals with socioeconomic and cultural change in Guanajuato.

FRANCIE R. CHASSEN-LÓPEZ is an associate professor of history at the University of Kentucky at Lexington and the author of a political biography of the Mexican labor leader Vicente Lombardo Toledano. She has published articles on prerevolutionary and revolutionary Oaxaca in *La revolución en Oaxaca, 1900–1930* (Instituto de Administración Pública de Oaxaca, 1985) and the journals *Eslabones, Historia Mexicana,* and *Revista Mexicana de Sociología.*

HEATHER FOWLER-SALAMINI teaches Latin American history and women's studies at Bradley University. She is the author of *Agrarian Radicalism in Veracruz, 1920–38* (University of Nebraska Press, 1978). Her essays about peasants, caudillos, and agrarian revolution in the Mexican Revolution appear in *Caudillo and Peasant in the Mexican Revolution,* edited by David Brading (Cambridge University Press, 1980); and *Provinces of the Revolution,* edited by Thomas Benjamin and Mark Wasserman (University of New Mexico Press, 1990).

JUDITH FRIEDLANDER is the Walter Eberstadt Professor of Anthropology and dean of the Graduate Faculty of Political Science and Social Science at the New School of

Social Research. She is the author of *Being Indian in Hueyapan: A Study of Forced Identity in Contemporary Mexico* (St. Martin's Press, 1975) and *Vilna on the Seine: Jewish Intellectuals in France Since 1968* (Yale University Press, 1990), and the coeditor of *Women in Culture and Politics: A Century of Change* (Indiana University Press, 1986).

Soledad González Montes holds a degree in anthropology and teaches in the Interdisciplinary Program for Women's Studies at El Colegio de México. Her articles appear in *Presencia y Transparencia. La Mujer en la Historia de México,* edited by Carmen Ramos (El Colegio de México, 1987); and *Las mujeres en el campo,* edited by Josefina Aranda Bezaury (Universidad Autónoma Benito Juárez de Oaxaca, 1988). She is the editor of *Hacia una antropología de género y las relaciones genéricas en América Latina* (El Colegio de México, 1993).

Florencia Mallon teaches Latin American history at the University of Wisconsin-Madison. She is the author of *The Defense of Community in Peru's Central Highlands: Peasant Struggle and Capitalist Transition, 1860–1940* (Princeton University Press, 1983) and *Peasant and Nation: The Making of Postcolonial Mexico and Peru* (University of California Press, 1994) as well as numerous articles on peasant politics, nationalism, the state, gender, and social theory. She is presently editing a volume on popular nationalism and state formation in Asia, Europe, and the Americas.

Maria da Glória Marroni de Velázquez is a professor of economics at the Benemerita Universidad Autónoma de Puebla. She has published several articles on agricultural production, social differentiation, and modernization and is currently completing her doctoral dissertation on the processes of change in the lives of rural women in Atlixco, Puebla.

JoAnn Martin is an assistant professor of anthropology at Earlham College. She is the coeditor, with Carolyn Nordstrom, of *The Paths to Domination, Resistance and Terror* (University of California Press, 1992). She has been conducting research in Morelos, Mexico, since 1984 and is currently writing a book that examines the impact of land privatization on the culture of Mexican politics.

Gail Mummert, a demographer and social anthropologist, is a research professor at the Colegio de Michoacán in Zamora, Michoacán, and the author of *Tierra que pica. Transformación de un valle agrícola michoacano en la época postreforma agraria* (El Colegio de Michoacán, 1994). Her articles on the incorporation of women into the labor market and the role of gender in Mexican migration to the United States have appeared in journals such as *Nueva Antropología* as well as in various collections published in Mexico.

Piedad Peniche Rivero is the director of the State Archives of Yucatán. She has worked as an anthropologist at research centers and archaeological sites in the Yucatán and Campeche and is the author of *Sacerdotes y comerciantes. El poder de los mayas y los itzaes en Yucatán en los siglos VII–XVI* (Fondo de Cultura Económica, 1990) as well as a number of articles on peonage during the Porfiriato.

Raquel Rubio Goldsmith teaches history at Pima Community College in Tucson, Arizona. She has also taught at the Mexican-American Studies and Research Center at the University of Arizona. She contributed to *Women on the U.S.-Mexico Border,* edited by Vicki L. Ruiz and Susan Tiano (Allen and Unwin, 1987); and *Between Borders: Essays on Mexicana/Chicana History,* edited by Adelaida del Castillo (Floricanto Press, 1990).

Elizabeth Salas is an associate professor of American ethnic studies at the University of Washington-Seattle and the author of *Soldaderas in the Mexican Military: Myth and History* (University of Texas Press, 1990).

Mary Kay Vaughan teaches in the Department of History and the Latin American Studies Program at the University of Illinois-Chicago. She is the author of *The State, Education, and Social Class in Mexico, 1880–1930* (Northern Illinois University Press, 1982) and numerous articles on the history of Mexican education, several of which focus on women's education. Her most recent articles appear in *Molding the Hearts and Minds: Education, Communications and Change in Latin America,* edited by John A. Britton, and *Rituals of Rule: Rituals of Resistance,* edited by W. H. Beezely, W. E. French, and C. E. Martin, both published by Scholarly Resources in 1994.